Recent Research in

The Lewin Legacy

Field Theory in Current Practice

Edited by
Eugene Stivers and Susan Wheelan

Springer-Verlag

Berlin Heidelberg New York London Paris Tokyo

Editors

Eugene Stivers
Susan Wheelan
Department of Psychoeducational Processes
College of Education, Temple University
Philadelphia, Pennsylvania 19122, USA

ISBN 3-540-96352-9 Springer-Verlag Berlin Heidelberg New York
ISBN 0-387-96352-9 Springer-Verlag New York Berlin Heidelberg

Library of Congress Cataloging-in-Publication Data. The Lewin legacy. (Recent research in psychology) Bibliography: p. 1. Lewin, Kurt, 1890–1947. 2. Field theory (Social psychology)
I. Stivers, Eugene II. II. Wheelan, Susan A. III. Series.
HM251.L47413 1986 302'.01 86-5756

© Springer-Verlag Berlin Heidelberg 1986
Printed in Germany

Printing and binding: Beltz Offsetdruck, Hemsbach/Bergstr.
2817/3140-543210

The Context of This Book

Kurt Lewin has influenced modern life as fully as John Dewey, Marx, Darwin, or Freud. The ideas and practices of organizational development, life space, leadership styles, force-field analysis, group dynamics, the t-group, feedback, and action research were generated or developed by this humane man and his students, both women and men.

On May 3rd and 4th, 1984 at Temple University the first International Kurt Lewin Conference was held. It brought together scholars, professionals and practitioners from the United States and abroad to celebrate Lewin's ideas and work, and to talk about and demonstrate current Lewinian theory and practice. Some local professionals, practitioners and students joined them.

This book is a main outcome of the Conference, and represents most of the presenters, unified by their lively common interest. A number of the original papers have been reduced to their present size for the sake of the book's clarity and coherence.

A large group of graduate students played a significant part in planning the Conference. Alice Jackson typed the book manuscript, and Claire Staffieri did the graphic work. Marcia Patton was editorial assistant.

Eugene H. Stivers, and
Susan A. Wheelan
Psychoeducational Processes,
College of Education
Temple University

A Personal Introduction

I have attended quite a few conferences and meetings devoted to the ideas of Kurt Lewin. Among these the 1984 conference at Temple was outstanding for its high quality. What made it so successful? Several things. The conference included a stimulating mix of generations. The first generation of women who obtained their Ph.D.'s in psychology in Berlin in the 1920's strike me as a remarkable group. Now in their 80's, they are characterized by enormous vigor and energy. They are still professionally active. Two of them - Tamara Dembo and Maria Rickers-Ovsienkina - joined us. Other participants in the Temple conference had been in Iowa in the 1930's and 1940's, or at MIT. Of course there were many who had learned about Lewin from their own teachers, and in some cases, their teachers' teachers. There was a good mixture of applied psychologists and academics.

Father said on several occasions that he did not want to found a school of psychology as such. Rather he wanted to introduce the field theoretical viewpoint and approach. I think he would have been stimulated by and enthusiastic about the many diverse areas to which Lewinian analyses, ideas, and concepts are applied today, as illustrated by this volume. He would have been pleased to see so many people applying basic theoretical concepts to important social problems.

Father loved to discover new things about America. When he first came to the States he took many photographs of the car carriers which transport eight new cars at a time across the country - apparently in Germany there were no such animals. At Temple, at first he would have been amazed to find T shirts in vibrant colors with his name boldly emblazoned upon them. But then, with his usual fondness for the unexpected inventions of the country he had taken to his heart, he would have been amused and delighted.

I heartily recommend this collection of "work in progress" to the reader. I look forward with anticipation to subsequent conferences sponsored by the Society for the Advancement of Field Theory.

Miriam Lewin
Manhattanville College

The Fertility of Kurt Lewin

The 1984 Kurt Lewin Conference at Temple University provided a rich contemporary memoir to the many dimensions of Kurt Lewin's genius.

The first section of this volume will help many connect with the historical roots of the Lewinian legacy, and help reconstruct some of the intellectual ferment of this launching period.

Other sections provide samples of some of the major areas of utilization and development of the Lewinian initiatives - mental health and group therapy, classroom learning process, organizational development, and community development and action.

Cutting across all these areas of applied group dynamics and field theory are the contributions of research and change methodology as illustrated by contributions on action-research, forcefield analysis, conflict analysis, gatekeeping functions, and the dynamics of cooperation and competition.

This conference, and subsequent volume, are clear evidences of the generational bridging and continuing vigor and fruitfulness of Kurt Lewin's outreach.

Ronald Lippitt
Ann Arbor, Michigan

An Overall View

Kurt Lewin, whose scientific contributions provided the background for the theory, research and practice described in this book, has often been called the major figure in the history of modern social psychology. Edward C. Tolman, himself a giant in psychological history, expressed such a view when he said that Lewin, the experimentalist, along with Freud, the clinician, would be remembered as persons who first made psychology a science applicable to real human beings and to real human society.

My own associations with Lewin began immediately after World War II. The end of the war had freed him from war-related research and made it possible for him to embark on an endeavor about which he felt deeply and for which he had high expectations. This was to be an effort to extend his theory and research to include the phenomena of group life, including those of intergroup prejudice and discrimination, from which he and his family had suffered in Germany.

The year, 1945, saw him preoccupied with establishing two research institutes that were to be the primary instruments of his new scientific thrust. One of these was the Research Center for Group Dynamics at MIT, and the other was the Commission on Community Relations of the American Jewish Congress. As research director of the latter I consulted with him on a regular basis from mid-1945 until his sudden death in 1947. In these exchanges I had the opportunity to experience at first hand the creativity for which Lewin was famous.

Lewin's growing concern with the psychology of groups and intergroup relations had been stimulated in two ways. The first was his prewar and wartime experience. He had left Nazi Germany as a result of discrimination against Jewish scientists. He devoted extensive time and resources to efforts to rescue family, friends and colleagues. In many instances he succeeded, only to lose his own mother in a concentration camp. He recognized that--however significant his studies of the dynamics of individual psychology--the rise of Fascism, the world war and the Jewish holocaust raised questions about human behavior that must be studied at the level of groups and society.

The second stimulus was two sets of subsequently famous experiments conducted in the late 1930s and early 1940s. One of these grew out of a dissertation on autocratic and democratic leadership by one of his students, Ronald Lippitt. This study and a follow-up experiment done by

Lewin with Lippitt and Ralph White revealed differences in group atmosphere and behavior associated with differences in leadership styles.

The second set of studies occurred during the war. In collaboration with Alex Bavelas he carried out the well known experiments on promoting the use of organ meats to relieve food shortages. Out of these wartime studies had grown a distinctly social-psychological concept, namely, that of "group decision." Group decision, it was learned, had more influence on individuals' actions than did decisions made separately by the individuals themselves.

Lewin's commitment to the psychology of groups and community action led him to seek university and organizational support to pursue further research. MIT provided a home for the research on the psychology of groups (the Research Center for Group Dynamics), and the American Jewish Congress made similar provisions for the research on intergroup prejudice and discrimination (the Commission on Community Interrelations). The research carried out in these institutes under the guidance of Lewin (and, after his death, by those who continued the work he had initiated) had considerable influence on the rapidly growing fields of social, organizational, and developmental psychology. Empirical findings on such topics as leadership, group cohesion, group goals, group standards, group pressures, cooperation, and communication within groups and organizations became the basis for the new field of group dynamics. Other studies dealing with organizational and community action directed against religious and racial discrimination added to knowledge of prejudice and intergroup hostility. Developments in "action research" methods concerned with facilitating the practical application of social science findings paralleled these substantive advances. A typology of varieties of action research emerged.

Had Lewin lived, it is safe to assume that these empirical developments would have been paralleled by an equally vigorous expansion of his field theory of individual psychology to the social-psychological phenomena of face-to-face groups, large organizations, communities, and political entities. As Albert Pepitone notes in his chapter in this book, the beginnings of such an extension were already evident. For example, Lewin had begun to deal with the task of conceptualizing the paths that objects and persons traverse through the social environment. He called these "channels" and noted the presence in these channels of "gatekeepers." A second example, described in a posthumous article published in the first issue of Volume 1 of the journal, Human Relations, is that of "quasi-stationary equilibrium" of group processes. Lewin called attention to the implications of this phenomenon for methods of promoting change in undesirable societal practices.

While such mini-theories are helpful in generalizing across a variety of person-environment relationships, they fall short of the goals that Lewin set for himself in field theory. We can be sure that he would have incorporated such mini-theories into a broader field-theoretical framework. Such had been the course of his progress in individual psychology, where he had integrated into a single over-arching system such components as individual goals, barriers to goal achievement, individual personality characteristics, representations in the present of past experience, subjective meanings of perceived environmental events, and behavioral intentions, as well as the means for understanding the interaction and interdependence of such components.

The recognition that Lewin's work had been cut short in the vital area of social relationships and group life was one of the factors that led the faculty and students of Temple University's Department of Psychoeducational Processes to convene an international gathering of social scientists interested in the contemporary implications of his work. This book records the proceedings of that meeting, the First International Kurt Lewin Conference, held in the spring of 1984. As Eugene Stivers and Susan Wheelan indicate in their Introduction, the range of topics at the conference was broad: the discussions covered historical, theoretical, research, and practical matters.

The success of the first conference stimulated two additional undertakings for the future. The first is to continue to hold biennial international gatherings of social scientists whose work has been stimulated in some way by that of Lewin. To this end a Second International Kurt Lewin Conference is scheduled for the fall of 1986.

The second undertaking is to form an international network to foster communication during the intervals between conferences. The general objective of the network is indicated by its title, Society for the Advancement of Field Theory. The society's stated aims are to revitalize and advance Lewin's field theoretical approaches to the development of social science. These are ambitious objectives. Nevertheless, their significance for social science and for the application of social science to society justifies our best efforts to achieve them. Lewin died too soon after shifting his focus to social-psychological phenomena to develop the full potential of field theory in this area. Hopefully, the efforts of the new society will provide social and intellectual support to others to take up where Lewin left off.

Stuart Cook
University of Colorado

The Creativity of Field Theory

The striking characteristic of the Lewin Conference, and of this volume which reflects it, is the extraordinary diversity of human experience and behavior encompassed by Lewin's way of thinking. More particularly, the evidence of the field theoretical approach pervades the astonishing variety of experimental and field research, conducted in a period of at least sixty years by Lewin and his students, and by students of their students, among distant places around the world. What is it about the Lewinian approach that gives it such impressive generality in its representations of human psychology?

As usually described, field theory is not a theory that explains any given behavior or kind of social relationship, not even a general theory such as a theory of learning or cognition. Rather, it is metatheory, a body of methodological perspectives on the representation of psychological reality, the relationship between psychological law and the individual case, the method to be used in the construction of concepts, and the meaning of scientific causality. Also associated with the field theoretical approach is the analysis of concept types, and the classification of the types into structural and dynamic. Arguably, it is the representational "work" of these two classes of concepts that has given the field theory approach its range and power.

Structural concepts have been used to represent the totality of behavioral possibilities constituting the life space; for example, the position of the individual with respect to goals, being in overlapping situations at the same time, membership in a group, location in a status hierarchy, and being surrounded by a barrier. Structural concepts have also represented the system of needs in the person, the organization of abilities, etc. Lewin's Principles of Topological Psychology (1936) is an introduction to a method of geometrically depicting such structures.

Dynamic concepts have represented goal-directed activity, the effects of frustration, decisions on level of aspiration, the rate of racial discrimination in a town during a period and other "quasi stationary" equilibria, behavior in conflicting goal and avoidance situations, the effects on a group of authoritarian leadership, and so on. Lewin's The Conceptual Representation and the Measurement of Psychological forces (1938) is a detailed exposition of the dynamic concepts of field theory. Concerning the conceptual linkage between the structural and dynamic, Lewin uses the structure of psychological paths, as measured by the "hodological" geometry he invented, as a basis for defining the direction and distance gradients of psychological forces.

One of the unique properties of field theory as far as empirical implications are concerned is that it represents the case in which structural conditions influence dynamics, as well as the reverse case in which dynamics affect structure. Thus, whether a person is inside or outside a barrier that surrounds a goal makes a decisive difference in the directional pattern of behavior. On the other hand, the spread of emotional tension across the boundaries of regions representing the organization of a person's abilities causes a breakdown of that organization; the person becomes dedifferentiated.

Although prodigiously fecund for so long and worked upon by so many talents, the ideas that can be generated from structural and dynamic representations have not been exhausted. Kurt Lewin left a rich conceptual legacy for the new Society for the Advancement of Field Theory to draw upon and to build upon creatively.

Albert Pepitone
University of Pennsylvania

Lewin, K. (1936). Principles of Topological Psychology. New York: McGraw-Hill.

Lewin, K. (1938). The conceptual representation and measurement of psychological forces. Contributions to Psychological Theory, Vol. I, No. 4. Durham, N.C.: Duke University Press.

Table of Contents

General introductions

Eugene Stivers and Susan A. Wheelan
The context of this book V

Miriam Lewin
A personal introduction VII

Ronald Lippitt
The fertility of Kurt Lewin IX

Stuart Cook
An overall view XI

Albert Pepitone
The creativity of field theory XV

Part I: Lewin, then and now

Introduction 1

Tamara Dembo
Approach as a description of the nature of scientific activity:
Some reflections and suggestions 3

Miriam Lewin
Kurt Lewin and American psychology: An ambivalent relationship 8

Robert Kleiner and Frank Maguire
Lewin's sphere of influence from Berlin 12

Vytautas Cernius
The man in transition: Kurt Lewin and his times 21

Matthias von Saldern
Kurt Lewin's influence on social emotional climate research in
Germany and the United States 30

Bernhard Wolf
Theoretical positions of Kurt Lewin and Egon Brunswick — controversial or complementary points of view? 40

Kurt W. Back
Lewin and current developmental theory 52

Albert Pepitone
Lewin and social science: A theoretical note 65

Part II: Practical Theory

    A. Therapy-mental health-interpersonal relations

        Introduction 70

        Susan Wheelan
        Kurt Lewin's influence on the field of mental health 72

Matti K. Gershenfeld
Understanding enrichment and therapy in marriage: The
legacy of Kurt Lewin 79

George Bach
Lewinian theory in clinical practice 91

Matti K. Gershenfeld
Kurt Lewin: Intergroup relations and applications in current
action research 95

Yvonne M. Agazarian
Application of Lewin's life space concept to the individual
and group-as-a-whole systems in group psychotherapy 101

B. Education

Introduction 113

Steven Krupp, Robert F. De Haan, Szabi Ishtai-Zee, Effie
Bastas, Karen Castlebaum, and Evelyn Jackson
Action research as a guiding principle in an educational
curriculum: The Lincoln University Master's Program in
Human Services 115

Gerald Biberman
Kurt Lewin's influence on business education 122

Emmy A. Pepitone
Children in cooperation and competition: The role of
entitlement and deservedness 128

Richard A. Schmuck
Participants as consultants to themselves 136

C. Organizational and human resources development

Introduction 145

Steven Krupp
The quality circle phenomenon 147

Jean H. Woods and Irene G. Casper
Using graduate students as consultants to teach action research to residence hall staff 158

Melvin L. Silberman
Teaching force field analysis: A suggested training design. 166

Jay M. Yanoff and William E, Bryan
Utilizing Lewinian principles for an institutional planning
process within a medical school 171

Edmund Amidon and Tim Doris
Organizational processes in a University department: A report
of an action research and organizational development
project 179

D. Community psychology and community action

Introduction 192

Leanne G. Rivlin, Maxine Wolfe and Matt Kaplan
Environmental psychology and action research: Lewin's
legacy 194

Jeanette Turner
Community action research in North Philadelphia 201

Stephanie Reynolds
Report of an action research project: The Hunting Park
community leaders survey — problems and prospects for
park preservation 208

David Bargal and Tsiyona Peled
A practical theory for optimal intergroup-initiated encounters: The Arab-Jewish case 213

E. Research lines

Introduction 221

Jeanne M. Plas, Kathleen Hoover-Dempsey and Barbara
Strudler Wallston
Support, reference, and gatekeeping functions within the
interpersonal field: Lewin contributions 223

Emmy A, Pepitone
A continuation of Lewinian research in the study of
cooperation and competition 232

Jerome S. Allender
New paradigm research 243

Eugene H. Stivers
A neo-Lewinian action research method 258

Rupert W. Nacoste
The effects of affirmative action on minority persons:
Research in the Lewinian tradition 268

Part I: Lewin, Then and Now

How was it in the first Lewin group in Berlin? What was it like to theorize and do research? <u>Tamara Dembo</u> remembers, and recommends a focus worth nurturing--<u>approach</u> as scientific activity.

"In some ways, Kurt Lewin had enormous influence on the development of psychology. Nevertheless, many of his fundamental ideas are poorly understood." "...we are now advancing to where Lewin was sixty years ago." With these sentences, <u>Miriam Lewin</u>, his daughter, asserts the themes that she develops in the second article. It is clear what she thinks about Lewin, then and now.

The next paper, by <u>Robert Kleiner</u> and <u>Frank Maguire</u>, takes an historical step backward in the service of demonstrating that Kurt Lewin was a widely known, well respected and influential figure in the world many years before he settled in the U.S. in 1933. Further, that he was a complete psychologist--theorist, methodologist, and practitioner. The urgency and sense of rediscovery in this article underlies Kleiner and Maguire's conviction that there is a presently unexplored historical subcontinent of Lewin's work and influence, before 1932.

<u>Vytautas Cernius</u> depicts the historical settings and the sweep of change that Lewin lived through. Are his works a response to the contextual drama of his life? Cernius asks readers to help decide.

<u>Matthias v. Saldern</u> aims specifically to survey Kurt Lewin's influence on social emotional climate research in Germany and the U.S., from the late thirties up until the present. His careful work finds that the influence network is extensive, but not always in the direction one would predict. He also suggests a substitute for the word "climate."

Now in a very careful focussed way, <u>Bernhard Wolf</u> compares the theoretical positions of Kurt Lewin (1890-1947) and Egon Brunswik (1903-1955), a social psychologist who was, like Lewin, prominent in Europe and America. Why Brunswik? Wolf is interested in helping define "Lewin, then," yes, but he is more interested in pursuing the question: In what specific way should the processes of person-environment interrelations be understood in psychological research? To serve this basic question he reveals the sharp immense distinction between the two views. What Wolf finally suggests could be called "beyond the Aristotelean <u>and</u> the Galilean modes of thought."

<u>Kurt W. Back's</u> theme is Lewin and current developmental theory. He does not address current theory until after he has first thoroughly and systematically reviewed the history of certain of Lewin's large-

scale scientific ideas. With sections on "Group dynamics" and "The Self" as a transition, Back then comes to the heart and conclusion of the paper--Lewin's Ideas and the Modern Logic of Development. "The developmental theories Lewin sketched apply not only for biological development, but for cognitive and emotional development, and for development of the self, of groups and even for social and economic development as well," Back asserts.

The final article is appropriately titled "Lewin and Social Science: A Theoretical Note." Albert Pepitone offers a way to summarize Lewin's ideas and take hold of salient and useful constructs. Tracing the change in his ideas during the forties, and the introduction of "phase space," Pepitone promises us that "when sufficiently diffused, the last creative contribution of Lewin may thus be useful in the restructuring of social psychology as a more integral part of social science."

Approach as a Description of the Nature of Scientific Activity: Some Reflections and Suggestions

Tamara Dembo

Clark University

Progress in psychology (and probably in any science) is not made in an orderly fashion, (i.e., stating a problem, choosing a method, and developing a theory). In reality, the course of everyday scientific activities is quite different. Precise steps are uncertain in an unknown area of thought. Therefore, tentative hunches are made, and then deviations from these notions take place. New ideas leading away from the major problem come to one's mind and may be followed for a while. Insights leading into blind alleys and insights about related problems emerge, complicating the original problem of investigation. The journal article report, that is, the description of the research, leaves out the above tentative steps and instead presents in a brief, orderly and logical form only three of the research constituents: the problem of investigation, method used to gather data, and concepts and their relations to each other. The orderly method of presentation was arrived at <u>after</u> the study was completed and after everything was known.

The traditional way of presenting results has its advantages: not only is it the most efficient way of acquainting the reader with new findings, but also it clearly designates three of the four necessary constituents of the research. The fourth, which manifests itself in the totality of events that occur while the study is being conducted, is not even mentioned. The trials and tribulations are not reported and neither are the piloting in thinking, preliminary tryouts, dealing with preconstructs and partial insights, and playing with important ideas which might have led away from the main focus of the investigation but which contained a kernel of importance for a point to be pursued. In reporting cooperative research involving two or more people, what is not given is the tugging and pulling which occurs between researchers, the intertwining of minds, the acceptance or rejection of the twists in a partner's thoughts, or the untangling of a misperception introduced by a partner which may seem peculiar but which may lead to a new way of looking at matters.

All of the above goes on daily in forming a study, but, I repeat, nothing of it is reported. The bulk of what was experienced during

the performance of the research, which is full of gems for beginning
related, additional, or new studies, is discarded. And with it is discarded much of what constitutes the specificity of the approach which
proved to be fruitful. Speaking concretely, what is lost is how the
study was made. The material which could be used to teach the next
generation of scientists how a particular researcher or group of researchers made their discoveries is not recorded. Also lost with it
is the feeling of excitement and pleasure in doing research and making
discoveries within a research group centered around a founder. Unfor-
malized also remains the structure and dynamics of the approach within
its specific situational atmosphere.

The Situation and Atmosphere in the Lewinian Group

It is advantageous for the development of a fruitful approach that
the prevailing interpersonal relations between the founder and followers
of an approach permit not only communication between them, but also the
free sharing of thoughts and ideas. The participants of a group will
be better communicators with each other on scientific matters the less
personally ambitious they are during the scientific work, that is, the
less they are concerned with who contributes a particular idea, or who
got it from whom in the process. As in music and other arts, involvement in the subject matter can, and does in many cases, become the
primary concern. This also happens among scientists and was characteristic of the Lewinian group. The intense scientific involvement of
Lewin and his followers in the beauty of the subject matter typically
overrode personal competitive feelings. In correspondence to the above,
the founder and his followers were on equal footing during their scientific discussions. Lewin was not the domineering "founder" in the
sense of a "leader," but Kurt, who always had excellent ideas, and
readily accepted ideas from coworkers. This describes the prevailing
situation with its atmosphere which was due to particular persons and
their particular interpersonal relations. Such an atmosphere also is
conducive to the enjoyment and remembrance of interpersonal occurrences
indicative of an approach.

To describe the approach without the founder of it is, of course,
one-sided. It is slanted toward the interpretations of the followers.
This has its disadvantages, but also some advantages. The disadvantages lie in the lack of knowledge of the approach as seen from the
founder's standpoint. The advantages lie in the stress on the views

from the coworkers' standpoints, who are the <u>carriers</u> of the approach
to their scientific progeny. The coworkers and their students, the
students of students, etc. will continue to use and benefit from the
original approach and its subsequent development. The original approach
is what took place during the coworkers' contact with the originator.
But there are also quite a number of Lewinians who adapted the approach
in listening to Lewin's lectures, participating in some meetings with
him, or who read some of his reports, articles, or books and thought
them over thoroughly.

During their work with the originator, the followers were in no
way uncritically following Lewin's ways of handling matters. The followers were actively engaged in research. They were team workers on
equal footing with Lewin and as such contributed to the approach.
While respecting the scientific know-how of Lewin and being inclined
to adapt his opinions as fully as possible, the followers' genuine
involvement in scientific research made them also contribute to the
approach their views, efforts, ways of understanding and interpretation, and ways of searching within the field. That means that what
the coworkers remember and describe as the Lewinian approach at present is very much tinged by <u>their views</u> and their attempts to move
forward. This again has its advantages and disadvantages. The disadvantage is that at present we do not have the "unadulterated" Lewin
approach, but, rather, different versions of his contributions as seen
by the people who worked with him. The advantage is that the different
reports on the approach show that different scientists got a lot of
diverse, fruitful views from the interchange with the originator which
they integrated within their own thinking and work. The resulting
views may be close to or very different from Lewin's unadulterated
views and statements. However, all followers are in the position of
being promoters of the Lewinian approach to succeeding generations and
do so.

It is, of course, a great disadvantage that we cannot get data on
the day-to-day work with Lewin observed at the time of its happening.
We cannot distinguish the personal contributions of Lewin from the
totality of the diverse interpretations of his approach made by his
students and coworkers. However, the latter is what we can determine,
and it is that which perhaps should be called the Lewinian approach in
operation today. It is the one which actually can and should be used
by Lewin's followers and taught to the next generations.

The generations of Lewin's students and coworkers who accepted
many of his viewpoints were people mostly chosen by Lewin as promising

scientists to be productive in their own way. They certainly contributed their own ideas and understanding to Lewin's approach, developing it with him, and they continue to develop and integrate it within their own approaches after having lost their founder. They participate in new scientific interpersonal relations with their own students and coworkers. Being Lewinians, they also value their own ideas. Valuing Lewinian ideas, they know that the line between what constituted Lewin's views and their own is not always sharply defined, and together they present one of the possible views of what the Lewinian approach is. The multitude of paired interpersonal views of the founder and a student or coworker builds the totality of data on the approach which we know of today. Available to us is what is remembered by Lewin's students and coworkers. Some of the views of some Lewinians might be contrary to the views of other Lewinians. Instead of rejecting these views as heresy, I believe the Lewinians have to determine the circumstances which led to this view, and this might even open some new avenues to understanding the approach. At present there is not one factual Lewinian approach, but a multitude of approaches. They build an integral approach to be determined and studied as the Lewinian approach today.

Studying an approach has another purpose which is gaining knowledge about the activity of performing scientific investigations. This would facilitate not only learning and teaching psychological achievement, but also performing new research. Furthermore, it would help in performing another major function of academic psychologists, how to solve practical problems. It would also increase the efficiency of scientific endeavors by paying more respect to the insights arrived at in preliminary steps and, therefore, not so easily discarded. This sometimes will eliminate rediscovery of the wheel over and over again.

Besides the above mentioned purposes, the mutual determination of the approach used by Lewinians, and discussion of it, contribute to cohesiveness. This is a valuable purpose in itself and also would help the promotion of Lewinian psychology and psychologists. The cohesiveness needs to be fostered by the group especially because the founder is gone, and the Lewinian group at present is dispersed geographically and needs closer communication and mutual support. Lewinians have experienced enough rejection, in spite of wide acceptance, and I believe are ready to work for the sake of the cohesiveness of the group. They are ready for it, and they will be able to enjoy the background of a common scientific ancestry, sharing the founder's ideas, while at the same time having the occasion of discussing their own ideas in congenial group meetings with other Lewinians, or in acting as independent, innovative, original scientists.

Kurt Lewin and American Psychology: An Ambivalent Relationship

Miriam Lewin

Manhattanville College

In some ways, Kurt Lewin had enormous influence on the development of psychology. Nevertheless, many of his fundamental ideas are poorly understood. Field theory was a radical and highly original step. Many of Lewin's students had no training in mathematics (other than statistics), in physics, or in philosophy of science. Undoubtedly, they had not read Cassirer, or much Gestalt psychology. It was, and remains, hard to understand Field Theory.

Field Theory offers an alternative view of science, genuinely different from the positivist, mechanistic determinism characteristic of both the behaviorist and psychoanalytic paradigms--traditions so taken for granted in the education of psychologists today that it is extremely hard for us to fully imagine another way, or to use it in our day-to-day research efforts.

To insist that all significant variables must be taken into account if we wish to predict behavior accurately, or to stress the importance of the context, or to say that personality and environmental factors interact to determine behavior, is to say what is virtually self-evident. Indeed, "interactionism" has been rediscovered at regular intervals since 1920. The power of atomistic thinking is demonstrated, however, by the fact that interactionism is no sooner rediscovered than it is once again cast in the familiar, comfortable, additive, "and summation" (Wertheimer) fashion which the Gestalt psychologists have criticized for so long.

Lewin held an interactionist viewpoint throughout his career; it was often endorsed by others--here is one Lewinian idea which did not seem very controversial--and yet it does not stick, as we shall see shortly. If this non-controversial point is so hard to grasp, how much harder it has been to fully integrate the more difficult aspects of Field Theory into our thinking.

Lewin avoided the American distinction between subjective and objective psychology from the start. Like other Gestalt psychologists, he rejected mind-body dualism. He is neither exactly a phenomenologist, nor an antiphenomenologist. It is assumed that thought and action are in the same realm of discourse, closely linked, and both subject to experimental treatment. A change in perception and cognition (a restructuring of the life space) normally precedes a change in behavior. The process flows in the other direction as well. When unable to solve a problem through action, individuals engage in fantasy solutions.

A few years ago, Henle (1977) commented that we are now advancing to where Lewin was sixty years ago. The contemporary status of these issues in American psychology is nicely illustrated by a review in The Sciences (Kaye, 1980) of Urie Bronfenbrenner's book The Ecology of Human Development (1979). The book takes a Lewinian approach and extends it to explore how mini-settings are nested within larger settings, and to conceptualize how the behavior of individuals is affected by these environmental contexts.

The book reviewer, Kenneth Kaye, represents a rather typical example of a modern psychologist unaware of the topics addressed by Lewinian psychology. What does he make of the book? Mostly, he is dumbfounded. The terms of the argument are so foreign to him that he is quite unable to comment on the issues raised by Bronfenbrenner at all, whether to praise or criticize. Instead he offers these comments: the meaning of a setting to the participants must come from past experience in similar settings. Conceptual analysis of the present setting is not taken seriously.

My second example will be a book by David Tresemer which reviews the mass of research on Fear of Success (1977). Matina Horner's work on "fear of success" (FOS) is in the direct historical line from Ferdinand Hoppe, a student of Lewin's in Berlin who researched the effect of success and failure on the level of aspiration. The line continues through numerous students of Lewin's in both Germany and the United States to Atkinson, McClelland and Horner.

Tresemer, like Kaye, assumes that the past is scientifically more important than are the characteristics of the present. FOS is "explained" if we can show a correlation between some childhood experience and current FOS level on a questionnaire.

It is important to clarify the fact that Lewin was not opposed to such explanations, which he called "historical" explanations. They have a legitimate place in psychology. However, he wished to emphasize--because they were then, and are now neglected--the importance of a second type of explanation which he called conditional-genetic explanation. From that viewpoint, FOS behavior is explained by conceptualizing the dynamic properties of the present experimental situation and the dynamic structure of the personality of the particular subject. It is necessary to accurately represent both the forces and the regions in the life space of the subject who, today, shows FOS behavior, and of the subject who, today, does not.

Tresemer sees no need to do this. He makes numerous assumptions which Lewin would not have made: that motives must be deep-rooted, originate in childhood, be almost impossible to change, and represent "unseen stable traits" (Tresemer, 1977, p. 49 and passim). Lewin assumed that motives can be central or peripheral, stable or fluid, easy or hard to change. He assumed that behavior changes readily if the total field of forces changes. Tresemer is so thoroughly grounded in the opposite assumptions that these possibilities hardly occur to him.

Tresemer states his position clearly:

> In the positivist scientific model used in modern social
> psychology, the inference of a truth for all humans
> in a specified group is made from a probability state-
> ment about how the average member of that group acts
> when compared with the average behavior in other groups.
> (1977, p. 174.)

Lewin would probably have called this an example of Aristotelean rather than Galilean scientific thinking. Persons are placed into specified groups or classes. The frequency with which members of the classification categories have certain traits is determined. The total field of forces within which the specific FOS behavior occurs is ignored.

Interestingly, Tresemer himself is disappointed in the results of this approach. "Why were the psychoanalytic and anthropological approaches so rich and interesting and understandable concerning fear of success while the conventional psychological methods were so barren?", he plaintively asks (1977, p. 174). After reviewing the large number of seemingly inconsistent studies of FOS, Tresemer concludes sadly that "positivist science has reached a dead end."

Lewin might agree and offer a suggestion. Go beyond fixed motives, classification, and statistical averaging. Look at the dynamics of the concrete individual case in its particulars. Formulate what is happening there in a carefully designed scientific language, if possible, one amenable to mathematical statement.

These illustrations probably represent quite well the reaction of many a mainstream psychologist on an average day, doing typical "normal research" within the current paradigm. The modern psychologist does not, of course, deny the Gestalt laws of perceptual closure. But when he is not self-conscious about what he is doing, we see that what comes naturally is still atomism, mechanism, reductionism, and the search for solely historical causes, not for systematic or contemporan-

eous causes. He still rejects context, interaction, systems, or Field
Theory. The language of concepts which he knows is still the language
of psychoanalysis and of updated associationism. It seems that the
viewpoint of Lewinian psychology is not yet integrated into general
psychology. The Lewinian message is only dimly heard as yet.*

---

*This paper is a short version of the main address given at Temple
 University to the First International Kurt Lewin Conference.

REFERENCES

Bronfenbrenner, Urie (1979). <u>The Ecology of Human Development: Experi-
    ments by Nature and Design</u>. Cambridge, Mass.: Harvard University
    Press.

Henle, M. (1977). The influence of Gestalt psychology in America,
    <u>Annals of the New York Academy of Sciences</u>, <u>291</u>, 3-13.

Henle, M. (1965). On Gestalt Psychology, in Wolman, B., <u>Scientific
    Psychology</u>. New York: Basic Books.

Hoppe, F. (1930). Erfolg und Misserfolg (success and failure), <u>Psycho-
    logische Forochung</u>, <u>14</u>, 1-62. Translated in De Rivera, J., op.
    cit., 455-493.

Kaye, K. (1980). Context in context. Book review, <u>The Sciences</u>, <u>20</u>,
    No. 2, Feb., 24-26.

Lewin, M. Psychological aspects of minority group membership: the
    concepts of Kurt Lewin, <u>in</u> Blass, T. (Ed.), <u>Readings in Social
    Psychology</u>. Itasca, Ill.: Peacock Pub., p. 197.

Lewin, M. (1979). The crisis of 1927 and the crisis of 1977, <u>Persona-
    lity and Social Psychology Bulletin</u>, <u>3</u>, 159-172.

Lewin, M. (1979). <u>Understanding Psychological Research</u>. New York:
    Wiley.

Tresemer, D. (1977). <u>Fear of Success</u>. New York: Plenum.

Wertheimer, M. (1970, 1979). <u>A Brief History of Psychology</u>, 1st ed.
    New York: Holt, Rinehart and Winston.

Lewin's Sphere of Influence from Berlin

Robert Kleiner and Frank Maguire

Temple University

Our experience in discussing Kurt Lewin with colleagues and students has been interesting. While we have not kept formal records of these informal conversations, we have come to a generalization. Those of us who began our professional training prior to the 1970's are likely to have a stock of Lewin's work in the United States; those who trained since the 1970's are likely to stare blankly at the mention of his name or identify it with few vaguely remembered concepts. But there has been a recent international revival of interest in Lewin (e.g. the Kurt Lewin Werkausgable in Heidelberg, Germany; the Lewin Conference at Temple University). We believe that the remarkable viability of the Lewinian system is the element that has kept it as an influence on some of us; we believe it is a recognition of this viability that has generated a renewal in social sciences given to self-examination.

This paper is an attempt to focus on a particular aspect of our much broader research project. We will demonstrate that Kurt Lewin was a widely known, well respected, and influential figure many years before he settled in the United States in 1933. Further, we will indicate that Lewin was a complete psychologist--a theorist, a methodologist, and a practitioner. It is not difficult to imagine that the isolationist intellectualism of the United States might have completely ignored the work of Lewin, as it has that of many European intellectuals, had a world crisis not forced emigration to this country. But Lewin, once here, could not be ignored.

Unfortunately, most of his early philosophical work on the nature of science has been ignored, and his research during the Berlin years has received selective attention. Even more unfortunately, Lewin's work in the United States has suffered a silence. Many of Lewin's ideas and concepts have become part of contemporary social scientific thought while the debt to Lewin goes unacknowledged. Much of our overall project is an elucidation of the intellectual debts owed by and to Lewin. Our present paper discusses Lewin as a German scientist who had wide international influence on Psychology quite early in the twentieth century, with particular interest in his influence on Soviet psychology.

Lewin, prior to 1933, had evolved an extensive web of personal and professional bonds. For purposes of our present discussion, we will focus on Lewin's associations within the field of psychology. Further, we will concentrate, with a few exceptions, on those psychologists who can be shown to have an early personal contact with Lewin and whose later work reflects that contact. The exceptions include Gordon Allport, Jean Piaget, and French psychology in general. The reasons for the inclusion of such exceptions will be clarified in the course of our discussion. Our presentation does not pretend to be an exhaustive survey. Our purpose is to substantiate wide influence. Because we are interested in breadth of influence, we have used geographical referents to order the discussion.

BELGIUM

Albert Michotte, a Belgian psychologist, first came into contact with Gestalt psychology in 1923 at the International Congress of Psychology at Oxford. There he met Kohler and Koffka. Michotte noted, at that time, many similarities between his own current views and those of Gestalt theory. While there is no clear indication that he met Lewin at this time or prior to it, Michotte was aware of Lewin in 1924. At that time, Michotte was experimentally investigating the problem of association. His results confirmed the views of Lewin concerning the eventual dynamic role of 'associations by contiguity' by showing that connections established in this way are not sufficient in and of themselves to bring about the arousal of the induced term following the mere occurrence of the inducing term (Michotte, 1952, p. 255). Later, at the International Congress of Psychology at Yale in 1929, both Lewin and Michotte delivered papers. By this time, Michotte had devoted considerable effort in researching and extending Gestalt principles. Lewin's work is very clearly important to Michotte's research efforts and, especially, to his interpretations.

As director of the Psychological Laboratory at the University of Louvain, a position which he held from 1905 until his death, Michotte influenced three generations of psychologists. His major publications indicate a Gestalt orientation and a general Lewinian influence. He had ample opportunity to present his orientation in a series of visiting professorships in England, France, Germany, Holland, Italy, Spain, Switzerland and the United States.

FRANCE

Lewin's influence in France is one of our immediate research problems. We are not yet satisfied with either the quantity or the quality of our information in the area and cannot yet attempt a definite statement. Nevertheless, there is evidence of Lewinian influence in French psychology. For example, Pierre Kaufmann shows a familiarity with nineteenth and twentieth century German psychology and with Lewin in particular. Alfred Marrow (1969, p. 59) cites the testimony of Claude Faucheuz on the influence of Lewin on French psychology. Much of Lewin's work has been made available in French, and Lewin had a few contributions published in French journals.

French psychology, then, is not an exception in terms of exhibiting Lewinian influence. It is an exception in that it represents a lacuna in the information available to the authors of this paper. More research remains to be done.

GERMANY AND AUSTRIA

The intricacies of the influences of German psychology on Lewin and of Lewin on German psychology are so complex and extensive as to require a paper, if not a book, in themselves. We are forced by considerations of time and space to be a bit more selective than we would like.

Among Lewin's most important alliances in Germany are those with members of the Psychologische Institut of the University of Berlin: Karl Stumpf, Max Wertheimer, Wolfgang Kohler, and Kurt Koffka. The latter three are generally considered to comprise the Gestalt school.

Koffka may be credited with the introduction of Gestalt psychology to the United States with an article published in the "Psychological Bulletin" in 1922. The travels of Kohler and Koffka also provided some early introduction of Lewin and his work to the United States. In 1925-1926, Kohler visited Harvard and Clark Universities. Koffka spent a year (1924-1925) as a visiting professor at Cornell, another (1926-1927) at the University of Wisconsin, and, in 1927, accepted a professorship in psychology at Smith College. He held this position until his death. The continual cross citations in the works of Kohler, Koffka, Lewin, and Wertheimer are good illustrations of the high regard in which they held each other.

In 1921, the journal "Psychologische Forschung" was founded by Kohler, Koffka, Wertheimer, Hans Bruhle and Kurt Goldstein. Essentially, it was the publishing arm of the Psychologische Institut at Berlin. More of Lewin's work was published in the "Forschung" than any other journal. It is also part of the ground of a close personal and professional relationship between Goldstein and Lewin which can be documented as early as 1926, and may well have begun several years earlier.

Another close relationship prior to 1933 was that between Lewin and Fritz Heider. The relationship, which began in Berlin, deepened and expanded in the United States to include Kurt and Gertrude Lewin and Fritz and Grace Heider. The translation of "Principles of Topological Psychology" is one of the many contributions made by the Heiders to psychology.

Lewin's influence was further spread through the writing and teaching of his students of the Berlin years most of whom became major influences in the continuing development of psychology and social psychology.

JAPAN

Two of Lewin's students, Kanae Sakuma and U. Onoshima came from Japan. Sakuma began his studies with Lewin in 1923 and co-authored a paper with him in 1925. Late in 1925, Sakuma abandoned his doctoral studies and returned to Japan. The abandonment, however, seems to have been no severe handicap. Upon returning to Japan, Sakuma developed a highly successful Psychological Institute at Kyushu University. The seed of Lewinian thought had been planted on fertile ground. Marrow, and several of our informants, report that a group of scholars had formed a Lewin study group in Tokyo prior to 1933. Lewin himself visited Japan in 1933.

SWITZERLAND

The most widely known Swiss psychologist is Jean Piaget. We have been unable to substantiate a direct relation between Lewin and Swiss psychology in general or between Lewin and Piaget in particular. While Lewin's work, prior to and after 1933, refers to Piaget's early descriptive work, Lewin is mentioned only in Piaget's later collaborative works. None of our present information, which is at best sketchy, places the two in the same geographical area at the same time. We have no more than an eliptical comment by Piaget which might be interpreted as indicating a personal acquaintance. More research is needed to clarify this area.

UNITED STATES

There are many contemporary American Psychologists and social psychologists who indicate Lewinian influence. Our immediate interest, however, is in those who knew and were influenced by Lewin prior to 1933. Notable among these are D.I. Adams, J.F. Brown, J.K. Frank, D. MacKinnon, E.C. Tolman and K. Zener.

Adams and Zener did not have Lewin in mind when they went to Germany to study psychology in the mid 1920s. It was under fortuitous conditions that they encountered Lewin in Berlin. Both soon took up study with Lewin. While neither Adams nor Zener are responsible for opening up new areas of psychology, they opened up channels for Lewinian thought. We owe to them inspired translations of eight Lewin papers which are compiled under the title "A Dynamic Theory of Personality."

Junius Brown is another important figure. Brown, like Adams and Zener, seems to have happened upon Lewin accidently. Brown, who went to Berlin in 1927, developed a deep interest in Lewin from the outset of his two years in Berlin. In 1929, Brown published "The Methods of Kurt Lewin in the Psychology of Action and Affection" in the "Psychological Review." The article was a further introduction of Lewinian thought to the United States. In 1936, Brown published "Psychology and the Social Order" which is a unique although naive attempt to merge Lewin and Marx. Brown and Lewin were in contact up to 1940 (Marrow, 1969, pp. 113-114). Brown's life after 1945 remains something of a mystery.

Jerome Frank, influenced by Brown's 1929 paper, went to Berlin with the specific intention of studying with Lewin. Since Frank came late to the scene, his study was interrupted by the events of 1933 and was continued at Cornell.

Donald MacKinnon also went to Berlin intending to study with Lewin. He returned to the United States prior to 1933 to work at the Harvard Psychological Clinic. MacKinnon took his Ph.D. at Harvard in 1933 and soon after accepted a position at Bryn Mawr. He maintained friendly relations with Lewin.

Edward Tolman first visited Germany in 1912 at which time he spent about a month studying with Koffka at Giesen. He returned again to Germany in 1923. It is at this time that Tolman became interested in Lewin's work. While Tolman is generally thought of as a Behaviorist, the influence of Gestalt theory in general and of Lewin in particular is evident in his work. Our review of Tolman's notes for lectures in psychology at Berkeley show a yearly increase in the time given to discussion of Lewin, a trend which is noticeable from the late 1920s.

Gordon Allport also spent time in Germany in 1923. While in Berlin, he studied with Stumpf, Wertheimer and Kohler, but did not encounter Lewin. He did, however, encounter the Lewinian approach and reports being impressed with its brilliance (Allport, 1947).

We can, then, demonstrate the early introduction of Lewin's work to psychologists in the United States prior to 1933 through several channels: visits to the United States by members of the Berlin Psychological Institute; publication in English by Koffka; the writings of J.F. Brown; the return and teaching of Americans who studied with Lewin in Berlin; the work of Americans who encountered Lewin or his work while visiting Germany, and, a point not yet mentioned, Lewin's own visits to the United States.

SOVIET UNION

We have found that if one were to rely solely on the bibliographical references made in the publications of such writers as Lewin, Goldstein, Vigotsky, Luria, Zeigarnik, and others (at least the material in English) one would never know the nature of the relationships between these important scholars, and the extent to which their ideas and work may have been mutually influential. They make few references to each other, and where they do refer to each other, the citations are of limited interest or appear peripheral to the discussion. Our question was whether they had more than a passing familiarity with each other. Certainly, if one were to look at Lewin's publications alone, this would not appear to be the case. Lewin (1951) mentions Vygotsky only twice and not at any length. He mentions Goldstein twice as well, and again not to any length. In Vygotsky's well known book, Thought and Language (1962), Lewin is not mentioned at all. Goldstein mentions Lewin in The Organism once.

Time and space do not allow us to discuss the Lewin-Goldstein connection other than in passing. We want to discuss the connections between Lewin and his group (sometimes referred to as the Berlin Group), and Vygotsky and his group (sometimes referred to as the Moscow Group). We will show that the two groups had parallel ideas, were quite familiar with each other's work, in fact knew each other personally, and their work complemented each other. The period of interest to us includes the years 1918-1933. The period for Vygotsky includes the years 1923-1934 (when he died at the age of 38).

In a recent book entitled Mind in Society (1978), a series of papers by Vygotsky were published posthumously. These papers had all been written prior to Lewin's emigration from Germany. In reading the first four papers, one can't help but be impressed with the similarity in thinking between Vygotsky and Lewin, particularly in the manner in which Vygotsky criticized Pavlovian Behaviorism and Psychoanalytic theory. The nature of his arguments were the same as those of Lewin. Then, in the paper "On Method," Vygotsky states most explicitly and clearly that he is following the ideas and thinking of Lewin in Berlin, particularly the argument presented against the Aristotelian approach and for the Galilean approach to science. In Luria's book The Nature of Human Conflicts (1932), the author repeatedly cited Lewin's work and its importance for their work in the Soviet Union. At one point, Luria said that their own research methods, early in their work, were not satisfactory but after they became familiar with the Berlin Group, they were able to improve the quality of their own research. The research methods developed by the Berlin Group are evident in the research of all of those who worked in the Moscow Group or were trained by them.

Clearly, then, the Moscow Group was very familiar with Lewin's ideas and the research conducted by the Berlin Group. The question is how did they become aware of the work? Did the Moscow Group or members of it read German? Was Lewin's work published in Russian? Neither of these explanations seems plausible. The most obvious explanation, for us, is that the two groups had direct personal contact. Lewin's first seven students were Russian women. The first student was Zeigarnik who received her doctorate degree in 1926, after studying with Lewin and conducting the classic experiment on the recall of completed and incompleted tasks. After finishing her studies, she returned to the Soviet Union and worked at the Psychological Institute of the University of Moscow with Vygotsky, Luria and other members of the Moscow Group. It seems most probable that she introduced Lewin's ideas and work to the Moscow Group.

The second contact between the groups was made by Luria. In 1927-28, Luria visited Berlin and spoke many times to Lewin's seminars.

During this period, they came to know each other very well. The third direct personal contact occurred in 1933. Lewin was invited to the Soviet Union to give a series of lectures. The invitation was extended by Luria; and Lewin stayed at the home of Vygotsky. Vygotsky and Lewin were very compatible during this time. Vygotsky died the following year.

Earlier in this paper, we made mention of Kurt Goldstein, a world known research psychiatrist who did pioneering work on the development of concrete and abstract thinking. Goldstein was not a member of the Berlin Group. However, Goldstein and Lewin were very good friends, particularly after Goldstein came to Berlin in 1926, from the University of Frankfurt. Goldstein came to know Luria when he was in Berlin and became familiar with the work of the Moscow Group. For years after they met, they corresponded about their work. Goldstein's work is frequently cited by members of the Moscow Group.

CONCLUSIONS

As part of our ongoing research on Kurt Lewin's life prior to his emigration to the United States, it has become most evident that extremely little was known about this scholar's interests and activities prior to 1933. Based on our research, we have been impressed with the extent of his international influence prior to his migration. In this paper, we have sought to accomplish two purposes. The first was to sketch out the names of internationally known psychologists, and the countries in which they resided, who were influenced by Lewin's thinking and research of that period. The second objective was to show the extent of his involvement with a group of (at that time dissident) psychologists in the Soviet Union. This Moscow Group, under the leadership of Vygotsky and Luria, came to be very influential in Soviet psychology in later years.

The findings of this phase of our research were based on extensive use of archival material from different parts of the world, oral interviews with scholars who studied with Lewin in the Berlin years, and published material. It is important to emphasize that we have only sketched and discussed his influence on psychology. Elsewhere, his other interests and influences will be discussed.

BIBLIOGRAPHY

Allport, G. (1947). "The Genius of Kurt Lewin" in Journal of Personality, V. 16, pp. 1-10.

Carnap, Rudolf (1978). "Memoirs of Hans Reichenbach." In M. Reischenbach and R. Cohen, Eds., Hans Reichenbach: Selected Writings, 1909-1953. Boston: Reidel Publishing Company.

De Rivera, Joseph (1976). Field Theory as Social Science. New York: Gardner Press.

Goldstein, Kurt (1939). The Organism. New York: Macmillan Company.

Goldstein, K. and Gelb, A. (1924). Uber Farbennamenamnesie nelist Bemerkungen uber des wesen der amnesleschen Aphasie uberhaupt und die Beziehung zivischen Sprache und dem Verbatten zur Umwelt, Psychol. Forsch., 6, 127-187.

Lewin, K. (1920a). Die Verwandtschaftsbegriffe in Biologie und Physik und die Darstellung vollstandiger Stammbaume. Berlin: Borntrager.

Lewin, K. (1920b). "Die Verwandschaftsbergrigge in Biologie und Physik und die Darstellung vollstandiger Stammbaume." Abhandlung zur Thoretischer Biologie 5, 1-34.

Lewin, K. (1920c). Der Ordnungstypus der genetischen Reihen in Physik, organismischer Biologie und Enwicklungageschichte. Berlin: Borntrager.

Lewin, K. (1922). Der Begriff der Genese in Physik, Biologie, und Entwicklungsgeschichte. Berlin: Julius Springer.

Lewin, K. (1926). "Uber Idee und Aufgabe der vergleichenden Wissenshaftslehre." Symposium, Vol. 1, #1, pp. 61-93.

Lewin, K. (1935). A Dynamic Theory of Personality, translated by D. Adams and K. Zener. New York: McGraw-Hill.

Lewin, K. (1951). Field Theory in Social Science. New York: Harper & Brothers Publishers, pp. 60-87.

Luria, A.S. (1932). Nature of Human Conflicts. New York: Liverwright.

Marrow, A. J. (1969). The Practical Theorist. New York: Basic Books, Inc.

Michotte, A. (1952). "Albert Michotte." In E. G. Boring, et al., Eds. A History of Psychology in Autobiography (Vol. 4). Worcester, Mass.: Clark University Press.

Vygotsky, L. S. (1962). Thought and Language. Cambridge: M.I.T. Press.

Vygotsky, L. S. (1978). Mind in Society. Cambridge: Harvard University Press.

The man in Transition: Kurt Lewin and his Times[1]

Vytautas J. Cernius

Temple University

THE BEGINNINGS

Kurt Lewin was born September 9, 1890 in Mogilno, Poland. Mogilno is a small town situated about mid-point between Poznan and the Visla, the river which flows from the Carpath Mountains into the Baltic Sea. Since the last partition of Poland in 1795 the little town had become part of Prussia. The official language, the law, the governing institutions were German. And so were many of the leading towns people. But the villages surrounding this small town, the nobility and the simple people in the town were Polish.

Among the ethnic Germans, Poles and officials from Germany, lived a small minority of Jews, who ran their little businesses, engaged in trades or in some other ways tried to make their living.

The Lewins were Jewish. They had a village store and a small farm. They dealt with Poles and with the Germans. They were aware that they did not belong to either group although there was more identification with Germans than with Poles. As Kurt himself is supposed to have said, he was aware that Jews were somehow different from most Germans (Schellenberg, 1978). One may speculate to what extent these early experiences of ethnic and group differences may have provided the impetus in his later years to explore ethnic and cultural differences and issues.

In this world of hard work, the progress and the promise of better life came from Germany. And so Kurt after attending the elementary school in Mogilno, went to Junior High School (1900-1905) at the Province Capital Posen (Poznan) and Kaiserin Augusta Gymnasium (1906-1909) in Charlottenburg, Berlin (Evered, 1984).

---

[1] Much of the biographical information was provided by Lewin's daughter Miriam, and his former students Kurt Back, Tamara Dembo, Ronald Lippitt, Maria Rickers-Ovsiankina, Albert and Emmy Pepitone, and Ralph White.

PRE-WORLD WAR I GERMANY

Kurt Lewin grew up in a Europe which after the Franco-German war of 1870-71 enjoyed long years of tranquility and peace. The Arts and Sciences flourished. Society exuded order, stability, progress and a hopeful future. People were hard working, striving for respectability, devoted to their country and the Monarch.

Europe seemed to be at the apex of civilization. Technology was coming up with marvelous inventions and improvements. Ships sped across the oceans, express trains rushed from one end of the continent to the other, telephone and telegraph linked the cities. Hunger, plague and other diseases seemed to be conquered. And even the aggression, which so frequently had led to war, seemed to have been curtailed into controllable, civilized channels. Thus, in 1899 at the initiative of Russian Czar Nikolaus the Hague Peace Conference was called together which led to the foundation of the International World Court in The Hague. This court was supposed to make judgements among nations so that a war would become unnecessary. Kaiser Wilhelm II, King George, Czar Nikolaus, Emperor Franz-Joseph II, and the industrialist and philanthropist Andrew Carnegie, contributed the building, furniture, and art objects to the Palace of Peace which was occupied in 1913.

And the Geneva Convention, which had been signed previously (1864) provided a code for the treatment of the sick and wounded and the prisoners of war and sought to protect hospitals. Yes, even aggression seemed to have been gotten under control so that war would become just an organized, fair-play game not unlike soccer.

Yes, Europe was on the edge of the Golden Age of Rationality. And especially the life in Germany seemed to be so well-ordered, stable, secure and full of hope. After all, Germany had the most educated population. Everybody could read and write. And was not education the cure to social evils? The civil service was most efficient, an envy of other countries. German products ("Made in Germany") were highly respected and desired through the world. Bismark (1815-1898), the Great Chancellor of Germany, ahead of everyone else, had laid the first foundations, for social security, unemployment compensation, and health protection. And so even the fears of illness, unemployment, and old age were diminishing. Life was good in Germany.

Kurt having finished the respected Kaiserin Augusta Gymnasium in Charlottenburg turned to University study. In the beginning, in the best German student tradition he did some university hopping. At first (1909) he thought of studying medicine. He went to Freiburg and enrolled in medicine and philosophy, but then switched to Munich and in 1910 changed to Berlin for philosophy and psychology. And here he stayed for nine semesters to finish with a doctoral examination September 10, 1914 (Evered, 1984).

WORLD WAR I

But Central Europe since August 1 was at war. And Kurt Lewin, who considered himself a German, rushed as a volunteer with all the other Germans to the army. The youth went enthusiastically into the war. Only a few months ago many of them with a guitar in hand were singing about their first love and discussing the meaning of life, but now they dropped the guitars and seized rifles. There was enthusiasm, newness and adventure. But by 1915 the slaughter began in earnest. The machine-guns and other modern weapons drove the fighting into the trenches. Here they killed and maimed and were killed and were maimed. Things and words began to have a different meaning. Kurt Lewin in his essay "Kriegsland-schaft" (Battlefield-scape), (Lewin, 1917), describes how the meaning of the surroundings changes as one moves from the safety of the back of the front closer to the frontline. Eventually, these observations led to the formulation of the "field theory."

As the slaughter went on, the frontlines moved back and forth and the group mentality began to be more and more absorbed either with the destruction of the others or being destroyed by others. The abstraction "the enemy" emerged. "The enemy" was depersonalized and dehumanized. It was "bad", "evil", a projection of one's own evilness, own destructiveness. It had to be destroyed. The group--the state--rewarded those who inflicted the most damage on the enemy. The "enemy" was bombed, gassed, burned and driven out of its houses. Physical violence became accepted. Individual responsibility, the deeds and misdeeds, the virtues, and beliefs of the individual did not count. He was judged only as a member of a group, a collective. He was "good" or "bad" simply because he belonged or not belonged to a particular national, religious, ideological group or social class. The complex assessment of an individual's conduct, his contributions to his family, community, humanity, and his crimes against others was now replaced by a simplified categorization of individuals into groups and viewing them as "bad" or "good" and therefore destined to be destroyed or preserved. The passport, the birth certificate, and the language spoken became the tickets to life. or death. During the war all of the states reduced individual freedom and rights. The state made the judgement which groups were to be hated and which to be loved. And the World War I slaughter went on, until in 1917 and 1918 first the Russian, then the Austro-Hungarian and German Empires began to collapse. The war ended (Johnson, 1983).

GERMANY AFTER WORLD WAR I

Kurt Lewin, the ex-lieutenant of the Kaiser army, the wounded veteran, found himself in the midst of the unstable turbulence of the Weimar Republic. In different parts of Berlin there were different political factions with more or less loyal armed groups. There were endless political discussions as to the most recent history and the future of Germany. And there were attempts by various groups to unseat the government and to capture state power. Democracy had won the war. Democracy preached pluralism, respect for individuals' rights, acknowledged political diversity and minority representation. But in Germany, democracy represented the defeat, the stab in the back where the politicians turned against the undefeated army and forced the defeat of Germany. There were so many different dreams: bringing the Kaiser back; making Germany the ideal democracy; making life possible inspite of the huge reparations to be paid, loss of territories, and rampaging inflation which soon became a financial disaster. And there were huge masses which subscribed to totalitarianism.

Kurt Lewin after the return from the army ended up working with Wolfgang Koehler, Kurt Koffka and Max Wertheimer at the Psychological Institute of Berlin. It was a lively, intellectually exciting and productive group. While the three of his colleagues continued to develop the Gestalt theory, Lewin, in addition to his theoretical work, began to extend Gestalt theory to issues of everyday life. He wrote about the development and psychology of children, rationalization of agricultural units, effectiveness of agriculture and industrial workers.

Kurt was a keen observer who placed what he observed into some theoretical framework. Thus, Bluma Zeigarnik's dissertation ("Zeigarnik Effect") owes its start to his observation in Berlin's coffee shops that a waiter remembers without any notes what everyone of the guest has ordered but forgets as soon as it is paid ("completed task") (Schellenberg, 1978).

The Berlin years were productive. Lewin wrote close to thirty manuscripts, some of them extensive, up to two-hundred pages (Evered,

1984). Many of them were published in German philosophical and psychological journals. He began to be known in Germany and abroad.

Meanwhile, Germany was going through emotional, social and economic spasms. There were riots, Nazi and Communist claims for power, the changing governments, unemployment, the erasure of the accustomed German law-and-order. England, France, and the USA were also caught in their economic and political problems. Political movements emerged which claimed to have solutions to problems. They said that they had the absolute social and political truth and were grabbing the power to take the masses to paradise if not today then for sure tomorrow.

In the natural sciences, however, in some respects the world of absolute truths and absolute belief systems collapsed on 29th of May 1919 when photographs taken on the coast of West Africa and in Brazil confirmed Einstein's Theory of Relativity. Among other things it proved that space and time are rather relative than absolute, dependent upon a particular set of elements and relationships. It took some time before the concept of relativity began to change the perceptions of the physical world and increase our understanding of the physical universe. But eventually the concept of relativity began to change our views of social reality as well (Johnson, 1983).

But this was not the case in Europe in the nineteen twenties and thirties. Strong passions were swaying the people. Democracy had won the war and was the new magical formula which was supposed to bring justice, eliminate oppression, and secure the well-being of the masses. And all the newly emerged nationalistic states spouted democratic governments, which proclaimed the rights of individuals and minorities. But only very few of the young European democracies actually did adhere to these promises. Czechoslovakia was a shining example of a flourishing democracy and Weimar-Germany too, although here democracy labored under the strains of a lost war, inflation, reparations, unemployment and the battle between the totalitarian groups--the Communists and the National Socialists. But there was still the "Weimarer Traum" (dream) of the idealized democracy and the rebirth of Germany. In Europe in general, especially in the new born states, democracy began to wither as more and more of the newly emerged national states succumbed to semiauthoritarian or authoritarian regimes.

The authoritarian regimes and the mass movements which claimed to be in possession of the Absolute Plan, the Absolute Truth, viewed the individual with suspicion and glorified the collectivity, the group and its leaders as the centralizations of wisdom, planning and action. These regimes and movements repressed those who thought differently, they re-

stricted or counted individual freedom to be irrelevant, and insisted
on patterns of interaction and living which emerged out of their theories. The Theory, The Belief triumphed. Lives and life patterns not
consistent with the Theory, the Belief were declared as non-existent.
The psychological and physical terror began to emerge.

The first one-party terror-state emerged in Russia. Some observers
of the Russian psyche note that Russians tend to believe that people
can not be trusted, that left to themselves they tend to be selfish,
irrational, given to the immediate pursuit of pleasure, unable to govern
themselves. They need authority to give direction, to control their
irrationality, to engage people in work for the mutual benefit. The
authority is to provide the reality principle and save the masses for
their redemption. These conscious and unconscious beliefs defined the
Czars' regime and after 1917 the Red dictatorship. The Red dictatorship
established itself in a rural, poor, and poorly educated society. Russia
was backward and had never developed societal mechanisms to bring about
evolutionary progress. The emergence of the communist regime was accompanied by the death of millions of people through starvation, exhaustion,
and bullets. Whole groups of people were declared as enemies, or were
sacrificed to implement various five-year plans. The old autocrats were
destroyed or declared non-existent but the new were even more ruthless,
fed by the zeal of the new converts.

There were political and social changes going on around and within
Germany. Life in Germany was interesting. In the post-War I years
Berlin, Munich and Frankfurt were places where arts and sciences flourished and new concepts and perspectives emerged. Berlin in particular
was the midpoint of Central Europe. This is where the East and the West,
the South and the North met. Herr Aussenordentlicher (extraordinary)
Professor of Philosophy and Psychology at the University of Berlin, Dr.
Lewin, was stimulated by what was happening around him. This was a very
creative period. He published and he conducted experimental studies to
be "one of the most distinguished group of empirical studies in the
psychological literature." Lewin became known and was invited to lecture
in England, France, Holland, Denmark, the U.S.S.R., and Japan.

THE NEW BEGINNING

In 1932 Lewin came as a visiting professor for a brief period of
time to Stanford University, in the U.S.A. In Germany the National

Socialists were pushing for power. On January 30, 1933, Adolf Hitler became the Chancellor of Germany. Kurt Lewin sought a job in the United States and in 1933 with his second wife and their young child moved to Cornell University (1933-1935), and later to the University of Iowa Child Welfare Research Station (1935-1944). Many of the best known American social psychologists were trained there by him. In 1945 he became the Professor, founder and director of The Research Center for Group Dynamics at the Massachusetts Institute of Technology (MIT). He died from a heartattack in 1947, at the age of 57 (Marrow, 1969).

So the man who was born in the German West-Prussian town of Mogilno (the town was part of Poland when he left Europe) studied in Freiburg, Munich and Berlin ended up in Newton, Massachusetts, U.S.A. Little did he or others anticipate that he was a precursor of a stream of millions of refugees and deportees of the late thirties and forties moving through Europe and other continents and looking for safety. And this stream did not stop with World War II. Much has happened since his birth. He reached the safety of U.S.A., but in Germany, Kurt Lewin's mother, most of his relatives and many of his friends perished. The Jewish community of Mogilno was wiped out. While all this was happening, while he was moving from place to place, what was going on inside of him? What thoughts, what feelings did he have? Did he redefine his own identity as he moved from country to country, from Europe to the U.S.A.?

The transition from the little Polish-Jewish-German town of Mogilno to Germany proper seems to have been easy. He was a success. He graduated from Kaiserin-Augusta Gymnasium in Charlottenburg, then completed his studies at the University of Berlin with a doctorate when he was 24. He volunteered for the German Army, was decorated with the Iron Cross, became a Lieutenant, and was a respected, wounded war veteran. After the war, he became a privatdozent and eventually an extraordinary professor at the University of Berlin. He published about 40 articles in German (Evered, 1984). None of the articles deal in any way with the experiential, the transitional aspects of his life. The only possible exception is the "Kriegslandschaft" (Battlefield-scape) article in which he apparently uses his own experiences as a soldier as he moves from the peaceful rear to the frontlines.

What was the transition for Kurt Lewin from Germany to the U.S.A.? After all it was forced upon him suddenly by the political events in Germany. It meant moving from a country where he felt at home, knew the language, had friends, and was valued to a new and strange country and a language which was foreign to him. It was a transition from being a citizen to being an immigrant and refugee. While all this was happening

what went on inside of him? How did he see himself? How did he feel?
Was he a Jew, a German, an American?

His years in U.S.A. were very productive. Out of this period there
are sixty publications (Evered, 1984). His papers dealt with everyday
social problems (change, food habits, conflict), topographical psychology, frustration and regression in children, field theory, aggression,
experimentation, leadership, dynamics of groups, philosophy of science,
and the re-education of Germany. Eight of the papers focus on minority
problems, issues of ethnic identity, and adjustment of minority members
in the U.S.A. He wrote about psycho-social problems of a minority group
(1935), social-psychological differences between the United States and
Germany (1936), bringing up the Jewish child (1940), self-hatred among
Jews (1941), action research and minority problems (1946), research on
minority problems (1946), Jewish education and reality (1944), and psychological problems in Jewish education (1949). Were these articles his
catharsis, his way of coming to terms with his own roots, his identity
in a new country? This question was presented to his former students:
Tamara Dembo, Kurt Back, Emmy Pepitone and his daughter Miriam. According to them Kurt Lewin was always very absorbed in the here-and-now problems of the situation, maybe his research, or a contractual project, or
a dissertation of one of his students. He never talked about his past,
his roots, or his identity. He was a Jew,--this was a fact--and he did
not spend much time on it. According to his former students, the articles dealing with with being a minority member were the result of the
contracts which he obtained from various Jewish organizations in the
U.S.A. And yet who knows what was going on inside this man in the early
morning hours when he was all by himself?

After all he was a man who had made the transition from Mogilno,
a small, poor village, to the illustrious halls of the Massachusetts
Institute of Technology and the tree-shaded streets of Newton, Mass.
He began his life in one century and ended in another. He was a man who
within the context of his time had to solve problems of living so that
he could survive and create. He grew from a youngster to a central figure of an extended group of men and women from many countries who seek
to understand the forces acting upon us so that we can remain masters of
our own fate.

REFERENCES

Evered, R. (1984). An Exploration of Kurt Lewin's Contributions to the Social Sciences. Philadelphia: Department of Psychoeducational Processes, Temple University.

Johnson, P. (1983). Modern Times, The World from the Twenties to the Eighties. New York: Harper and Row.

Lewin, K. (1917). "Kriegslandschaft", Zeitschrift fur angewandte Psychologie, 12, p. 440-447.

Lewin, K. (1935). "Psycho-Sociological Problems of a Minority Group," Character and Personality, 3, p. 175-187.

Lewin, K. (1936). "Some Social-Psychological Differences between the United States and Germany," Character and Personality, 4, p. 265-293.

Lewin, K. (1940). "Bringing up the Jewish Child," Menorah Journal, 28, p. 29-45.

Lewin, K. (1941). "Self-hatred among Jews," Contemporary Jewish Record, 4, p. 219-232.

Lewin, K. (1944). "Jewish Education and Reality," Jewish Education, 15, No. 3.

Lewin, K. (1946). "Action Research and Minority Problems," Journal of Social Issues, 2, p. 34-46.

Lewin, K. (1946). "Research on Minority Problems," The Technology Review, 48, No. 3., pp. 163-164, 182 (Jan.).

Lewin, K. (1949). Psychological Problems in Jewish Education, published by the Jewish Education Committee.

Marrow, A.J. (1969). The Practical Theorist, The Life and Work of Kurt Lewin. New York: Basic Books.

Schellenberg, J.A. (1978). Masters of Social Psychology, Freud, Mead, Lewin and Skinner. New York: Oxford University Press.

Kurt Lewin's Influence on Social Emotional Climate Research in Germany and the United States

Matthias v. Saldern

Center of Educational Research, Landau, Federal Republic of Germany

Social emotional climate research is not new in Germany. Many of the older scientists already wrote about problems like group climate or atmosphere. No doubt, the importance of social climate was recognized many years before the first questionnaire concerning this subject matter was constructed. Social climate is a typically psychological problem, because it is significant for human behavior.

Climate can be defined as the shared experiences of members in a group. With other words, social climate exists whenever every individual of a group constructs the same subjective environment in a common objective one. This is the basic definition; obviously others can be found in the literature (Withall, 1949; Chemnitz, 1978).

Sometimes climate is characterized as the "personality" of an environment (Moos, 1979). This comparison is quite illustrative, because the common judgement of many persons concerning the individual is defined exactly in this way. The word climate came from meteorology, but it is originally based on a Greek word which was used by Aristotle to describe the height of the sun.

Unfortunately this word has been transferred into human sciences. Climate implicates a long-term subjective world of the individuals of a group. But if the researcher is interested in fast changes of the subjective environment, "weather" might be the more appropriate term (Diederich, 1984).

In spite of the existence of earlier European philosophical thought concerning subjective definitions of the world, the social emotional climate research itself has come to Germany from the United States. There were especially the two American research groups around Moos and Walberg, who are both well known in Germany. These two groups again influenced an Australian research project (Fraser, Fisher) as well as a number of German scientists (Fend, Kahl, Dreesmann). The problem is that these projects were not led by theoretical considerations, but by well-known questionnaires of Moos and Walberg. Accordingly research was to a large extent "theoryless."

Empirical results available at this point show that the subjective view of the world can be utilized as a valid predictor for individual and group behavior. At this point attempts are being made in younger research projects to find out the theoretical foundation for these results so to speak a posteriori (v. Saldern, 1984).

Theoretical Foundations of Social-Emotional Climate Research

There is no question about the importance of Lewin's definition of the environment as a subjective one. But in the scientific world he was not the first who tried to include this definition into a broad theory of human behavior.

An early group at the University of Chicago created a theory which is well-known as Symbolic Interactionism. One of the founders of this was W.I. Thomas, after whom the wide spread Thomas-Theorem was named: If men define situations as real, they are real in their consequences (Thomas & Thomas, 1928). So the definition of a situation is a construction of reality (Ball, 1970). The most important aspect of climate research is the fact that the environment is only similar for all persons in a group as long as they all construct the social reality in the same way.

Next to W.I. Thomas stood C.H. Cooley, who tried to find synthesis between the pure behaviorism (Watson) and the pragmatism in its American form (Helle, 1977). Already in 1926 he distinguished between objective environment and social reality. Thomas and F. Znaniecki (1981) enlarged upon this thought in the following way: the person is the subjective factor, society the objective one. The person is able to change the objective environment by means of action. The empirical research of Thomas and his colleagues about Polish people who immigrate to the United States shows that the process of adjustment to the new culture is one of the most interesting group processes someone can explore.

G.H. Mead, the most prominent figure of Symbolic Interactionism, did not publish very much. His student H. Blumer (1969) however reviewed the theory of Symbolic Interactionism in a way which shows the parallel to Lewin's theory:

1. A person acts because of the meaning of the objective world.
2. The meaning of this world results from the interactions with other persons. Meaning is a social product.
3. A person can change meanings by communicating with himself or with others.

The link between Lewin and Thomas can be found in their common definition of situation. Lewin defined environment or situation as a subjective one, Thomas and the later Symbolic Interactionists tried to express the same idea with the term "meaning of the world."

Another aspect is common to both of their concepts: the difficulty to distinguish between the subject and the object in the methodological transfer into empirical research. This is obviously one reason why both theories open the way to action research and to ethnomethodology.

It has been shown that Symbolic Interactionism is the older theory compared to Lewin's, with some similar assumptions which can be the basis for climate research. It would be very interesting historically to find out whether Lewin knew the work of W.I. Thomas. One year before Lewin was born (1889), Thomas visited Berlin, the later domain of Lewin. There is no known indication that Lewin ever had contact with the early Chicago School. According to my knowledge he never cited Thomas or other Symbolic Interactionists.

There are several other theoretical concepts which have had an influence on social climate research. In the following some of these concepts are described and compared to Lewin's ideas.

Sometimes the scientific impact of Lewin's theories did not find its way to social emotional climate research directly, but rather indirectly via later theories.

At first glance the environmental psychology of J.F. Wohlwill (1970) seems very interesting for social climate research. Wohlwill prefers a simple model in which human behavior is explained by the objective environment and the person. At the same time the person is influenced by the environment. On the other hand the environment is determined by the behavior of a person.

Wohlwill criticizes certain concepts, for example those of Lewin, because the subjective environment confounds person and objective environment: if environment is a function of behavior and again behavior a function of environment, nobody can distinguish between the two. Accordingly, Wohlwill wrote about the "circularity of behavior and environment" (Wohlwill, 1973; Becker, 1978).

As will be described in detail later, some theoretical concepts include the objective environment as an exogene variable. The problem is, how to conceive the objective world as it is. Since the famous German philosopher Immanuel Kant, it has been generally accepted that world is subjective per se.

So an important question in psychology has been answered in detail by philosophers of science. Some articles of Lewin show that he was interested in these problems, which were not necessarily an integral part of his own discipline. Lewin was well informed about the Vienna Circle ("Wiener Kreis"), where philosophical problems were discussed informally. The question to what degree and when Lewin's work was influenced by this group, would be of great interest here.

Another very interesting theory comes from R.G. Barker (1968), who was Lewin's colleague and received the Kurt-Lewin-Memorial-Award in 1963. Barker's "ecological psychology" (which should not be confused with the same term as it was used by E. Brunswik) characterizes Lewin's theory as an "encapsulated psychology," because it ignored extra-personal factors. Barker himself concentrates his research on these factors. His main environmental unit is called "behavior setting", an attempt to describe and explain the connection between behavior and environment (Synomorphy). This "bio-physical unit" (Barker's wife was a biologist) forces many individuals to a very similar behavior. Thus Schoggen defines the behavior setting as an "environmental force unit." Empirical results show that Barker was able to describe human communities precisely with this concept. But this was done with a very high methodological expenditure and not on the basis of a sound theory (Barker himself calls ecological data atheoretical).

Barker's deterministic approach shows in the sense of Lewin that the comparison of many individuals can lead to extra-personal values and determinators of human behavior. This is, of course, a fruitful result for social climate research. The sociological norm-concept supports this result as well. There is one central point among others where we can find a decisive difference between Lewin and Barker: whereas theory was most important for Lewin, it was irrelevant for Barker.

In recent years the discussion of Lewin's and Brunswik's (1943, 1955) theories has come to the foreground (see Wolf, 1983).

The main difference between these two scientists can be found in their definition of environment. Brunswik prefers to work with the "distal stimulus" as it exists physically. So Brunswik's criticism in respect to Lewin is, that the latter was not able to systematize environment and its different meanings. The description of Brunswik's theory is given by Bernhard Wolf (another paper in this section). No doubt Brunswik's concept could have been as successful as Lewin's in the United States. But Brunswik could not adjust to the new situation as an immigrant as well as Lewin did. Also he had problems in learning the language of his new country. The formulation of his theory

as well as his thought concerning experimental design and philosophy
of science are of great interest for present research.

The impact of Brunswik's theory, however, could not be as far-
reaching as Lewin's because the transfer from theory into practice can
be carried out more easily in Lewin's concept. There are only a few
empirical research projects published which refer to Brunswik. Some of
these projects (Jessor & Jessor, 1977) even come to interpretations which
show great parallels to Lewin's concept.

Another theory to describe and explain human behavior is the need-
press-concept of H. Murray (1938). His influence on social climate
research was similar to that of Lewin's, especially in the thirties.
He recognized early that psychology was not able to explain human behavior if the environment was not included. Murray's concept is a kind
of early interactionism of environmental influences (press) and personal
necessities (needs). Needs and press are related to each other in sets,
which are called "themes." The new idea of Murray was the distinction
between the objective environment (alpha press) and the environment
as it is seen by the person (beta press). Beta press and the needs
lead to behavior, which is a result of the difference in relation
between the two.

G. Stern (1970) made an important contribution to Murray's concept:
the beta press is divided into consensual and private beta press. Whenever persons of one group experience the same beta press, it is a
consensual one, in other cases it would be called private beta press.
Stern's idea is obviously important for social climate research, because, with it, the group itself has become a subject of research.
This concept can be accepted in the sense of Lewin: The objective
environment is outside of the person and not directly related to human
behavior.

Some empirical work based on Murray's concept has been carried out
in Germany. It is not solved, however, how the connection between press
and needs works. Murray himself left it open. There are also some
other reasons, why Lewin's theory is more effective. Murray did not
consider that a need can lead to a specific view of the environment.
Accordingly needs and press are not independent factors. The distinction is therefore an artificial one.

Considering this realization we have once again to rely upon Lewin.

A scientist who considers himself to have followed in Lewin's
footsteps is U. Bronfenbrenner. He characterizes Lewin as a giant in
social sciences. Bronfenbrenner's aim is to specify the topological
regions developed by Lewin, which were formulated, however, only in a

very abstract way. Each of Lewin's regions has a value of its own;
Bronfenbrenner tries to describe these in a hierarchical structure of
systems. The basic system is the microsystem, which can be described
as the subjective world of a person. The others given by Bronfenbrenner are the meso-, exo- and macrosystem. The mesosystem is a set
of settings, which are important for the person (family, peers). The
exo-system includes mass media, working world and so on. The macrosystem is the culture or political system in which a person lives.

Bronfenbrenner's units are valuable in order to describe the
behavior of any person. If someone tries to explain the difference
in the behavior of two students in a class, the microsystem is more
important than, for example, the macrosystem. Thus the value of this
concept can be seen in the intercultural comparison of human behavior.
Considering this it can be seen as an extension of Lewin's theory. For
social climate research the microsystem is the most important unit,
which again is, in some respect, only a reformulation of Lewin's ideas
concerning cognitive development in an impressive way: the development of a person is the development of the way a person sees his/her
environment. In social climate research we find only few longitudinal
studies, but it seems that the results of these few support the above
hypothesis.

One concept which belongs to the psychology of thought seems to
be very useful for the discussion of person-environment interaction.
It is called the "concept of isomorphy." The authors (Derter, Dreher
& Dreher, 1977) criticize the various theories in the psychology of
thought, because according to them these theories exclude the environment from thought processes. Oerter et al. define the objective
environment as the "objective structure," whereas its cognitive representation is called the "subjective structure." So they prefer the
same dichotomy as Murray, for example. When two elements of the
objective and subjective structure correspond, then this is an "isomorphism." Isomorphism can be accomplished by means of action. Beyond
the subjective structure in the person there is internal value which
is similar to the needs defined by Murray. Both influence the "executive," which itself can change the subjective structure and lead to
behavior.

The basic idea of this concept is not a new one. It is, however,
not necessarily of greater value than the need-press model has been
for the explanation of human behavior.

It is only natural that social climate research cannot neglect
the well-known dispute called the interactionism-debate. Everybody

is familiar with the three concepts for the explanation of human
behavior: personalism, situationalism and interactionism. No doubt
the first two were not very useful and a step backwards compared to
Lewin's ideas. The early interactionism had a purely mechanical view
of the problems, a view which was not productive. The later inter-
actionism--the dynamic one--undoubtedly rediscovered Lewin or the
Symbolic Interactionism by including the subjective situation in explaining human behavior (see books and articles by Endler and Magnusson).
Again it should be interesting to ask why scientific simplifications
like personalism, situationalism and the early form of interactionism
could have been of such a great influence.

A last scientific group of theories to be discussed are the social
learning theories of Rotter (1955), Mischel (1968) and Bandura (1979).
These theories do not work when the subjective situation is excluded.
The difference to Lewin is the more differentiated analysis of the
processes of how the definition of the situation is developed. Lewin
talked about a field "at a given time" and thus restricts the definition of a situation to a certain point of time. Social learning theories
assume that the definition of the situation depends on the individual
learning history. With this they are a welcome completion of Lewin.

This short discussion of different theories shows that there are
enough resources for social-emotional climate research. Most of these
theories are undoubtedly influenced by Lewin's definition of the situation. Theories which are in opposition to Lewin's cannot easily be
transferred into practice. Some theories can be seen as a welcome
addition to Lewin's concept.

All of the discussed theories contain statements about individuals
and their view of the environment. Social emotional climate, however,
is a construct, which applies to groups and not to one individual.
So it must be taken into account that the above theories can be a first
step, but are not a sufficient theoretical foundation for social emotional climate research. The second step necessary here would be the
explanation of why different individuals come to the same subjective
environment. This leads us to the problem of group dynamics and processes, which is an another broad area and therefore excluded here.
Another interesting question is, whether the theories applicable to
social-emotional climate are explicitly used in present research
projects.

Lewin's Empirical Contribution to Social Emotional Climate Research

It has always been stressed that Lewin's contribution to social emotional climate research was primarily a theoretical one. It may be appropriate to raise the question whether Lewin and his collegues contributed empirical results as well. One important article by Lewin, Lippitt & White (1939) stands for many empirical studies of this group. In "Patterns of aggressive behavior in experimentally created 'social climates'" the authors investigate and discuss human behavior in different social emotional climates. This research project may have been motivated by the political events in Lewin's mother country.

It has been said before that Moos created the term "personality" to describe the climate of a group. The above mentioned article, however, shows that this way of reducing the complex information about a group was used already before Moos. Here Lewin et al. talked about the "individuality of the club."

At first glance, this article is not associated with social emotional climate research, but primarily with leadership style investigations. Lewin and his group created a new research strategy, which initiated many publications and follow-up research projects in this area.

Up to the famous book by Duncan & Biddle (1974) climate was synonymous with leadership style. It was even later that social emotional climate research became an independent discipline.

Another very important part of the large and famous work done by Lewin is his social research in factories. Lewin and his group are the founders of organizational climate research (see Schneider). It can be observed that today there are two traditions of social emotional climate research: one applies to the domain of education, the other to the field of industrial management. Both traditions have the same theoretical background, but did not have any stimulating effects on each other. Today theories and empirical studies in organizational climate research are far more differentiated than in scholastic research. It cannot be denied that the sources of this differentiation can be found in the early work of Lewin in organizational research.

In summary, the characterization of Lewin as given by Bronfenbrenner as a "brilliant giant" can be strongly supported when we analyze social emotional climate research today.

REFERENCES

Ball, D.W. (1972). The Definition of the Situation: Some Theoretical and Methodological Consequences of Taking W.I. Thomas Seriously. Journal for the Theory of Social Behavior, 2, 61-82.

Bandura, A. (1979). Sozial-kognitive Lerntheorie. Stuttgart: Klett.

Barker, R.G. (1963). On the Nature of the Environment. Journal of Social Issues, 19, 17-34.

Barker, R. G. and Associates (Edts.) (1978). Habits, Environments, and Human Behavior. San Francisco: Jossey-Bass.

Becker, F.D., Bossert, S.T. (1978). Ecological Theory of Teaching. San Francisco: Far West Laboratory for Educational Research.

Blumer, H. (1969). Symbolic Interactionism: Perspective and Method. Englewood Cliffs.

Bronfenbrenner, U. (1977). Lewinian Space and Ecological Substance. Journal of Social Issues, 33, 199-212.

Brunswik, E. (1943). Organismic Achievement and Environmental Probability. Psychological Review, 50, 225-272.

Brunswik, E. (1955). Representative Design and Probabilistic Theory in a Functional Psychology. Psychological Review, 62, 193-216.

Chemnitz, G. (1978). Das sozio-emotionale Klima in Schulklassen. Dissertation, Johannes-Gutenberg-Universitat Mainz.

Diederich, J. (1984). Schulklima - Konzeptuelle Implikate einer Analogie. In: Ingenkamp, K. (Ed.), 59-68.

Dreesmann, H. (1982). Classroom Climate: Contributions from a European Country. Studies in Educational Evaluation, 8, 53-64.

Endler, N.S. (1973). The Case for Person - Situation Interactions. Canadian Psychological Review, 16, 12-21.

Fend, H. (1977). Schulklima. Weinheim: Beltz.

Fisher, D.L., Fraser, B.J. (1983). A Comparison of Actual and Preferred Classroom Environments as Perceived by Science Teachers and Students. Journal of Research in Science Teaching, 20, 55-61.

Fraser, B. J. (1980). Research in Classroom Learning Environment in the 1970's and 1980's. Studies in Educational Evaluation, 6, 221-223.

Jessor, R., Jessor, S.L. (1973). The Perceived Environment in Behavioral Science. American Behavioral Scientist, 16, 801-828.

Kahl, T.N. (1977). Unterrichtsforschung: Probleme, Methoden und Ergebnisse der empirischen Untersuchung unterrichtlicher Lernsituationen. Kronberg: Scriptor.

Lewin, K., Lippitt, R., White, R.K. (1939). Patterns of Aggressive Behavior in Experimentally Created Social Climates. Journal of Social Psychology, 10, 271-299.

Magnusson, D. (1974). The Individual in the Situation. Studia Psychologica, 16, 124-132.

Magnusson, D. (1981). Toward a Psychology of Situations: an Interactional Perspective. Hillsdale: Lawrence.

Mischel, W. (1973). Toward a Cognitive Social Learning Reconceptualization of Personality. Psychological Review, 81, 252-283.

Moos, R., Gerst, M. (1974). University Residence Environment Scale Manual. Palo Alto: Consulting Psychologist Press.

Murray, H.A. (1938). Explorations in Personality. New York: Oxford University Press.

Oerter, R., Dreher, E., Dreher, M. (1977). Kognitive Sozialisation und subjektive Struktur. Munchen: Oldenbourg.

Rotter, J.B. (1981). The Psychological Situation in Social-Learning Theory. In Magnusson, D. (Ed.), 169-178.

Saldern, M. v. (1983). Das Sozialklima als gruppenspezifische Wahrnehmung der schulischen Lernumwelt. Unterrichtswissenschaft, 11, 116-128.

Saldern, M. v. (1984). Sozialklima - ein historisch-theoretischer Abrib. In Ingenkamp, K. (Ed.), 47-58.

Schneider, B. (1972). Organizational Climate: Individual Preference and Organizational Realities. Journal of Applied Psychology, 6, 211-217.

Schoggen, P. (1978). Environmental Forces on Physically Disabled Children. In Barker, R.G. and Associates (Eds.), 125-145.

Stern, G.G. (1970). People in Context. New York: Wiley.

Thomas, W., Thomas, D.S. (1928). The Child in America. New York: Knopf.

Thomas, W., Znaniecki, F. (1981). The Polish Peasant in Europe and America. In Furnham, A. & Argyle, M. (Eds.), 7-11.

Walberg, H.J. (Ed.) (1979). Educational Environments and Effects: Evaluation, Policy and Productivity. Berkley: McCutchan.

Withall, J. (1949). The Development of a Technique for the Measurement of Social-Emotional Climate in Classroom. Journal of Experimental Education, 17, 347-361.

Wohlwill, J.F. (1970). The Emerging Discipline of Environmental Psychology. American Psychologist, 25, 303-312.

Wolf, B. (1983). On the Assessment of Learning Environment. Studies in Educational Evaluation, 9, 253-265.

Wolf, B. (1984). Kritik der bisherigen Klimaforschung. In Ingenkamp, K. (Ed.), 105-118.

Theoretical Positions of Kurt Lewin and Egon Brunswik – Controversial or Complementary Points of View?

Bernhard Wolf

Center of Educational Research, Landau, Federal Republic of Germany

This paper concentrates on the _theoretical_ work of two psychologists who were extremely different in some respects - and at the same time astonishingly similar.

The development of psychological theories is a significant feature of their approaches although their scientific activities - especially Kurt Lewin's - were much more varied. The presentation of some essentials of the theoretical debate between Lewin and Brunswik will proceed in three steps: (1) A comparison of their biographies, especially of their educational background, will show a lot of remarkable parallels along with considerable differences which can be exemplified by their personality structures. (2) The distinction between their theoretical points of view can be best demonstrated by their only public disputations following their lectures during the "Symposium on Psychology and Scientific Method." This symposium was part of the "Sixth International Congress for the Unity of Science" at the University of Chicago in September 1941, which was carried out by Egon Brunswik, Clark L. Hull, and Kurt Lewin (Brunswik, 1943; Hull, 1943; Lewin, 1943a). (3) Reasons why this potentially fruitful controversy was not utilized for scientific progress can be found in both persons. Lewin as well as Brunswik appreciated parts of the other's seemingly strange system but the establishment of a common theory as a compromise solution was never really attempted. It is my conviction that a complementary assembly of some elements of both fundamental psychological theories is not only possible but would be highly desirable.

COMPARISON OF BIOGRAPHIES

Kurt Lewin was born thirteen years before Egon Brunswik, and he died eight years before him: both much too early. Their families moved from the provinces into a capital while the two boys were still at school. After graduation from high school (Abitur) - at the usual age of 18/19 - they started an academic career which was typical for the German speaking regions of central Europe at those times.

The end of both their studies in psychology was then marked by a doctorate (Dr. of Philosophy); and some years later a second university examination for selected persons, the postdoctoral teaching qualification (Habilitation, which permitted them to use the title Privatdozent) opened the way to being appointed to a professorship (here at the early age of 31/32).

Their psychological institutes at the universities of Berlin and of Vienna, respectively, were renowned places before the Nazi rule started. Lewin's most prominent colleagues were Wolfgang Kohler, Max Wertheimer, Kurt Koffka, and at the beginning, Carl Stumpf. Brunswik worked at an institute headed by Karl Buhler with colleagues like Charlotte Buhler, Hildegard Hetzer, Lotte Schenk-Danzinger, Else Frenkel, and Paul Lazarsfeld.

Unfortunately some sort of rivalry between Karl Buhler and some Berlin Gestalt-psychologists--not unknown even in the scientific world of those times--interfered with the plans of some researchers' intentions to come into contact with each other. Fritz Heider who was not only a postgraduate research student during the twenties in Berlin but who also knew the Vienna institute very well (he was asked in 1927 to become a Buhler-assistant) informs us about some of his activities to promote the Vienna-Berlin dialogue (Heider, 1983).

This effort, however, to facilitate connections between the two institutes was only a drop in the ocean. The strict separation of Vienna and Berlin before 1933 may be one reason for the sharp distinction between the two forward-looking theoretical approaches of Lewin and Brunswik, a distinction which is still existing today.

Besides these structural components some marked differences in both men's personalities existed which became clearly evident during their later life in the United States.

Kurt Lewin was a highly extrovert person who always assembled a team of talented coworkers stimulating a mutual process of research productivity. The extent of his activities and restlessness is incomparable (Marrow, 1969). His way of living and working is unconceivable if you consider the various severe injuries caused by anti-Semitism.

Egon Brunswik was an introvert, sometimes a rather depressive person who found only few coworkers in Vienna as well as in Berkeley and became a more or less isolated scientist in later times (Tolman, 1956).

Both men were totally engaged in psychology as a science, both brought about completely new ideas some of which came 'too early' if you consider the Zeitgeist of that time. Both wished to become U. S. citizens and were engaged in the development of a more democratic behavior (cf. Marrow, 1969; Adorno et al., 1950).

Both did not submit to the obligation of 'publish or perish': the number of pages of their scientific literature is not gigantic.

Another important connection between Lewin and Brunswik is their immense interest in philosophy, something which is significant for their entire work. It is no accident that they met at a Congress for the Unity of Science in Chicago (1941) because Brunswik, strongly influenced by the Vienna neo-positivists, was a member of the board of trustees of the Institute for the Unity of Science, and because Lewin was always engaged in the philosophy of science.

Although Lewin did not get the well-deserved recognition as full professor at a famous university, his research principles and results constitute an integrated and pervasive part of present psychology. In contrast to this Brunswik's ideas are hardly known and therefore play only a minor role in psychological thought of today. The disregard of Brunswik's ideas is partly due to the fact that his papers--in German as well as in American--are almost incomprehensible.

This disadvantage could not be counterbalanced by secondary literature (Postman & Tolman, 1959; Hammond, 1966), especially because some of these interpretations altered Brunswik's concept itself.

The biographical outline will be concluded by the reference to some personal friends of both Lewin and Brunswik.

As mentioned above, Kurt Heider came into contact with Lewin in Berlin and with Brunswik in Vienna. Brunswik remarked several times that Heider's "Ding und Medium" (1926; translated 1959 as "Thing and medium") was one important foundation for his own "psychology in terms of objects" (Brunswik, 1934). During the American years Grace und Fritz Heider met the Lewins several times and the Brunswiks only a few times. The influence of both persons on Heider's work is best documented in his lifework "The psychology of interpersonal relations" (Heider, 1958).

A second significant bridge between the two is Edward C. Tolman who spent some months in 1933-1934 at the Vienna institute where he quickly made friends with Brunswik. Their ideas, independently developed in different research areas (Tolman, 1932; Brunswik, 1934), were so well matched that they published an excellent joint paper (Tolman & Brunswik, 1935). Tolman helped Brunswik to get a Rockefeller Fellow-

ship for Berkeley in 1935-1936, and to become assistant professor there
in 1937 (one year before the Nazi rule in Austria). As it is commonly
known a lot of contacts existed between Lewin and Tolman, as well.

Lewin's attempts, assisted by Tolman, to found the Research Center
for Group Dynamics nearly led him to Berkeley where Brunswik already
worked.

The third colleague connecting Lewin and Brunswik was Roger G.
Barker who, during the later part of his career (after 1947), tried to
integrate some elements of the theories of Lewin, Brunswik, and Heider
into his "Ecological Psychology" (Barker, 1968, 1963).

This biographical outline will facilitate the understanding of
the following arguments.

THE ACCESS TO BEHAVIOR IN SCIENTIFIC PSYCHOLOGY: LIFE SPACE OR OBJECTS OUTSIDE OF THE PERSON?

One favorite topic of both theoretical approaches can be illustrated
with the following question: In which specific way should the processes
of person-environment interrelations be understood in psychological research?

The answers to this question given by both scientists diverged
immensely. The sharp distinction between Lewin's and Brunswik's approaches could be demonstrated in several ways by utilizing a great
number of pairs of concepts or structural or dynamic models. Here only
two of these disparate points of view are presented paradigmatically.

The first aspect refers to the unit of psychological analysis in
respect to content.

In the center of Lewin's system you will find the life space which
is composed of (a) mainly the psychological characteristics of a person
"at a given time," and of (b) his/her psychological environment at the
same time (cf. Heider, 1959; Wolf, 1983). His model primarily consists
of psychological elements. Rules for measurement which were developed
in nonpsychological sciences are excluded from analysis. Environmental
characteristics not perceived by a person are not relevant for scientific
psychology except for a "boundary zone" of the life space (Lewin, 1943a,
1943b, 1944, 1947). The meaning of the relation of this nonpsychological boundary zone to the dominant life space was never clearly explained.
His meeting with Brunswik in 1941 induced Lewin to think about the
status of "psychological ecology" (Lewin, 1943a) as an additional part
within his theory. This term, however, was not defined as clearly by

him as by Brunswik who had used the term "psychological ecology" (Brunswik, 1943) before as an integral and essential constituent of his theory. At all event the two "psychological ecologies" are not synonymous.

The focal point of Lewin's theory is the purely psychological life
space. The person-environment relation is directed by percepts, as
indicated by the arrows in figure 1.

Lewin's idea of the behavioral determinant "life space" is timeless, i.e. without reference to the reality of the past or future (except for the idea one has of the past or future). Figure 1 only shows
the framework of life space which should be sufficient here; it is not
supposed to be a differentiated description.

No doubt Lewin's theoretical restrictions were surpassed by his
empirical and action-research realizations (cf. Brunswik, 1952, p. 79),
but his doctrine of "exclusively psychological aspects within psychological research" has been influential up to now.

The influence of Lewin's theoretical counterpart, Brunswik's
"psychology in terms of objects," on present scientific psychology has
been astonishingly weak. This is not only due to personal features of
Brunswik as mentioned in the biographical outline above, but mainly to
the divergence in their understanding of the role which the active person
plays. Lewin's active person in his/her life space is endowed with the
potentiality "to change the world" because the percepts solely or at
least mainly determine the behavior results. Individual percepts are
so powerful in Lewin's theory that they form the main elements for the
construction of reality. This axiom not only reflects Lewin's biography
but also a certain cliche in American thought. Brunswik's active person, called "organism" in his work, pursues the aim of finding adequate
solutions for the problems as they arise in the broad system of a person in his/her environment.

Brunswik's concept of environment is very extensive: it contains,
for example, geographical and historical as well as far remote, distal,
and proximal objects (Gegenstande). Definitely all the objects that
could be relevant for the person in order to reach or at least to come
close to "functional attainment" or "achievement" (using Brunswik's
words) can be included in the analysis. The non-psychological environment (objects outside of the person) plays a decisive role in his access
to human behavior.

One part of these objects, sometimes called "attained objects" or
"intended results," is highly relevant for the person because it marks
preliminary or final aims of behavior.

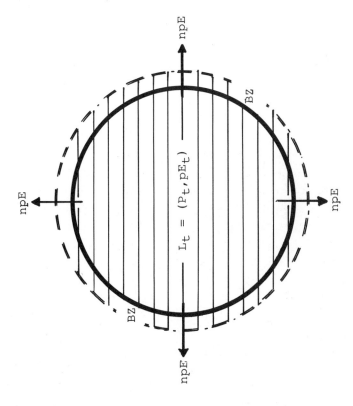

Figure 1   Life Space as a Central Unit of Behavior Research (Lewin)

npE: non-psychological Environment (outside of Lewin's theory)
BZ: Boundary Zone (part of npE, close to L_t)
L_t: Life space at a given time (t) consisting of:
P_t: Person characteristics at a given time (t)
pE_t:psychological Environment (outside of Lewin's theory)

$$L_t = (P_t, pE_t)$$

Therefore Brunswik's psychology can be characterized by a teleo-logical component, similar or nearly equal to Tolman's assumption of a purposive component (Tolman, 1932).

A second part of these objects guides the person in approaching his/her adjustment to the aimed objects. This adjustment combines passive and active processes in which the person is involved. With the words of Jean Piaget we would speak of accomodation and assimilation.

Figure 2 tries to illustrate this theoretical model using the same symbols as in figure 1 (Brunswik, 1939; Wolf, 1983). Again it is only a simplified framework including only some "ramifications" of the environment which could become significant for the person and should be taken into consideration. The horizontal axis in figure 2 represents the difference in distance from the person (organism) in respect to time and other aspects. The importance of the respective environmental factors changes along with the "longitudinal sequences of events." The whole system must be considered as highly dynamic because the contents of all parts of non-psychological environment will be modified perma-nently.

A special place for the objects aimed at does not exist. The goals of behavior will be primarily found in the region of distal effects (B) or in that of far reaching results (C).

Brunswik summed up these facets of his theory in the Chicago-discussion (Brunswik, 1943, p. 271): "By representing an organism's or species' achievement system in terms of attained objects and results, such a psychology would in a sense be without the organism (i.e., would neglect all but a few focal details of organismic structure and intra-organismic processes), yet would let us know much about the organism (i.e., its relationships to the environment, in both cognition and action)."

Brunswik's active person embedded in a space of objects is endowed with the potentiality "to adjust--more or less--to some of these ob-jects." If this specific point of view reflects the quality of Bruns-wik's scientific achievement his ideas should receive more attention. For his adjustment to the object "psychology" could be a vantage point for future research.

The second aspect to be singled out here refers to the formal side of psychological analysis.

Lewin is a typical representative of--what he called--the Galileian mode of thought in psychology searching for strict laws which can explain behavior completely (Lewin, 1931; Bischof, 1981). Brunswik shortly classifies this approach as follows (Brunswik, 1952, p. 77): "Gestalt-

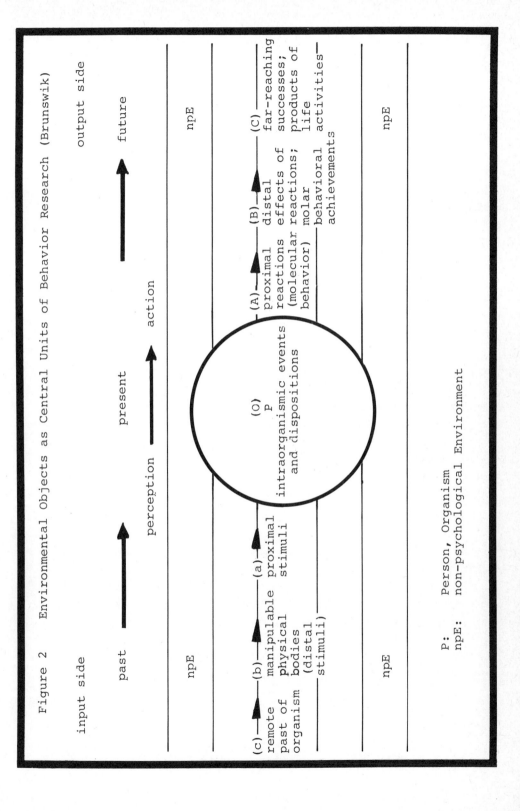

Figure 2   Environmental Objects as Central Units of Behavior Research (Brunswik)

input side   output side

past   present   future

perception   action

(c) ─── (b) ─── (a)   (O)   (A) ─── (B) ─── (C)
remote   manipulable proximal   P   proximal   distal   far-reaching
past of physical   stimuli   intraorganismic reactions   effects of   successes;
organism bodies   events   (molecular   reactions; products of
         (distal   and   behavior)   molar   life
         stimuli)   dispositions   behavioral activities
                                                        achievements

npE   npE   npE

npE   npE   npE

P: Person, Organism
npE: non-psychological Environment

psychological, molar behavioristic, and formal-nomothetic features are combined in the theories of Lewin." Law-finding, nomothetic strategies aimed at univocal relations are constituents of his theory. Lewin succeeded in overcoming the Aristotelian mode of thought (Lewin, 1931) but he burdened psychology with formal limits which were developed in physics some centuries ago. His demand (in respect to content) for a psychological research which is composed of purely psychological components was a real progress for human sciences while his demand for a Galileian mode of thought has proved to be questionable.

My reservation here is not typical. Undoubtedly the majority of leading figures in the academic psychological world consider the principle of law-finding to be an essential theoretical aspect. Nevertheless: these general and timeless laws sometimes resemble the stone Sisyphus had to wrestle with!

The probabilistic nature of Brunswik's theory—often misunderstood by secondary literature, even by Lewin (1943a, p. 308), seems to be the greatest obstacle to a present recognition of his ideas. An approach based on uncertainty and equivocality (Brunswik, 1952)—with strong connections to some of Heider's contributions (Heider, 1958)—may be the long awaited light at the end of the tunnel. Up to now the idea of an organism which very quickly tries to combine insecure, preliminary, inconsistent, and even contradictory clues to one solution has been fascinating. Brunswik's way of differentiating between "perception" and "thinking" (Brunswik, 1966) is one interesting facet of this formal access. The best metaphor to illustrate his "probabilistic functionalism" is the "lens" which can receive a lot of divergent information and at the same time focus a lot of possible reactions on one attainment (output).

The aim of behavior, called functional attainment, asks for the principle of "vicarious functioning." This principle alone has initiated a variety of experimental and quasi-experimental investigations.

A NEW ACCESS TO BEHAVIOR: LIFE SPACE AND OBJECTS OUTSIDE OF THE PERSON

In spite of the theoretical controversy discussed above, complementary combination of both models would not only be possible but desirable. Both approaches can be regarded as "encapsulations" restricted either to person-oriented and psychological aspects or to subsets of the non-psychological environment. The shortcoming in the arguments of Lewin could be made up for by some of Brunswik's proposals, and vice versa. The need for complements was expressed concisely by Brunswik's phraseology (Brunswik, 1943), classifying Lewin's theory as "post-perceptual and pre-behavioral,"--cf. figure 1,--whereas he classified his own as "perceptual and behavioral"--cf. figure 2-- ('behavioral' here means something like 'the response of the organism').

During the Chicago symposium in 1941 Brunswik tried to integrate the two controversial points of view. He attempted "to show that the 'relationship' of the positions of the three speakers of the meeting was complementary rather than contradictory" (Brunswik, 1943, p. 271). Brunswik gave Lewin's work his full attention, and although he plainly critized some basic assumptions he admired Lewin's ability in other respects. This can be illustrated in the following statement: "In his topological psychology, furthermore, Lewin has probably developed the most adequate conceptual tool for dealing with the central layer" (Brunswik, 1943, p. 267; 'central layer' here means 'life space').

A mutual completion of both theories seems to be necessary at present. Brunswik's 'empty person' could be enriched by integrating Lewin's percepts of persons, e.g. for the recognition of their goals.

On the other hand, Lewinian psychology should open up to Brunswik's priority of purposes for the explanation of behavior, and to the superiority of provisional results based on probabilities.

Both theories prefer dynamic points of view, i.e. process models. Explicitly in the theoretical statements (Brunswik) or implicitly in the experimental procedure (Lewin; cf. Brunswik, 1952, p. 79) the principle of "vicarious functioning" has come to the fore. We should take advantage of the possibility to combine both strategies. Science has to look for unusual solutions at times, and psychology should enlarge its knowledge by permitting manifold sources and links in behavior analysis.

The reintegration of some of the modern and sophisticated thoughts of Egon Brunswik into psychology of the present which has been greatly influenced by Lewin would be a promising step. We should not ignore the last sentence of Brunswik's symposium paper: "But in the end, it seems that none of the various aspects just discussed can be dispensed with in a completely rounded-out system of psychology" (Brunswik, 1943, p. 271).

REFERENCES

Adorno, T.W., Frenkel-Brunswik, E., Levinson, D.J., & Sanford, R.N. The authoritarian personality. New York: Harper, 1950.

Barker, R.G. (1963). On the nature of the environment. Journal of Social Issues, 19, 17-38.

Barker, R.G. (1968). Ecological psychology. Stanford: Stanford University Press.

Bischof, N. (1981). Aristoteles, Galilei, Kurt Lewin - und die Folgen. In W. Michaelis (Ed.), Bericht uber den 32. Kongress der Deutschen Gesellschaft fur Psychologie in Zurich 1980. Gottingen: Hogrefe, 17-39.

Brunswik, E. (1934). Wahrnehmung und Gegenstandswelt. Grundlegung einer Psychologie vom Gegenstand her. Leipzig and Vienna: F. Deuticke.

Brunswik, E. (1939). The conceptual focus of some psychological systems. Journal of Unified Science (Einheitswissenschaft), 8, 36-49.

Brunswik, E. (1943). Organismic achievement and environmental probability. Psychological Review, 50, 255-272.

Brunswik, E. (1952). The conceptual framework of psychology. Chicago: The University of Chicago Press.

Brunswik, E. (1966). Reasoning as a universal behavior model and a functional differentiation between "perception" and "thinking." In K.R. Hammond (Ed.), The psychology of Egon Brunswik. New York: Holt, Rinehart, and Winston, 487-494. (Lecture of 1954.)

Hammond, K.R. (Ed.) (1966). The psychology of Egon Brunswik. New York: Holt, Rinehart, and Winston.

Heider, F. (1926). Ding und Medium. Symposium, 1, 109-157.

Heider, F. (1958). The psychology of interpersonal relations. Hillsdale: Lawrence Erlbaum (Reprint).

Heider, F. (1959). On Lewin's method and theory. Journal of Social Issues, Supplement Series, 13, 3-13.

Heider, F. (1983). The life of a psychologist: An autobiography. Lawrence: University Press of Kansas.

Hull, C.L. (1943). The problem of intervening variables in molar behavior theory. Psychological Review, 50, 273-291.

Lewin, K. (1931). The conflict between the Aristotelian and Galileian modes of thought in contemporary psychology. Journal of Genetic Psychology, 5, 141-177.

Lewin, K. (1943a). Defining the "field at a given time." Psychological Review, 50, 292-310.

Lewin, K. (1943b). Forces behind food habits and methods of change. Bulletin of the National Research Council, 108, 35-65.

Lewin, K. (1944). Constructs in psychology and psychological ecology. University of Iowa Studies in Child Welfare, 20, 1-29.

Lewin, K. (1947). Frontiers in group dynamics: II. Cannels of group life; social planning and action research. Human Relations, 1, 143-153.

Marrow, A.J. (1969). The practical theorist: The life and work of Kurt Lewin. New York: Basic Books.

Postman, L., & Tolman, E.C. (o959). Brunswik's probabilistic functionalism. In S. Koch (Ed.), Psychology: A study of a science. Volume 1. New York: McGraw-Hill, 502-564.

Tolman, E.C. (1932). Purposive behavior in animals and men. New York: Century.

Tolman, E.C. (1956). Eulogy. Egon Brunswik: 1903-1955. American Journal of Psychology, 69, 315-342.

Tolman, E.C., & Brunswik, E. (1935). The organism and the causal texture of the environment. Psychological Review, 42, 43-77.

Wolf, B. (1983). On the assessment of learning environment. Studies in Educational Evaluation, 9, 253-265.

Lewin and Current Developmental Theory

Kurt W. Back

Duke University

COMPARATIVE THEORY OF SCIENCE

Lewin's early writings, including his first book, "Der Begriff der Genese in Physik, Biologie und Entwicklungsgeschichte" (the Genese) shows concern with large-scale theory, which may be an unexpressed basis for later work. The center of this work was an exposition of the comparative theory of sciences (Metraux, 1982-3).

THE FRAMEWORK OF THE GENESE

In several papers and drafts of papers Lewin expounded the comparative theory of science (Metraux, 1982-83); following his usual procedure, he avoided a formal definition of what comparative theory of science is. He rather gave negative definitions: it is not history, sociology, or philosophy of science; nor is it logic or methodology. The favorite way of explaining the meaning of the term in this tradition is the ostensive definition, giving an example of an investigation in the comparative theory of science, showing the meaning in use. This Lewin did in the Genese, where he investigated one way in which sciences describe their objects of discussion. He posed the question: What do we mean when we say that an object is still this object at a different time?

Lewin starts the discussion with minimum assumptions: any structure or object at any particular moment of time is considered to be a separate object. Thus, structures which exist at different times are fundamentally as different as structures in different places. The relationship to be studied associates structures at different times; it is a genetic relationship, saying that in some ways one derives from the other. Lewin called this relation Genidentity and set out to determine its place in different sciences.

Here, as well, Lewin refused to give a formal definition, but persisted with the ostensive description, that is, definition through pointing and thorough use. We shall follow his procedure. As close as he came to a definition was, "We shall, to avoid confusion, call the relation between structures which derive existentially from each other, Genidentity" (p. 62).[1]

This question leads to a consideration of what "the same" and dif-ferent" mean in different sciences. As in comparative theory of science, he lists the characteristics of genidentity, but mainly negatively. It is independent of similarity: for instance, an egg and chicken may have genidentity, although they are structurally and perceptually dif-ferent; while two eggs may be identical in many respects, but are not genidentical. The egg and chicken differ in time, the two eggs in space. Genidentity means something different according to the facts about objects of study in a particular field. It is not a logical re-lation, like logical identity, but an empirical relationship. The na-ture of genidentity in each field must be understood before one can deal with theory or empirical research in a field. One must know what a physical object or an individual is and how one can recognize the object at different times. Every scientist (or layman) does so, of course, intuitively. Lewin endeavors to make these definitions expli-cit as a basis for his comparative theory of science. This discussion may then lead to clarification of terms and procedure in each science. He discusses comparative study in general, but the procedure is best indicated by this example, in the same way as genidentity is defined best by example. He discusses genidentity in four contexts: physics, inheritance, individual development and phylogenetics.

Physics: Genidentity in the world of physics (which includes chem-istry) is ultimately determined by the law of conservation of matter. Writing in the dawn of the age of relativity theory, Lewin acknowledged that his analysis is limited to the extent of applicability of the law of conservation. Thus, genidentity is defined here by ascertaining that the matter--in any transformation--is present in the objects under con-sideration. Here he introduces the concept of total genidentity which means that all the aspects of one object are included in the others. In the further discussion Lewin is principally concerned with establish-ing the logical properties of genidentity and total ("remainderless") genidentity. Thus, genidentity in physics is symmetrical, therefore independent of time. It is not important whether one starts from an earlier or later point (which he calls "cut") in the series of exis-tence of matter. It is also continuous: one can always make a deter-mination of the matter under consideration between the two points which one has considered. It is infinite in both directions: there is no earliest or latest point of matter; therefore there is no preferred point for describing the object, no point in time which gives the essential definition.

Like much conceptual analysis these propositions seem to be self-evident and not very useful. However, they need to be stated; they also act here as the baseline from which the nature of biological objects can be distinguished. In passing, it may be noted that Lewin, in contrast to other gestalt psychologists, does not accept structural form in inanimate objects as being of special consequence (Kohler, 1920). On the contrary, he states the theorem "Every real part of a physical structure and each complex of structures can--as far as genidentity relations are concerned--be seen again as a physical structure," i.e., there are no natural or preferred physical structures or gestalts.

Biology: In biological structures, however, the situation is different. Biologists are concerned with special structures, namely organisms, and Lewin now discusses the question: What do biologists mean by the nature of the organism, whose nature is here defined as genidentity? The example of the chicken and egg shows that preservation of matter is out of the question, nor are any particular structures or relationships preserved. The solution is here not as simple as it was in the case of physics, especially if one wants to avoid any vitalist or teleological answers. Lewin here proposes three different kinds of genidentity, corresponding to different scientific problems. (We must remember that his aim is to establish a comparative study of science.) They are: ancestral (aval) genidentity, the identity with ancestors; individual identity, the identity through the life course; and phylogenetic genidentity, the identity through evolution and through change of species. Each of these genidentities is related to different questions, inheritance, development, and evolution of species; all of them differ in their logical properties from physical genidentity, but they also differ among each other.

Ancestral genidentity: Ancestral genidentity derives from the biological fact that every organism is a combination of its ancestors. Thus there is a kind of identity between the organism under consideration, the probandum, and any of its ancestors, and this is captured by the concept of ancestral genidentity. Total genidentity in this case is the relation of the probandum to all its ancestors. One of the principle characteristics of this genidentity is that it is not continuous, but stepwise; each step is a generation. In addition the generations define the sequence, not the flow of time: different generations may be contemporary, while the same generation may extend over more time. In fact the same organism may appear in different generations through

mating of relatives; this introduces loops, contrary to the unidirec-
tionality of time. Ancestral genidentity is symmetrical, but even total
genidentity is not necessarily transitive: if the middle term is in
the earliest generation then transitivity fails: two individuals may
be descended from the same ancestor without being in the same line of
descent. Thus the system of relationships is very complex and Lewin
devotes a whole section to several systems of graphic representation
(pp. 230-240). Human society has devoted some efforts to simplify this
definition of genidentity by introducing different kinship systems,
making classes of relationships.

Another characteristic of ancestral genidentity is that it is
bounded on one side; there is a youngest generation, namely that of the
probandum; the sequence is open, however, on the other end: there is
no oldest ancestor. This circumstance also gives a unique point of
reference, namely the probandum, the organism whose ancestry is to be
established. This is the point of reference from which the generations
are counted. If a family tree is divided we obtain new structure, a
new family tree which has possibly a new reference point, its own youngest generation. Parts as well as wholes have structured relationships.

Individual genidentity: The life course of the individual organism
is another focus of the life sciences. The identity of the individual
seems to be well defined and not problematic, but one must remember
that Lewin at this writing was not primarily concerned with human subjects or even higher animals, but tried to encompass the whole realm of
living beings, especially the more primitive ones where identity of
the organism is not so easily determined. In propagation of plants,
for instance, does the individual persist in the cuttings, or is the
individual life span continued only in the stem plant? Questions of
this kind show the need for formal analysis. Individual genidentity can
be characterized as continuous and bounded at both ends (birth and
death). A dead organism is not anymore a part of the individual genidentity sequence, although as a physical body it is part of a physical genidentity sequence and may be in many respects defined to be "the same"
as the living organism. This is another example of the dependence of
genidentity on the particular science and its difference from logical
relations of identity or similarity.

It is also symmetric and time dependent. Because of conjugation
of some organisms, full transitivity is not established, even in total
genidentity. Two cells which conjugate are totally genidentical with
the fused cell, but not genidentical with each other: If the middle

term is the latest one, transitivity is not necessary, the opposite
condition from ancestral genidentity.

Both limit points of the organism are favored places in analysis
which can be uniquely defined and are points of reference; indeed, the
last point is really the proper point of reference, because the point
of death defines one individual uniquely; by contrast, the earliest
point may define the birth of several individuals. Thus, individual
genidentity is best defined by its latest point; any earlier cut has
meaning in relation to this cut. This does not imply, however, a teleological point of view which would say that life is determined by its
last point. Lewin takes care to point out that this analysis of genidentity makes it possible to account for the future in an organism without
any teleological premises, simply by looking at the complete genidentical
sequence as one unit (pp. 205-208).

Phylogenetic genidentity: The final meaning of genidentity is the
one of evolution or the relationship between different species and sub-
species. In a way this is the complement of ancestral genidentity;
phylogenetic genidentity treats descent from a common ancestor or group
of ancestors (in the case of creation of a new species through crossing).
It is therefore limited at the oldest end, but not at the youngest; but
the oldest end is not a unique probandum, but can be a conglomeration
of any size. As the unit is the species, not the individual, it is
continuous and we cannot speak of generations. As it is continuous,
it flows with time and loops are not possible. Lewin contrasts this
sequence with the two other biological sequences by saying that here
the determining factor is not "organizations" but "life" (pp. 258-261).
We have here the history of the manifestation of life; however, this
aspect of biological existence which he calls organismic biology, is
not an historical science: It does not treat the actual history of
species or individuals but conceptual transformations.

THE GENESE AND LEWIN'S LATER WORK

The main themes of the Genese give a background to the most difficult and most valuable parts of Lewin's further work. The comparative
aspect of his plan moved to the background when he became more and more
concerned with a particular science, psychology. As we know from
gestalt theory, however, the background determines the meaning of the
foreground. In his conceptual work, Lewin investigates those aspects
of psychology which had counterparts in other sciences. It seems that

he did not lose his original aim, the comparative investigation of
terms which are useful in all sciences. By concentrating on these concepts and by using a vocabulary which could be applied to other sciences,
his psychology frequently appeared to have a non-psychological character.
Ironically, it has appeared to many to be reductionist, to reduce the
theory of psychology to that of physics, while he carefully tried to
distinguish the meaning and use of concepts within the context of different sciences; he did that even within psychology, distinguishing
between what he called sensory psychology and psychology.

Two other difficulties in his work are also clarified to a degree
in these early writings: the relation between development and history
and the relation between structure and forces.

DEVELOPMENT AND HISTORY

In his discussion of genidentity, Lewin frequently employs definitions which imply a lawfulness in time; this happens, for instance, when
he defines sequences as unbounded in one direction or states a sequence
of events. He acknowledged, however, that this definition does not
apply to individual cases. Thus the infinite extension of the phylogenic identity into the future is only conceptually so; in actuality all
the descendants of a species may die out individually. The differentiation of ancestral genidentity and phylogenic genidentity is purely conceptual and refers to the same historical events. The same distinction
is especially important in the discussion of individual genidentity:
the fate of an individual is not described by any of the definitions of
structural identity; particularly death as defined here is a regular
event at the end of genidentical development; in actuality it may occur
at any time and not in the way in which the definition of the cut in
the sequence is conceptualized.

The distinction between the conceptual analysis of genidentity and
the historical description is shown best in Lewin's later works in the
studies of regression and retrogression (Barker, Dembo, & Lewin, 1941).
He distinguished between scientific developmental laws which define
the changes in the genidentity of the person or subsets of the person
and historical description where the specific circumstances of the particular organism is taken into account. A frustrating situation which
makes the organism retrace its steps will be looked at as regression,
if the retracing goes along the general principles of organismic development, and retrogression if it involves the individual's own history.

This distinction leads also to a corresponding division between experimental and clinical method. The experimentalist tries to establish how the important aspects of structure affect a predictable change; the individual is considered to be only an example of this structure. The clinician is concerned with the particular history of the individual and its effect on present conditions: he can help the individual in this correction, but will have trouble in establishing a general theory, not having used a definition of general validity in the first place. The experimentalist has the corresponding opposite strengths and weaknesses. In both cases we can posit an optimal development (orthogenesis) (Werner, 1957), and study the effects of deviations from this standard.

An example of this difference can be found in the current controversy about childhood seduction in psychoanalytic theory (Masson, 1984; Storr, 1984). Freud's claim that most neurotic patients imagined the seduction is attacked by evidence and speculation that child abuse has existed. From the point of view of devising a theory of development the fact whether seduction was real or imaginary is not very important, a question of degree in inducing the deformation of the personality. From a clinical point of view the actual historical circumstances are vitally important for an evaluation of the individual patient and for further procedures.

STRUCTURE AND FORCES

The elaboration of the concept of genidentity also throws light on Lewin's distinction between geometry and dynamics; his next two books (Principles of Topological Psychology and A Dynamic Theory of Personality) stressed this distinction. Genidentity is only preserved in structures. In fact, in this volume he considers only physical objects, including cells, groups of cells and organisms. Here one can speak of permanence and of the ways in which the persistence of a structure can be identified. Forces, on the other hand, arise from time to time and are the accidental vicissitudes to which these structures are exposed. They can be measured at different times but they have no identity as such and hence no permanence (pp. 291-293). One important task in each science is to identify the structures and their natural laws and the ways in which they can be affected by different forces. Again, Lewin distinguishes himself from Freud, who identifies forces--instincts, drives--and who assumes their persistence: the distorted reappearance of forces is seen as a base for neuroses. By contrast, Lewin avoids

distinguishing between types of forces and even naming them. Neither
does he distinguish between need and temporary intentions, calling the
latter quasi-needs. This enables him to treat experimental instructions
as valid examples of general needs and so develop his methods and his
general theory. His dynamics are based on a general concept of force,
which is defined by strength and direction only. As he used a type of
geometry to define structure so he used here the mathematical concept
of the vector.

EXTENSION OF THE GENESE

   While Lewin pursued a comparative study of science, he did not
extend this study to the sciences with which he actually worked. Indicated extensions are: first, going beyond the individual into social
units, especially to find genidentity of groups, second, the extension
from physical to psychological units, in the same way as Lewin's own
topological psychology designed structures of the self and its subdivi-
sions. In both cases one could gain new insight into current questions
of the meaning of developmental theory in different fields, extending
the analysis to non-palpable units.
   Group dynamics. Lewin himself did much to establish the legitimacy
of the reality of groups. Groups can be talked about and represented
as units; scientists, as well as practitioners, can work with groups.
Groups may have their own laws of development and much effort has been
expended to trace their development and also to define the beginning
and end of groups. Dare one call them birth and death? Similar usages
are established for larger units, social classes, ethnic groups, nations
and cultures and specialized units such as families or community groups.
These social structures have been described in detail, their reality
defended and separate issues have been studied. An approach to the
general questions which Lewin raised in the Genese may be fruitful at
the current time. Looking at genidentity in this context one can ask
how the term is used, how this genidentity differs from its use in
other fields and how we can use the same organizing principles which
had been used in other fields to social structures. Lewin's own work
on the theory of group dynamics went into this direction; however he
did not return to his original comparative approach. This approach
would contrast with systems theory in the same way as his original
work contrasted unified theory of science. Then he had separate principles for each level, while here the specific meaning for each structure

would be analyzed in its own right. Questions of continuity and transitivity, while seemingly abstract, would give valuable insights.

The self. The application of comparative theory of science to social structures is so vast, extending as it does to almost all of social science, that it has to stay here as a programmatic statement. A more modest start can be indicated in a field which has been more analyzed in a unified way, namely the psychological dimensions of the person, and especially the study of the self.

In conformity with the procedure of the Genese, we might ask whether self-genidentity is reflexive, transitive and bounded. Some of the questions would be quite easy to answer: for instance, self-genidentity can be said to be reflexive: if a self is genidentical with one at a later date, this later one is identical with the first. Other questions, including transitivity, are more difficult to answer; they depend in part on the question of how we recognize a self. Is a self coexisting with the individual? Does it start and stop at the same time? Can an individual have several selves, either contemporary or in succession? The last question would include considerations of multiple personality (or in a milder form, different roles) or the acceptability of complete abrupt changes. If the self could split or amalgamate, the genidentity here would not be transitive: two cuts would be genidentical to a third--the original before the split--but not to each other. On the other hand, under practically any definition, the self would be continuous, as the organism is; on the question of time connectedness we would again be dependent on the definition of the self: If we accept parts of the individual as separate selves, one could develop faster than another, and different phases would then be independent of a strict time sequence.

THE GENESE AND MODERN LOGIC OF DEVELOPMENT

The self develops parallel to the individual development of the organism. The analysis of the genidentity of the self would follow the analysis which Lewin had used for his individual genidentity; in fact, he did in his psychological work use representations of structure for psychological events which looked like cellular conglomerates. Propositions about individual differences, (e.g. between children and adults, or normal and mentally deficient individuals), refer to structural properties, not the content of consciousness. These properties are universal in different sciences, and thus amenable to comparative theory. Although Lewin defined some of these properties, such as number of units, strength of boundary or types of connectedness, he avoided a general theory of these properties in comparison with their use in other sciences.

The value of Lewin's approach lies in identifying those aspects of any structure which can be compared over the whole range of science; one must repeat that this is a comparative theory, not a unified one. The use of any concept in a particular context must be empirically justified. The structural aspects of the self, or of personality, are very general and can be discussed independently of individual experiences: they are scientific and not historical. Thus they fit with the contemporary desires of psychologists to work on general theories of cognitive and personality development and of sociologists to ascertain general theories of the self. The first requirement is to ascertain the structural units and to find the empirical correlates in a particular science.

These are almost random thoughts in response to Lewin's exact specifications in the comparative study of science. They direct attention to an important problem: How can we define the psychological nature of the individual, that is, the unit which makes it possible to compare psychology with other sciences? This question attacks the nature of psychology itself as a science, as some model of human action which can be compared with other sciences. (In a different context we may note that Thomas Kuhn (1970) practically excluded psychology and social sciences from his definition of scientific development by saying that they had no paradigm.) Although Lewin did much to define psychology as a science in its own right, he never returned to a comparative study which assured psychology a place in the company of other sciences. Work on the self-concept and individual development has assumed new importance in our time and one might make now an attempt to show the direction in which such an extension of Lewin's work may take.

It must be stressed again that Lewin's procedure was to accept the legitimacy of scientists' work and to ask how they employ their terms. Thus he was not compelled to define the structure which had genidentity; however, this question cannot be avoided when we turn to psychological entities which are not directly perceivable. Here we have to ask how Lewin and his colleagues employed the term. In the meantime, however, biologists have been asking questions of the same kind: How do we know or are entitled to say that one structure is like another? Waddington (1957) has coined the term chreod for this concept, from the Greek "necessary path": That is, we have here a structure or entity whose path is determined in some way but whose individual constituents may change drastically; in addition, this path would not be followed in any particular instance; circumstances may force deviations from the path, but the chreod will return toward this path as soon as disturbing influences are removed. (Waddington was thinking originally of embryonic development.) It is notable that Lewin used almost the same Greek term (hodos = path) to define a new theoretical field, namely hodology. Thus a chreod remains a theoretical construct and at the same time an empirical structure: We can define the observations which we need to determine the existence of a chreod, but at the same time theory gives us the definition of the necessary path which will not be realized in individual cases, but remains the model of the process under investigation (Back, 1976).

A similar idea underlies other theories of development; we need only mention Werner's (1957) concept of orthogenesis or Piagct's (1971) epigenetic model. In all of these discussions a definite direction and aim is specified. But, with Lewin we can see here that no teleological assumptions are involved: The path is just described in a definite sequence, which can have a beginning and end point--or even other transition points which are specially favored--but one does not need to assume a vital force or an aim to reach for this sequence to occur.

The refined concept of path which biologists have come to use is one aspect of a definition which may lead to the genidentity of the self; the other part of the chreod, necessity, has been given a new foundation in logic. The meaning of necessity, as contrasted to such terms as possibility or truth, has been actively under investigation (Lewis, 1973; Lewis & Langford, 1932). Neither necessity nor possibility refer to actual observations; both to a consideration of what could have happened. Could we imagine a world with the same laws of nature where an event which we have observed could not have happened (or an event which has not occurred could have happened)? If we cannot do so, then the event was necessary; if we can then the event which we are talking about is possible; in our system it could or could not have happened. In current logical analysis these thought experiments are referred to as possible worlds (Loux, 1979; Lewis, 1973). Within a given universe of discourse, then, a possible event or sequence is one which occurs in all of them. Thus we can talk of laws of development for physical as well as for mental entities where we can define a necessary path or a path in all possible worlds (Back, 1980; 1984).

The theory of possible worlds includes another feature which helps us in the problem of genidentity of the self: this is the need for determination of the corresponding individual in different worlds, or as it has been called, the question of counterparts (Lewis, 1971). In

order to do so, one must define the essential traits of the structure
under consideration which enable us to transpose an individual into
another world. The more different the situation of the other world
is, e.g. in historical or cultural terms, the fewer traits of the
structure can be used: it would be easier to reconstruct a person in
a different city than in a different country or in the distant past.
This variation is, however, just as true for a biological structure
as for a psychological one, such as the self. In constructing counterparts we have an exercise which makes it practicable to speak of the
genidentity of the self.

The advances in theoretical biology, logic and mathematics have
given a firmer foundation for some topics which Lewin almost intuitively
arrived at. The development theories which he has sketched apply not
only for biological development, but for cognitive, emotional development
and for development of the self, of groups and even for social and
economic development as well. In all these fields sufficient research
and theory has been assembled to analyze the common usage of terms which
formed Lewin's method in his comparative study of science. He hinted
at this approach in his later work in psychology; but the foundations
are here now to extend and complete his work for the social sciences,
in which his interest rested.

---

[1]Page references are given to the edition of the Genese in Metraux, 1983.

REFERENCES

Back, K.W. (1976). Personal characteristics and social behavior: The-
    ory and method. In R.H. Binstock & E. Shanas (Eds.), Handbook of
    aging and the social sciences (pp. 403-431). New York: Van No-
    strand Reinhold.

Back, K.W. (1980). Uprooting and self-image: Catastrophe and contin-
    uity. In C. V. Coelho & P.I. Ahmed (Eds.), Uprooting and develop-
    ment (pp. 117-129). New York: Plenum.

Back, K.W. (1984). Possibility, probability and necessity: Logical
    analysis of developmental theories. Academic Psychology Bulletin,
    6, (pp. 157-170).

Barker, R., Dembo, T., & Lewin, K. (1941). Frustration and regression:
    An experiment with young children. University of Iowa Studies in
    Child Welfare, 1, xv & 314.

Kohler, W. (1920). Die Physischen Gestalten in Ruhe und im Stationaren
    Zustand. Erlangen.

Kuhn, T.S. (1970). The structure of scientific revolutions. Chicago: University of Chicago Press.

Lewis, C.I., & Langford, C.H. (1932). Symbolic logic. New York: Dover.

Lewis, D. (1973). Counterfactuals. Cambridge, MA: Harvard University Press.

Loux, M.J. (Ed.). (1979). The possible and the actual. Ithaca, NY: Cornell University Press.

Masson, J. (1984). The assault on truth: Freud's suppression of the seduction theory. New York: Farrar, Straus & Giroux.

Metraux, A. (1982-83). Kurt-Lewin-Werkausgabe, Band 1-2: Wissenschafts theorie I-II. Bern, Switzerland: Huber.

Piaget, J. (1971). Biology and knowledge. Chicago: University of Chicago Press.

Storr, A. (1984, February 17). Review of Masson, The assult on truth. New York Times Book Review, p. 1.

Waddington, C.H. (1957). The strategy of the gene. London: Allen & Unwin.

Werner, H. (1957). Comparative psychology of mental development. New York: International University Press.

Lewin and Social Science: A Theoretical Note

Albert Pepitone

University of Pennsylvania

Early in his career, Lewin's statements of field theory encompassed both metatheoretical assumptions concerning the nature of concepts and causality--as in the well-known paper contrasting Aristotelian and Galileian "modes of thought"--and a small set of constructs that could represent the dynamic processes and structural relations required for a scientifically sufficient psychological explanation of human behavior. Such field constructs were used pervasively and generatively in the analysis and interpretation of the Psychologische Forschung experiments carried out during the 1920's and early 1930's (De Rivera, 1976). In the Iowa decade beginning in 1935, Lewin's thinking and research moved directly into the province of social psychology, and accordingly there is a greater emphasis on constructs more suitable for representing social fields--for instance, "powerfields" and goals induced by "values." In the final MIT period, Lewin introduced innovative conceptual tools that were never part of the original body of field theory.

The shift in perspective as Lewin moved from individual to social psychology was not abrupt, and spatial representations were never explicitly dropped, but with the 1944 Iowa Monograph, it becomes clear that theory had to go beyond the individual life space and even beyond the conceptual representation of the group to comprehend the influential realities of human ecology and culture.

What especially accelerated this evolving broader perspective was the research on food habits. To answer the question of "Why people eat what they eat?"--a priority issue for developing a national strategy to cope with wartime food shortages--Lewin proposed that we had to "know how food comes to the table and why." What he called "psychological ecology" comprises the various "channels" through which different foods flow from their source to the table and consumption. Such channels are determined by the economics of the market place, transportation facilities, the climate, the law, and other objective factors. The study of psychological ecology is necessary for the specification of what is and what is not possible in the life spaces of individuals, and this is a primary step toward answering the leading question.

Lewin's channel theory includes not only what constitutes the channel but what is chosen to be in it or excluded at decision points along the way, by housewives and other "gatekeepers." Ethnic, economic class, religious, and other groups have different gatekeepers, different capacities to buy, as well as different preferences and taboos in foods. Psychological ecology, therefore, not only requires a study of material properties of the environment but a study of the values and beliefs of groups, to define not only what is possible for individuals but what is prescribed and prohibited by the groups to which the individuals belong or are identified with. Thus, a theoretical case is made for group dynamics, an area of social psychology to deal with the essential questions of what normative values and beliefs are relevant to the flow of foods through the channels and how they are influential.

There is, of course, another case for the study of the dynamics of groups: such forces can be controlled and converted into agents of change. Any practical goal in modifying food habits would have to involve members of groups and awareness of the norms being maintained by them. The connection between theory of group dynamics and social action is especially close for Lewin; indeed, in his analysis of changing attitudes and conduct, theory and the strategy for change are one and the same argument. Thus: if the attitudes and conduct that need to be changed are not distributed across individuals at random but are patterned in ways that coincide with the boundaries of some group, then change involves replacing the old culture of that group, in which the undesirable attitudes and conduct are maintained, with a new culture. Theoretically, individuals tend to accept the standards of their groups about how to behave and what attitudes to hold because their personal experience is limited and because they exert pressure on one another to conform. Practically, re-education involves creating conditions for the voluntary relinquishment of those standards--a process of "unfreezing"--and the acceptance of new norms, with the likelihood of acceptance being increased whenever a strong "we-feeling" is created.

Much of the research in group dynamics centered on such influence processes within the group--for example, the source and direction of uniformity pressures, the effects of cooperative and competitive goal structures, etc.--but there were, and still are gaps in knowledge important for both theory and action which can only be filled by observation and conceptual analysis of the socio-cultural and ecological context of groups extended backward in historical time. For example, little is known about how norms of a certain kind develop; some groups enforce authoritarian values, some groups value the work ethic, some groups maintain norms that prescribe competition, some have beliefs about the powers of the evil eye, etc. How do these particular cultural

systems evolve and how are they maintained? It is true that people with
similar values tend to affiliate with one another and form enduring
groups, but where do the values they bring to the group come from? The
most accurate general statement that can be made is that such shared
normative systems that make up a group's culture are based on human
biology and the conditions of the objective environment in which groups
function. To give the latter its singular weight, although individual
human nature contributes to what is universal in culture, differences
in cultural norms cannot be explained by individual psychology.

Lewin envisioned this broader social science perspective for group
dynamics, and in his last, posthumously published paper, presents a new
conceptual approach. In what is appropriately called "Frontiers in
Group Dynamics" he suggests some of the considerations that led not only
away from the individual life space but extended the study of group life
into the domain of social science. He illustrates one limitation of
the individual life space analysis in representing changes in the relations between husband and wife. The husband wants to predict the behavior of his wife and vice versa. The expectations that each has of
the other's behavior is represented in their respective life spaces.
The actual behavior of the two creates new objective situations for
them which then determine the new life spaces. The behavior of the
pair derived from these "second round" life spaces creates for each a
new objective situation, and so on. Though it is difficult to see how
changes in interpersonal relations could be understood otherwise, such
a subjective-objective circular procedure for each life space clearly
becomes prohibitively complex when more than two individuals are involved.

The analysis of individual life spaces is not necessary, however,
for every kind of inquiry. Lewin reaffirms the field theoretical tenet
that the group is a dynamic whole with properties of its own, different
from other-sized units, but no less real. Accordingly, the behavior of
groups may be conceptually represented without reference to individual
life spaces.

The field theoretical representation of groups has problems of its
own, especially when more than one group is involved and when the theoretical question has to do with change. For the latter purpose, field
theory presupposes a specification of the possible activities or positions in which the group can be located and an arrangement of them in
a group space so that direction of movement can be apriori defined.
In discussing this field approach to change in the group life space,
Lewin proposes the same model used at the individual and interpersonal

level. Thus, change in the group's position follows the group "perception" of the situation, and the behavior of the group now changes the
objective situation. In this model, field theory "covers" the representation of the group life space at given times, and the derivation of
behavior from it. The idea of group "perception" is a shorthand way of
noting that the goals, values, and other dynamics present in the life
space affect the members' definition of their situation which is different from the way the situation is defined objectively. Field theory,
however, does not cover the effect of the objective environment on the
group life space; the change in the life space mediated by the group's
behavior is indeed beyond the scope of field theory. Thus, the determination of the group life space, both the topological structure of
possible movements and the group dynamics can only rest on theories of
how other groups, the larger culture, and the ecology affect the contents of the life space. To discern and theorize about these "boundary"
conditions were major reasons for the introduction of the phase space
method.

This non-field theoretical method, borrowed from physics, centers
on quantitative shifts in social processes that are conceived as quasi
stationary equilibria. More precisely, a phase space is a system of
coordinates in which the driving and restraining forces that maintain
and change behavior, events, products, etc. are represented and analyzed
as to their effects on such social processes. Lewin presents phase
space analyses of a variety of phenomena and their regulatory forces
over time: the level of productivity in a factory, the frequency of
aggression in childrens' groups, the amount of racial discrimination in
small towns, etc. One could add as suitable for phase space treatment:
changes in crime rates, shifts in public opinion, suicide rates in
different societies, and indicators of various economic processes. At
the level of the individual, one could analyze variations in mood,
number of altruistic acts at different periods of the year, and so on.
These examples describe a general feature of the method: it may be used
to analyze all the forces that are implicated in a social process re-
gardless of the unit in which those forces are actually observed. Thus,
one can study the behavior of individuals, groups or larger social units
such as the community or society. There is also the potential of
interunit transfer. For example, the forces that are affecting the
productivity of a group may be "translatable" into forces that raise
or lower the tension on individuals in different roles; events in the
lives of individuals may determine shifts in the indicators of intergroup conflicts; and fluctuations in the business cycle may cause changes

in the suicide rates of different ethnic groups. Translation of course, requires theory that specifies the function by which forces at one level of analysis affect those at another. Indeed, phase space analysis pre-supposes considerable theoretical and empirical knowledge to identify the relevant forces and to combine them so as to yield predictable effects on the equilibria. Nonetheless, as a method of analysis, the catholicity of phase space with respect to the kinds of forces that can be represented and dealt with encourages broad-gauged analyses of social phenomena and is surely promotive of Lewin's strongly held view that productive and cumulative knowledge about social behavior can only come with an integrated social science that speaks in the same conceptual language. Phase space analyses also suggests that social psychology cannot be based on individual or group behavior exclusively but on the mutual _relation_ between the two units of analysis studied in particular cultural and ecological contexts. When sufficiently diffused, the last creative contribution of Lewin may thus be useful in the restructuring of social psychology as a more integral part of social science.

REFERENCES

DeRivera, J. (1976). _Field Theory as Human Science_. New York: Gardner Press.

Lewin, K. (1935). The conflict between Aristotelian and Galileian modes of thought in contemporary psychology. In _A Dynamic Theory of Personality_. New York: McGraw-Hill.

Lewin, K. (1944). Constructs in psychology and psychological ecology. _University of Iowa Monograph_, xx, 1-29.

Lewin, K. (1947, 1951). Frontiers in group dynamics. _Human Relations_, 1, 2-38. Also in D. Cartwright (Ed.), _Field Theory in Social Science_. New York: Harper.

Part II: Practical Theory

Section A: <u>Therapy - Mental Health - Interpersonal Relations</u>

Lewin's contribution to the field of social psychology is clear.
The answer to the question, what is Lewin's influence on the field of
mental health, (and more specifically psychotherapy) has not been clearly
described. <u>Susan Wheelan</u> addresses this question and from her interviews, experience and literature survey gives an account of Lewin's direct
and indirect influence on etiology and treatment, especially modes of
group therapy. She closes with a quotation from the report of a task
force of The American Psychiatric Association, which says in part:
"Psychotherapy owes to (Lewin's) t-group much of its systematic understanding of such factors as group development, group pressure, group
cohesiveness, leadership, and group norms and values."

The next article describes the legacy of Kurt Lewin in the area of
marriage enrichment and therapy. <u>Matti Gershenfeld's</u> keynote phrase is
"what makes Lewin so impactful is that he uses a few concepts, and
through their use breaks down a complex problem." She then elaborates
the Lewinian approach to understanding marriage as a group, which leads
her to describing marriage enrichment programs and therapeutic methods
based on Lewinian understanding.

<u>George Bach</u>, a well known pioneer in some forms of psychotherapy
says "I want to acknowledge that the field-theoretical-Gestalt orientation I applied in my work as an individual and group psychotherapist
opened my eyes to many new options in dealing with our patients' problems.
In his article he blends personal reminiscences of Kurt Lewin with a
succinct history of certain Lewinian ideas, down to an intriguing current one. Bach explains, "My studies of and participation in group dynamics research made me aware of the importance of rituals and their therapeutic utilization in group therapy."

"Whatever a person does or wishes to do, he must have some 'ground'
to stand upon. This is probably the primary reason why he is extremely
affected the moment this ground begins to give way." With these words
as a theme, <u>Matti Gershenfeld</u> again addresses social situations using
Lewin's concepts. She chooses to focus on work done with women in life
transition stages, geographically mobile Black middle class families,
and newly unemployed middle class persons. She discovers a paradox
in her analysis of the social conflicts and problems--that with greater
free movement there is a corresponding greater tension.

Yvonne Agazarian's goal is to describe the way she conceptualizes all groups and specifically how that applies to therapy groups. First she deals with the application of Lewin's Field Theory to group psychotherapy. Then she conceptualizes the development of a psychotherapy group in the framework of the Life Space, with each phase represented as a region with a sub goal. Finally she demonstrates how to apply a force field to the analysis of group behavior for the determination of group phase and possible therapist interventions. Her concluding illustration of therapeutic issues focuses on the member-role and the group-role of the scapegoat in a group. The article is a fitting finish to this first section of Part II.

Kurt Lewin's Influence on the Field of Mental Health

Susan A. Wheelan

Temple University

Lewin's contribution to the field of social psychology is clear. Schellenberg (1978) credits him with enormous influence and states that at least half of America's most prominent social psychologists in the 1950's and 1960's were his students or close associates (p. 77). Back (1972) outlines his influence on both the academic study of group dynamics and the applications of his research and theory to organization development and human relations training (p. 99). His influence on the conduct of psychological research has been discussed at length by numerous writers.

Less clearly described is Lewin's influence on the field of mental health and more specifically, psychotherapy. What Lewinian ideas were most influential in the mental health field? What areas of the field were most influenced by Lewin? Who were the conduits of Lewinian concepts? This paper will attempt to provide preliminary answers to these questions.

Jerome Frank (1985) does not believe that Lewin influenced the field of mental health per se. Rather, he sees Lewin as influencing certain individuals. Frank also noted that many Lewinian concepts (the focus on the here and now; attention to context) are pivotal to the field but not necessarily attributed to Lewin. Similar ideas occurred in different people about the same time.

Lewin, himself, acknowledged his participation in a larger scientific revolution. This shift first occurred in the physical sciences when the work of Michael Faraday, James Maxwell, and Albert Einstein challenged Newtonian science and its concommitant determinism. Their work, and that of others, led to the emergence of field theories in the physical sciences.

The impact of this new way of thinking was not limited to the physical sciences, however. Durkin (1972) states that,

> "Necessity gave birth to quantum mechanics and relativity theory, which led, in turn, to a radical change in the prevailing scientific outlook and paved the way for systems thinking--At last the relationship between personality as a whole, its function in society, and society itself could be studied in good scientific conscience" (p. 11).

Levi-Strauss, Chomsky, Piaget, Brunner, Von Bertalanffy and Lewin
are among the early scientists who embraced systemic thought and altered
the course of social science research and theory. Consequently, it is
difficult to trace the specific contributions of Lewin among the prolifer-
ation of systemic theories and concepts. This is especially true in the
mental health field, since Lewin's primary focus was elsewhere. However,
traces of his influence are discernible. For example, Yalom stated that,

> "Although Lewin was not a psychotherapist, his impact on
> psychotherapeutic practice should not be underestimated.
> In addition to therapists who were more formally his students,
> he spoke frequently at meetings of psychotherapists and his
> work was well known by the British and American psychiatric
> community" (p. 150).

IMPACT ON ETIOLOGY

In order to develop methods to remediate problem behaviors, clini-
cians must first attempt to understand the etiology of normal as well as
abnormal behaviors. Much of Lewin's writings deal directly with issues
related to normal and abnormal development. His works describe environmental influences in child behavior and development (1931a, 1946); child
development (1929, 1930, 1937, 1941a, 1941b, 1942) and normal and abnormal intellectual development (1931b, 1940).

In order to understand the behavior of an individual, Lewin asserted,
one must know the totality of forces operating in that individual's psychological field. It is the total field, not the elements in isolation,
that produces behavior. This theoretical formulation is ever present
in Lewin's writings about child and personality development. It is also
a predominant notion in modern day psychologists' understanding of human
development but, more often than not, is attributed to social learning
theorists rather than to Lewin.

Much fruitful research has been generated by Lewin's early work that
has enhanced our understanding of human behavior. His students, such as
Dembo, Ovsiankina, Zeigarnik, Back, Pepitone, Redl, Hartmann and Brown
have all continued research and application of Lewin's ideas to understanding the behavior and development of individuals.

It would not be accurate to say, however, that Lewin had a tremendous impact on theoretical and research based understandings of individual human behavior. Many of his concepts are in common usage and
specific references to his work can be found. And yet, even the most
careful perusal of current developmental, personality or abnormal psychology texts will turn up little reference to Lewin or his students. The

ideas are there but attributed to other schools of thoughts. As Frank (1985) says, "Many people came up with similar ideas at the same time."

IMPACT ON TREATMENT

It is in the area of treatment, that Lewin's influence is felt most directly. Specifically, Lewin's work has influenced family therapy and group therapy. The need to examine behavior in its context, gave rise to treatment modalities that utilized groups (family and stranger) as a method of remediation.

Nathan Ackerman began working with families in the 1930's. Looking back on his career and the parallel development of family therapy, he stated that:

> In the perspective of the history of mental science, the emergence of the principles of family diagnosis and treatment is an inevitable development. It is the natural product of the coalescence of new conceptual trends in a number of fields: cultural anthropology, group dynamics, and communication (Ackerman, 1970, p. 6). (emphasis mine)

Ackerman acknowledges the emerging field of group dynamics as one of the prime influences on the development of family therapy. Current family therapy terminology abounds with references to concepts first identified by Lewin, his students and colleagues. Concepts such as norms, structures, communication patterns, cohesion, subgroups, scapegoats, types of conflict (the double bind) form the basis for understanding and altering family dynamics.

Group therapy, as a treatment modality predates Lewin's years of influence. The first reference to the use of a group mode of treatment was in 1906. Pratt used a group to increase compliance with the treatment of consumption (Corsini, 1957). Moreno's first publication on group treatment appeared in 1911. He remained the strongest influence on group psychotherapy through 1935. The six persons most often cited as the founders of group therapy are, Pratt (1906), Adler (1964), Moreno (1911), Burrow (1953), Lazell (1921), and Marsh (1931).

Marsh's motto--by the crowd have they been broken; by the crowd shall they be healed--expresses the belief of most early (and current) group psychotherapists. Methodology, however, remained psychoanalytic in the main. Little or no field theoretical influence was felt for many years. In fact, Corsini's (1957) Bibliography of Group Psychotherapy 1906-1956 does not make reference to Lewin until 1939. Beginning with that reference, however, names associated with Lewin appear in force (Bales, 1942; Redl, 1942; Bach, 1948; Frank, 1950 etc.).

A cluster of models developed that have come to be known as group dynamics therapy groups. Representatives of this approach include Bion (1950), Durkin (1957), Foulkes (1965), Ezriel (1973), Whitaker and Lieberman (1965), Agazarian and Peters (1981), Bach (1957), and Frank (1957).

METHODS OF GROUP THERAPY

Corsini (1957) credits Bach with giving impetus to the use of group therapy by providing evidence that the group method can work as well as individual treatment (p. 16). Bach is also credited with being instrumental in applying Lewin's field theory to group psychotherapy. Jerome Frank (1957) conducted the early research on group dynamics in group therapy groups.

Early discussions and investigations into the dynamics of therapy groups led to heated disagreements. The group dynamics advocates acknowledged the similarity of therapy groups and other task groups. They investigated ways to utilize naturally occurring group processes to facilitate change in members. They also sought ways to manipulate these processes to further therapeutic goals. Other psychoanalytically oriented group therapists (Slavson, 1940; Wolf and Schwartz, 1962) saw the study of group dynamics as fine in schools and clubs but not as occurring or useful in therapy groups (Kadis et al, 1963). This remains an issue to this day as evidenced by the presence of only two general models that utilize group dynamics out of 10 presented group therapy models in Shaffer and Galinsky's (1974) book.

Most of the group dynamics therapists are psychoanalytic in how they see individual personality but sought to develop an approach to treatment that utilized social psychological research on group processes and dynamics. It was natural, therefore, for them to turn to field theory as the most useful conceptual framework for their work. Thus, these models represent a combination of psychoanalytic theory and field theory. The proportions of each vary from model to model but each acknowledges a debt to Lewin.

Many people see Wilfred Bion's work as unrelated to Lewin and Field theory. However, Shaffer and Galinsky (1974) state that:

> General systems theory, ... was just beginning to be developed
> at the time that Foulkes and Bion were applying their experience
> with British army therapy groups to civilian groups ...
> Instead these men found Lewin's field theory, which may be
> viewed as an earlier prototype of general systems theory, to
> be the most suitable conceptual framework for their purpose. ...
> P. 5)

Yalom further solidifies the connection between Bion and Lewin by noting that Bion's analyst prior to World War II (Rickman) was very familiar with Lewin's works. Later, Bion worked with Melanie Klein. The influence of Klein and, through Rickman, Lewin, are evident in Bion's theoretical framework (Yalom, 1970, p. 150).

Whitaker and Lieberman (1965) are examples of the continuing influence of Lewin and Bion on the development of group therapy models. Their mentor, Herbert Thelen and they were active with both NTL which has direct links to Lewin, and Tavistock with direct links to Bion. Agazarian and Peters (1981) were students of David Jenkins who studied with Kurt Lewin. Also, they are both analytically trained and Yvonne Agazarian has studied at Tavistock as well. While biographers of Lewin often point out the marked lack of influence Freud had on Lewin, his intellectual offspring combine the two and see them as compatible.

Perhaps the most convincing statement of Lewin's influence on group psychotherapy is made in the following statement:

> T-groups, springing from the field of social psychology (and specifically Lewin's field theory), have behind them a long tradition of research in group dynamics. No comparable body of knowledge has been generated by group therapy, a field notoriously deficient in any systematic research. Thus, what is presently known of the basic science of group psychotherapy stems almost entirely from social-psychological research with task groups and t-groups. Psychotherapy owes to the t-group much of its systematic understanding of such factors as group development, group pressure, group cohesiveness, leadership, and group norms and values.
> (Task Force on Recent Developments in the Use of Small Groups of the American Psychiatric Association, Encounter Groups and Psychiatry [1970], p. 23.)

REFERENCES

Ackerman, N. (Ed.) (1970). _Family Process_. Basic Books.

Adler, A. (1964). _Social Interest: A Challenge to Mankind_. (J. Linton and R. Vaughan, Trans.) New York: Capricorn.

Agazarian, Y. & R. Peters (1981). _The Visible and Invisible Group_. Routledge & Kegan Paul.

Bach, G. Theoretical and Technical Explorations in Group Methods of Psychotherapy. _American Psychologist_, 3, 346.

Bach, G. (1954). _Intensive Group Psychotherapy_. New York: Ronald Press.

Back, K. (1972). _Beyond Words: The Story of Sensitivity Training and the Encounter Movement_. New York: Russell Sage.

Bion, W. (1959). Experiences in Groups. New York: Basic Books.

Burrow, T.N. (1953). Science and Man's Behavior: The Contribution of Phylobiology (W.E. Galt, ed.). New York: Philosophical Library.

Corsini, R. (1957). Bibliography of Group Psychotherapy 1906-1956. New York: Beacon House. Psychodrama and Group Psychotherapy Monographs, No. 29.

Corsini, R. (1957). Methods of Group Psychotherapy. New York: McGraw-Hill.

Durkin, H. (1972). In Sager and Kaplan (Eds.), Progress in Group and Family Therapy. Brunner/Mazels.

Durkin, H. (1957). Towards a common-basic for group dynamics: Group and therapeutic processes in group psychotherapy. International Journal of Group Psychotherapy, 7(2), 115-130.

Durkin, H. (1964). The Group in Depth. New York: International Universities Press.

Ezriel, H. (1973). Psychoanalytic Group Therapy. In L. Wolberg and E. Schwartz (Ed.), Group Therapy: 1973. New York: Intercontinental Universities Press.

Foulkes, S.F. (1965). Therapeutic Group Analysis. New York: International Universities Press.

Frank, J.D. (1957). Some determinants, manifestations and effects of cohesiveness in therapy groups. International Journal of Group Psychotherapy. January, 7(1), 53-63.

Frank, J.D. (1961). Persuasion and Healing. Baltimore: Johns Hopkins University Press.

Frank, J.D. (1985, May). Personal Interview.

Kadis, A. et al (1963). A Practicum of Group Psychotherapy. New York: Harper and Row.

Lazell, E.W. (1921). The Group Treatment of dementia proecox. Psychoanalytic Review, 8, 168-179.

Lewin, K. (1930). Expression movements of children. In W. Stern (Ed.), Psychology of Early Childhood. New York: Holt.

Lewin, K. (1931). Environmental Forces in Child Behaviour and Development. In C. Murchison (Ed.), Handbook of Child Psychology. Mass: Clark University Press.

Lewin, K. (1937). Experiments in Frustration and Regression in Children. Psychological Bulletin, 34, p. 754-755 (with Barkett & Dembo).

Lewin, K. (with Lippitt and White). Patterns of Aggressive behavior in Experimentally Created "Social Climates." Journal of Social Psychology, 10, p. 271-299.

Lewin, K. Personal Adjustment and Group Belongingness. Jewish Society Service Quarterly, 17:4, p. 362-66.

Lewin, K. Changes in Social Sensitivity in Child and Adult. Childhood Education, 19, p. 53-57.

Lewin, K. (1935). A Dynamic Theory of Personality. New York: McGraw-Hill.

Lewin, K. (1936). Principles of Topological Psychology. New York: Mc-Graw Hill.

Lewin, K. (1951). Field Theory in Social Science. New York: Harper & Bros.

Marsh, L.L. (1931). Group therapy by the psychological equivalent of the revival. <u>Mental Hygiene</u>, <u>15</u>, 328-349.

Moreno, J.L. (1911). Die Gotthert als Kommediant. Vienna: Anzengruber Verlag.

Pratt, J. (1906). The "home sanitorium" treatment of consumption. <u>Boston Medical Surgical Journal</u>, 154, 210-216.

Redl, F. (1942). <u>Group Emotion and Leadership</u>, p. 5, 573-596.

Redl, F. (1944). Diagnostic Group Work. <u>American Journal of Ortho-psychiatry</u>, <u>14</u>, 53-67.

Schellenberg, J. (1978). <u>Masters of Social Psychology</u>. New York: Oxford University Press.

Shaffer, J. & Galinsky, M.D. (1974). <u>Models of Group Therapy and Sensitivity Training.</u> New Jersey: Prentice-Hall.

Slavson, S. (1940). Group Therapy. <u>Mental Hygiene</u>, 24, 36-49.

Task Force on Recent Developments in the Use of Small Groups of the American Psychiatric Association. <u>Encounter Groups and Psychiatry</u>.

Whitaker, D.S. & Lieberman, M. (1965). <u>Psychotherapy Through the Group Process</u>. New York: Atherton Press.

Wolf, A. & Schwartz, E.K. (1962). <u>Psychoanalysis in Groups</u>. New York: Grune and Stratton.

Yalom, I. (1970). <u>The Theory and Practice of Group Psychotherapy</u>. New York: Basic Books.

Understanding Enrichment and Therapy in Marriage: The Legacy of Kurt Lewin

Matti K. Gershenfeld

Temple University

While many think of Kurt Lewin as a small group researcher, as the originator of the t-group movement, and as having an impact on social and organizational change, the work of Lewin related to marriage is little known. Moreover, Lewin is not to be thought of only as a social psychologist who had an impact on the historical beginnings of marriage and family therapy. Rather, the genius of his approach to resolving problems can be effectively utilized today. He helped in increasing our understanding of defining marriage and in designing for marriage enrichment programs (or educational programs in the areas of learning skills related to marriage). Further, for therapists, Lewinian concepts help to conceive treatment plans for couples.

What made Lewin so impactful was that he used a few concepts, and through their use could break down a complex problem. The concepts are well known. They include a person in a region of the life-space, movement through regions toward a goal, overlapping regions, being grounded, being in a group, attractiveness of the group, and ways to think about resolution of conflicts utilizing the previous concepts. Lewinian concepts can be used as effectively today as when he conceived them. They can be used to break down the complexities of marital problems to a level where they can be innovatively and freshly understood.

The prime presentation of Lewin's concepts on marriage is in <u>Resolving Social Conflicts</u> (Lewin, 1948) in a chapter, "Background of Conflict in Marriage," written in 1940. This chapter in the usual Lewinian style builds an understanding of marriage, the special properties of the marriage group, and eventually discusses methods for a solution of its conflicts. This chapter can be the basis for working with the general concept of marriage so that couples understand marriage differently. It can be used in designing marriage enrichment, or skill-building programs, and it can be used as the basis for designing therapy for a couple. Also, Lewinian concepts are applicable in creation of an approach for the first interview, for diagnosing the problems of the couple, and for methods for helping them understand not only where the problems lie but with concomitant data for resolving the problems.

Lewinian concepts can also be used in making decisions about the prime
interventions which might be made to increase the possibilities of
successful marriage. In this paper, an effort will be made to demonstrate how Lewinian concepts can be used in some of the above named
situations for being helpful to a couple.

UNDERSTANDING MARRIAGE

One method of learning is what Lewin calls "cognitive restructuring"
(Lewin, 1951). Here, how we think about marriage is changed from how
marriage is usually thought about. Marriage is not to be viewed as an
institution with rules to which a person adjusts. There are no assumptions about knowing roles, or prescribed roles; there are no assumptions
about goals--right or wrong. Lewin would say, "Marriage is a group situation, and as such shows the general characteristics of group life."
Marriage is like other groups and "a group is more than, or more exactly,
different from the sum of its members. It has its own structure, its
own goals, and its own relations to other groups. The essence of a
group is not the similarity or dissimilarity of its members, but their
interdependence. A group can be characterized as a 'dynamical whole'--
this means that a change in the state of any subpart changes the state
of any other subpart. The degree of interdependence of the subparts
of members of the group varies all the way from a loose 'mass' to a
compact unit. It depends, among other factors, upon the size, organization, and intimacy of the group." (Lewin, 1948, p. 84.)
     The smaller group may be part of a more inclusive group. The mar-
ried are generally a part of a larger family, and that family might be
a part of a community or a nation. Further, an individual is usually
a member of many more or less overlapping groups. He might be a member
of a professional group, a political group, or a luncheon group; in
addition to being a member of the family. The potency of any of these
groups, that is the degree to which a person's behavior is influenced
by its membership in them, may be different for the different groups to
which he belongs, as in Figure 1 (Lewin, 1948, p. 85). For one person,
business may be more important than politics. For another, a political
party might have higher potency. The potency of various groups varies
with a momentary situation in which a person finds himself. When a person is at home, the potency of the family is generally greater than when
he or she is in the office. Marriage usually has a high potency within
the world of an individual or in Lewinian terms, "his life-space."

How a person is grounded, very much influences his or her security, sense of belonging, and feeling of comfort. The group a person belongs to is one of the most important constituents of this ground. If a person does not feel clear belongingness in a marriage, it influences his sense of belongingness in all other areas of his life. And finally, the group is part of the life-space in which he moves about. His status in the group, the amount of space of free movement within it, and similar group properties are important in determining the life-space of the individual. It is then clear at the outset how much marriage means in the life-space of the individual.

Let us explore then, "How does an individual adapt to a group?" It is to be understood that belonging to a given group does not mean that the individual must agree in every aspect of the group. He need not concur fully with the goals, regulations, style of living, and thinking of the group. The individual has his or her own personal goals. He needs a sufficient space of free movement within the group to pursue those personal goals and to satisfy his individual ones. The question of a group member is, "How is it possible to sufficiently satisfy one's own individual needs without losing membership and status within the group?"

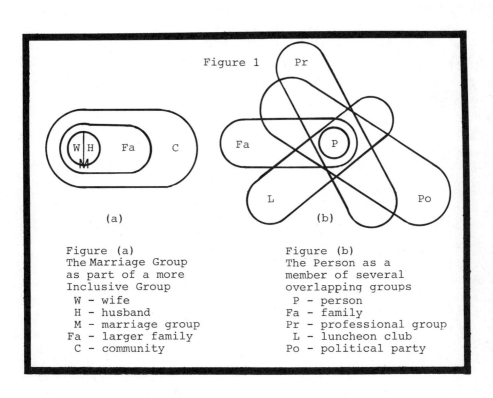

Figure 1

(a)

(b)

Figure (a)
The Marriage Group
as part of a more
Inclusive Group
  W - wife
  H - husband
  M - marriage group
Fa - larger family
  C - community

Figure (b)
The Person as a
member of several
overlapping groups
  P - person
Fa - family
Pr - professional group
  L - luncheon club
Po - political party

If the space of free movement within the group is too small, in other words if his independence of the group is insufficient, the individual will be unhappy. If the group limits free movement of members too severely, there will be too much frustration and he will leave.

Finally, there are great differences in how individual and group needs are reconciled. The restrictions set up by the group may leave the individual much or little freedom. The restrictions may be based upon discussion and common consent of members of the group, or may be imposed by fiat or an autocratic decree.

These concepts lay a groundwork for understanding marriage; marriage is a group and there are group properties as in all other groups. Members join a marriage (group) voluntarily, because this group will meet their needs and they expect to derive more satisfaction from belonging than not belonging.

There, further, is the Lewinian idea that a group will create its rules for meeting the needs of its members, and that rules developed by common understandings are likely to be more successful than rules imposed from without. These concepts carry an understanding that people are not newly hatched in a group called, "marriage" but rather that they have had previous group experiences as in their family of origin, and that this influences the atmosphere, the context, and the styles of behavior. These previous groups will influence the present groups; understanding the original family group is helpful for understanding norms to be established in the new group and problems which might emerge in this new group. It emphasizes the concept that marriage is to meet the needs of its members, so that the group will be attractive to its members. And, these needs must be clarified because membership in each group is unique.

There is a further understanding that an individual is part of several overlapping groups and that there needs to develop methods for a person to successfully belong and also cope with these multiple memberships. Especially, there needs to be a clarification of how important this marriage group is to each member.

Defining marriage as a group in this way underscores that each person has legitimate individual needs, needs for space of free movement. And, there needs to be specified how he or she will relate to this group. This conceptualization can have enormous impact for a couple getting off givens or guilt. It means getting off passivity and being threatened by change. Rather there is emphasized a process in which each couple clarifies what their marriage group will be.

THE SPECIAL PROPERTIES OF THE MARRIAGE GROUP

In addition to an understanding of marriage as a group with group properties, Lewin also develops the special properties of the marriage group. It is understood that the character of a marriage group within a particular culture will vary with nationality, race, occupation, and class. However, there are certain properties characteristic of most marriage groups within our culture. Two concepts are of special importance. The first is the smallness of the group, and the second is that the group touches central regions of the person.

First, the smallness of the group. The marriage group contains two adult members and perhaps one or more children. Because of the small number of members in the group any move by one member will, relatively speaking, deeply affect the other members and the state of the group. In other words, the smallness of the group means that there are not other members, nor other needs to be considered; and so the smallness of the group means members are very influenced by each other as to the quality of the group, the atmosphere of the group, and the tension within the group. Group members are highly interdependent.

The second central factor is that marriage touches the central regions of the person. Marriage is closely related to the central layer of the person, to his or her values, fantasies, social and economic status. Unlike other groups, marriage deals not with one or another aspect of the person, but his entire physical and social existence. Marriage means a desire for the least social distance. These factors produce a closely integrated social unit. That results on one hand to a high degree of identification with a group, and a readiness to commit energy to achieve the group goals--to stand together; on the other hand such a closely integrated unit increases the sensitivity to the shortcomings of the partner or oneself.

So then special group properties include; the attractiveness of the group, the small number of members, and the group involving central regions of the person. Effects of these properties mean tremendous influences and interdependence, being especially vulnerable and finally being especially sensitive to shortcomings of the partner or the self. Thinking of marriage in this way can greatly influence how partners deal with the creation of responsibilities and rules in their marriage, understanding of the affect each has on the other, and a recognition that how they act toward each other may be quite different from how they might act in other groups (with the boss, with colleagues, with friends, or with relatives).

CREATING ENRICHMENT PROGRAMS

Marriage is very different today from what it was in previous generations, and Lewin would say that it is important that "group members"
in a marriage group learn how to be in this kind of relationship. Lewin
extensively describes different kinds of learning. He uses a particular
example noting that we know how to live in a situation of autocracy, but
that we need to learn democracy. The analogy, learning to go from autocracy to democracy, is similar to the learning involved in going from a
role-related marriage in which the man (like Clarence Day in the "Auto-
crat of the Breakfast Table") gives orders, to learning in a contemporary
marriage in which there are equal members who express their needs and
where decisions are made as in a democracy.

So to learn how to be in a modern marriage (like learning democracy)
"means, first, that the person has to do something himself instead of
being passively moved by forces imposed on him." (Lewin, 1951, p. 76.)
"It means, second, to establish certain likes and dislikes; that is,
certain valences, values, and ideologies." (Lewin, 1951, p. 76.) That
would mean creating certain experimental situations or creating learning
situations in which people have an opportunity to experience their likes
and dislikes. "It means, third, to get acquainted with certain techniques such as, those of group decision." (Lewin, 1951, p. 76.)

From this discussion and the understandings developed previously
on marriage, it can be easily derived that there need to be educational
courses and workshops to teach people how to learn how to be members in
a modern marriage. Programs of this nature related to marriage are typically referred to as, "Marriage Enrichment Programs." In such programs
which are usually conducted in groups, there would be opportunities for
couples to "experiment" and observe themselves and others, and to learn
their likes and dislikes, their values and ideologies as different from
other couples. They would acquire a "we feeling" and a sense of being
a group (couple) distinctive from other couples. They would be actively
involved in their own learning and not be passive. Finally, they would
learn certain techniques like expressing their feelings and values, and
clarifying their style of decision-making in addition to practicing interpersonal skills within the group. An example of an exercise which
might be used in an enrichment program follows.

"EXPECTATIONS"

In the following exercise, each person is given a copy of the sheet, "Expectations of Myself, My Partner, and My Family." (See Figure 2) Participants are instructed to fill out the sheet as follows: In the center there is a circle with a heading, "MINE."

1. Briefly, list five expectations you have of yourself in relation to your family.

On the left there is a large rectangle

2. Insert your PARTNER'S name and list five expectations your
   partner has of you.

On other parts of the sheet there are five squares

3. List a significant member of your FAMILY by name and three
   expectations they have of you.

Now, look at each item. If you accept that expectation--draw a line from that expectation to you, having it end with an arrow at the circle which is you. Do that for each person. If you do not accept that ex-pectation, draw a line through the expectation.

Now, group with two other people. Examine your sheet and analyze with whom you get along well, and why. Next, analyze with whom you have the most difficulty, and why. Finally, select one person and think about how you will deal with the expectations they have of you that you do not want to meet; expectations that you do not willingly accept. Each per-son takes a turn discussing their sheet, having the two others be con-sultants.

The discussion can be continued, either between the couple at home, or the group can continue to be consultants for each other. In serving as the couple's consultants, group couples help the "target" couple deal with expectations people have of them that they do not want to meet and which only increase the tension in their marriage and family.

The preceding exercise is derived from Lewin's examination of gen-eral considerations of conflict within a marriage. He talks of needs to be met in a marriage and one of the factors which leads to conflict and a reduction of security (or ground in a marriage) is the "variety of contradictory nature of needs to be satisfied within marriage." (Lewin, 1948, p. 91.)

In summary, then, Lewinian concepts on marriage, and learning how to be a group member in a central core group, lend themselves to a wide variety of training designs. Just as Lewin's concepts had such impact and served as the basis of small group research, so Lewin's concepts,

Figure 2

EXPECTATIONS

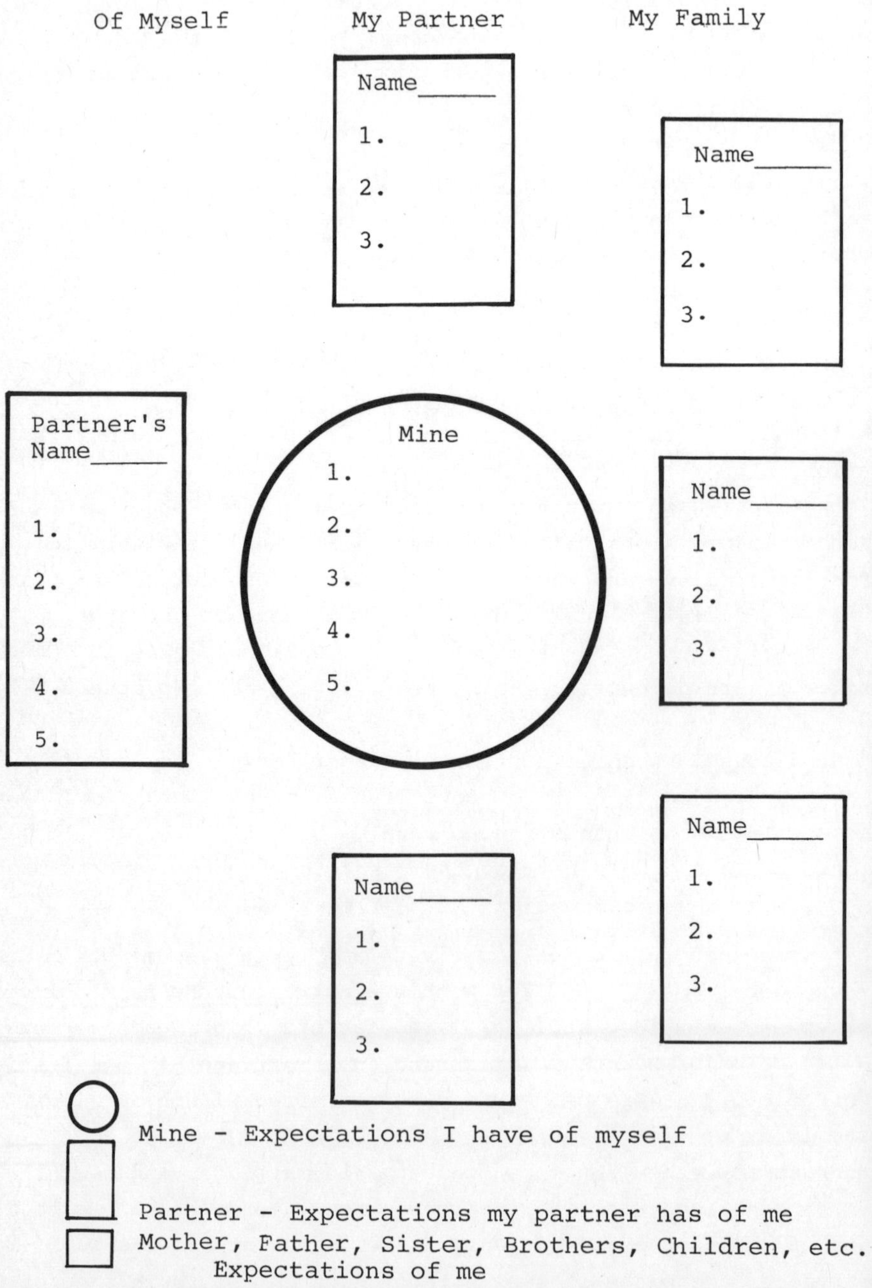

Of Myself   My Partner   My Family

```
┌─────────────┐
│ Name_____  │
│             │
│ 1.          │
│             │
│ 2.          │
│             │
│ 3.          │
└─────────────┘
```

```
              ┌─────────────┐
              │  Name_____ │
              │             │
              │ 1.          │
              │             │
              │ 2.          │
              │             │
              │ 3.          │
              └─────────────┘
```

```
┌────────────┐          ╭───────────╮
│ Partner's  │        Mine
│ Name_____ │       ╱  1.         ╲
│            │      │   2.          │
│ 1.         │      │   3.          │
│ 2.         │      │   4.          │
│ 3.         │       ╲  5.         ╱
│ 4.         │        ╰───────────╯
│ 5.         │
└────────────┘          ┌─────────────┐
                        │  Name_____ │
                        │             │
                        │ 1.          │
                        │             │
                        │ 2.          │
                        │             │
                        │ 3.          │
                        └─────────────┘
```

```
                                  ┌─────────────┐
                                  │  Name_____ │
                                  │ 1.          │
                                  │             │
┌─────────────┐                   │ 2.          │
│  Name_____ │                   │             │
│             │                   │ 3.          │
│ 1.          │                   └─────────────┘
│             │
│ 2.          │
│             │
│ 3.          │
└─────────────┘
```

○ Mine - Expectations I have of myself

▢ Partner - Expectations my partner has of me

▢ Mother, Father, Sister, Brothers, Children, etc.
    Expectations of me

in the area of marriage, lend themselves to an extensive variety of learning experiences. These would encourage participants to recognize their own needs and their partner's needs in conjunction with recognizing the basic sources of attractiveness and the tension systems related to their marriage.

THERAPY METHODS

Lewin's concepts on marriage also lend themselves readily to creation of an approach in therapy when the conflicts in a marriage require professional help.

Diagnosis

In the initial diagnostic interviews, questions should help to clarify some of the central issues Lewin raises in terms of expectations, dominant needs, degree of satisfaction or non-satisfaction of meeting these needs, style of dealing with satisfaction or non-satisfaction. Further, it allows examination of tension systems in a state of hunger or satiation, and exploration of needs in the central area of sexual needs. Also, the social ground of an individual in terms of marriage group constituting a social home is explored from a phenomenological perspective. These factors as individually felt, and their major influences on need satisfaction in marriage, are of prime importance in acquiring basic data needed for resolving marital difficulties in therapy.

It is significant that in the process, each partner hears the other's responses to the questions; there is developed an atmosphere of listening, and a collection of data which is phenomenologically based. There is a learning of the process of discussing information, and utilizing it to achieve desired group goals. It is as if the therapist's role is to be another group member whose prime role is to be a facilitator, generating continued interest and energy in the group.

The concepts on which the diagnostic interview questions are developed are derived from the discussion of general consideration about conflicts in marriage. (Lewin, 1948, p. 90-98.)

Treatment

In the treatment phase, there are also a number of approaches which would be derived from Lewin. The therapist, in the therapy process seems to create a general atmosphere of acceptance, listening, and encouraging thinking of each person having needs to be met. Lewin emphasizes, "We have mentioned that the frequency and seriousness of the conflicts in marriage depend mainly on the general atmosphere of the marriage. For the solution of conflicts, the atmosphere again seems to be the most important factor." (Lewin, 1948, p. 101.)

Another approach in treatment might be to teach participants a model for talking to each other as in Relationship Enhancement Therapy. (Guerney, 1977.) Here couples are taught three modes:

1. one of listening
2. one of speaking
3. mode switching; going from listening to speaking, or the reverse.

Here too, the emphasis is not on problem resolution, but rather on the process of a couple expressing their needs and learning how to understand their partner and build from this understanding. It is interesting to note that this would be directly in the Lewin model, and that recent research cited by Guerney has indicated that this model has been the most successful in comparison with other models. (Giblin, 1985; Ross, Baker & Guerney, 1985.)

A third approach in treatment derived from Lewinian concepts might be utilization of a problem solving approach involving the couples. They would act as process consultants and their data for discussion would be answers from the initial interviews. They might then indicate their highest priorities for need-satisfaction. Then, they might develop a force-field analysis and jointly create methods for resolving their problems and changing their behaviors.

They might become their own organization consultants, perhaps practicing as consultants to another couple to build skills in applying these methods to themselves. A method to encourage such an approach might be a three-couples group, with couples naming an area of difficulty to be resolved, having each couple take from the reprints of their interview data one that applies to them and then having other couples serve as consultants, as facilitators for their resolution of the problem--and their serving as consultants to the other couples. In this situation, a group size of three couples is utilized for a particular reason. It is designed so that one couple has the problem, one couple is the consultant, and one couple observes the process and interaction between the focus (problem) couples.

Lewinian concepts can readily be utilized as a basis for creation of diagnosis of couple problems and therapeutic approaches for resolving these problems. Each of the treatment approaches described emphasize the fact that the couple are a part of a unique small group who have feelings about the importance of the group in their lives, and ideas of how their needs should be met within the group. Conflicts arise and can be resolved in the process of helping couples clarify their needs and developing a perspective of their partners also being in the group with legitimate needs for remaining and seeking satisfaction in the group.

INTERVENTION

A question often raised is, "When is the best time to make an intervention to help a couple be successful in a marriage?"

Lewin would say that the time for intervention into a marriage is shortly after the couple marry and experience a real group. On the subject he says, "The sensitivity of the group to the move of each member is especially great in the early period of the marriage. Like a young organism, a young group is more flexible. As husband and wife come to know each other, a way of handling their marriage problems gets established. To alter these established ways may become difficult over time..." "In the young marriage the situation is not clear in regard to the balance between one's own needs and those of the partner. That leads to typical conflicts, but at the same time allows greater flexibility for their solution." (Lewin, 1948, p. 101.)

It is fascinating to note that forty years after his death, Lewin's suggestion of an intervention as being needed early in a new marriage is just taking hold. Even in this area, he had a unique vision and approach to resolution of problems which has much to say to present therapists and is innovative and fresh today. Currently, a major thrust is in intervention strategies with young couples new in a marriage. This is derived from a recognition that the prime time for divorce in the United States is three years into a marriage. An early intervention is therefore necessary if couples are not to become so conflicted that divorce becomes the only resolution.

SUMMARY

While Lewin's work is well known in small group research, in t-groups, and in organizational development; his work related to marriage is almost totally unknown. Yet, Lewin's concepts of marriage, as a small group with unique properties, contributes to understanding marriage as a particular system to be understood as a specialized small group. His concepts can also be applied fruitfully in creating educational programs for couples. These concepts are also uniquely useful in developing an approach to therapy; both in the initial diagnostic phases and in development of treatment strategies. Finally, Lewin's concepts are applicable in determining when the most efficient time for making an intervention with a couple would be. The genius of Kurt Lewin extends the use of his concepts to understanding and resolving problems in marriage.

REFERENCES

Giblin, P.   (1985).   Communication from Bernard G. Guerney, Jr., President, IDEALS. Penn State University, University Park: PA

Guerney, B.G., Jr.   (1977).   Relationship Enhancement: Skill Training Programs for Therapy, Problem Prevention and Enrichment.   San Francisco: Jossey-Bass.

Lewin, K.   (1951). Cartwright, D.   (Ed.), "Field Theory and Learning," in Field Theory in Social Science: Selected Theoretical Papers. New York: Harper & Row, pp. 69-72, 76.

Lewin, K.   (1948). Lewin, G.W.   (Ed.), Resolving Social Conflicts: Selected Papers on Group Dynamics. New York: Harper & Row.

Lewin, K.   (1948). Lewin, G.W.   (Ed.), "The Background of Conflict in Marriage," in Resolving Social Conflicts: Selected Papers on Group Dynamics.   New York: Harper & Row, pp. 84-102.

Minuchin, S.   (1974).   Families and Family Therapy. Cambridge, Mass.: Harvard.

Ross, Baker & Guerney (1985). Communication from Bernard G. Guerney, Jr., President IDEALS. Penn State University, University Park: PA

Lewinian Theory in Clinical Practice

George Bach

Bach Institute for California

My text, <u>Intensive Group Psychotherapy</u> (1954), was dedicated to "the remembrance of my teacher, Kurt Lewin, pioneer of group dynamics and the experimental study of human relations." Here is a brief quote from the preface: "One aim of this book is to explore the possibility of applying Lewin's theory and research findings to the clinician's task of effecting personality and behavior changes." By combining the two disciplines of field theory group dynamics and psychotherapy, new solutions to the many problems of clinical practice, as well as new conceptual tools and techniques, emerged.

At the outset let me make it clear that I am not the only nor the first clinician whose philosophy and practice was significantly influenced by Lewin, before and after his premature death in 1947. For instance, Jerome Frank, a former Lewin student introduced the "Humanistic" orientation in clinical psychology, before Maslow, Buhler, Carl Rogers, and other more recent champions of the currently popular humanistic orientation became influential.

Kurt Lewin did not guide or supervise my own early clinical work beyond being my first thesis advisor. After Lewin had left for M.I.T., Robert Sears, the learning theorist, guided me through to the completion of my Ph.D. Thesis: "<u>Young Childrens' Play Fantasies</u>" published in 1945 as an APA Monograph (#272). My thesis dealt with development of anger and aggression in very young children. This topic was of interest to both learning theorist and field theorist alike. Sears was a spokesman for the now classical frustration/aggression hypothesis while the innovative field theorist, and Lewin scholar, Tamara Dembo, had earlier clarified the dynamics of anger and aggression as a function of the totality of life space forces, beyond being a reaction to frustration. The interaction within my thinking of historically oriented learning theory concepts and the historical orientation of Kurt Lewin and his student Tamara Dembo, was of germinal significance in the emergence of my clinical concern to find a way to creatively utilize human aggression, particularly in the context of marital and parental family life, and school. In view of the current, keen interest in the clinical management of child and spouse abuse, as well as student and teacher abusive behavior patterns, the wide popularity of my "creative aggression" ("fight training") approach to these socially urgent problems should come as no surprise.

Since I have published on this topic extensively, I need not repeat my ideas and methods concerning the management of anger and aggression here. But I want to acknowledge that the field-theoretical-Gestalt orientation I applied in my work as an individual and group psychotherapist opened my eyes to many new options in dealing with our patients' problems in the practice of psychotherapy.

Now I shall try to share briefly with you some cogent examples of the clinical utility, the practical value of the Lewinian orientation in the practice of psychotherapy. This utility is further enhanced when one integrates the latest notions of cognitive behavior therapy, with a Lewinian orientation.

The practical usefulness of field theory fulfills an adage Kurt Lewin repeated frequently to us, graduate students of the University of Iowa in the early forties: "The most practical thing in Psychology is a good Theory." The major interest of professional therapists is to master clinical techniques or "interventions" which facilitate the natural human desire to improve their lot in life, both within and outside their inner selves. Facilitating healthy growth and changes for the better are the obvious foundations of effective clinical practice. But long before we can attempt to change anything, we have to understand the intrinsic nature of the human personality who turns to us for consultation. The phenomenological-cognitive approach by Lewin, becoming sensitive to the topology of the individual life space, is invaluable during the early, so-called "diagnostic" phase of our work while we are understanding the process by which every individual draws cognitive maps which guide much of his/her behavior and way of dealing with "outside forces" (Lewin's Alien Hull Concept). The emphasis of current here-and-now situational forces (beyond speculations of the remote, historical so-called "causes") I have found most useful in clinical practice especially since our patients are acutely concerned with how to handle current situations and current interpersonal dynamics, such as conflicts.

Kurt Lewin's work can be historically viewed in terms of certain phases, each phase focused on psycho-social problems central to that phase.

His early phase focused on phenomenological processes such as anger, resumptions of unfinished tasks, level of aspiration, decision-making, satiation, regression. Every one of the Lewinian researchers during this first phenomenological phase is of great value to students of the dynamics of personality functioning in general and cognitively oriented therapists, like myself, in particular.

Some writers categorize Lewin's group-dynamics discipline as largely irrelevant to the practice of group psychotherapy. I differentiate myself, in general, from this position. Even though nobody formally trained me on how to apply the field theoretical orientation to clinical practice, I felt an urge within me to use what I had learned from Lewin in my early clinical work.

My studies of and participation in group dynamic research made me aware of the importance of _rituals_. Of course I did not invent the idea of the therapeutic utilization of group-rituals. Rituals, as my friend and colleague, the late cultural anthropologist Gregory Bateson pointed out to me, are used in all cultures to train and reinforce role-behavior and thereby, perhaps incidently, deal with fears and anxieties of all sorts. For example, fears of the stranger are managed by hospitality rituals, and fears of aggression are reduced by peace-rituals such as the American Indian sharing a pipe smoke.

The specifically therapeutic use of small group rituals was widely practiced in ancient Greece. I visited recently the remains of several sanctuaries of Acelpaius--the Greek God of Healing.

In our time the best known therapy ritual is the psychodrama technique invented by the late J.K. Moreno who in seeming paradox used the highly structured role-playing procedures to promote spontaneity. The seemingly adversary, mutually exclusive relationship between ritual structure and spontaneity is my favorite research-study topic. I have learned under what conditions "Bad" rituals present barriers to spontaneous behavior, creativity and freedom, and I now can recognize the characteristic of "Good" rituals which promote and facilitate spontaneity and free expression. Understanding the difference between spontaneity-furthering and spontaneity-hindering rituals should be of central concern to psychotherapists. There are many conditions in and out of therapy in which spontaneity can be enhanced through ritualized behavior. Elsewhere, I review some research observations, but here further discussion of this topic would lead us too far afield.

REFERENCES

Bach, G.R. (1954). _Intensive Group Psychotherapy_. New York: Ronald Press.
Bach, G.R. with P. Wyden (1968). _The Intimate Enemy_. New York: Morrow.

Bach, G.R. with H. Goldberg (1974). Creative Aggression. New York: Avon. (a reprint with a new introduction was published in 1985 by Anchor Books-Doubleday, New York.)

Bach, G.R. (1956). "Freud's time-bound group concepts." Group Psychotherapy: 4, 301-304.

Bach, G.R. (1974). "Constructive aggression in growth groups," Ch. 7 in A. Jacobs (Ed.), The Group as an Agent of Change. New York: Behavioral Publications.

Bach, G.R. with R. Deutsch (1970). Pairing. New York: Wyden.

Bach, G. R. with L. Torbet (1982). A Time for Caring--Dynamics of "Networking". New York: Delacourt Press.

Bach, G. R. with L. Torbet (1983). The Inner Enemy--How to Fight Fair with Yourself. New York: William Morrow.

Lewin, K. (1948). Resolving Social Conflict. New York: Harper and Row.

Kurt Lewin: Intergroup Relations and Applications in Current Action Research

Matti K. Gershenfeld

Temple University

INTRODUCTION

Lewin would say that the background is important for any perception and the "meaning of every event depends directly upon the nature of its background." ..."the background itself is not often perceived, but only the 'figure' or 'event'." (Lewin, 1948; p. 145) Whatever a person does or wishes to do, he must have some ground to stand upon. This is probably the primary reason why he is extremely affected the moment this ground begins to give way.

One of the most important constituents of the ground on which the individual stands is the social group to which he belongs and one of the basic characteristics of belonging is that the same individual generally belongs to many groups. For instance, a person (p) may belong economically to the upper middle-class (uMCl)--perhaps he is a prosperous merchant. He may be a member of a small family (F) of three persons which is part of a large family group (lF). The person may also be a third generation American of Irish ancestry, may be a Republican, may be a Catholic. (See Figure 1).

During most of his life, the adult acts not purely as an individual, but as a member of a social group. The different groups a person belongs to are not equally important at a given moment. There are occasions when belonging to a group is doubtful or not clear for the individual. A person entering a gathering may have a moment of doubt whether he belongs there. He might be a newcomer to a club. He is uncertain about whether he is being accepted. The unclearness of the situation, this uncertainty in behavior. The person does not feel at home and will therefore be more or less self-conscious, inhibited, and be unsure about how to act.

Uncertainty of belonging is due to the fact that the individual is crossing from the margin of one group into another (coming from an outer-group to the gathering or to the club). This uncertainty is typical of the nouveaux riches or of other persons crossing the margins of social classes. It is typical, furthermore, of members of religious or national minority groups who try to enter the main group. It is characteristic of individuals crossing the margin between social groups that they are

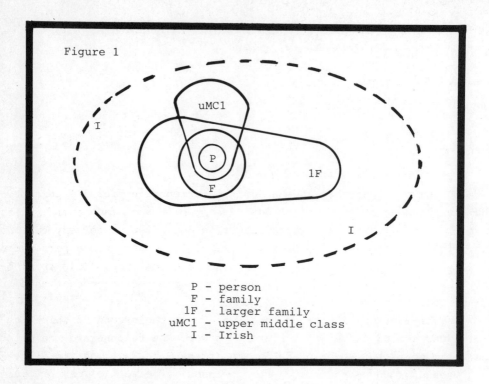

Figure 1

P - person
F - family
1F - larger family
uMC1 - upper middle class
I - Irish

not only uncertain about their belonging to the group they are ready to
enter, but also to the group they are leaving.

APPLICATIONS

This formulation just described of the Lewinian concepts of ground
and figure of the social group influencing a response has been very helpful. It has been helpful in three projects in which the Lewinian analysis helped me understand the problem and create a method of thinking
about it. The first of these projects is, "Transition Stages for Women,"
a program which focused on women 30 to 50.

Transition Stages for Women

In working with women for the last fifteen years, I have been impressed with how much better educated women are now. They have opportunities for a variety of lifestyles, and have opportunities to work
in the labor force or not. My assumption was that, with more options,
psychological health for women would go up, since there were many acceptable modes of behavior. There were no longer the boundaries between
women's and men's work, or "a woman's place." The research, in fact,
has been the reverse; there is not increased psychological health among

women. There is a much greater increase in alcoholism among women, in depression among women, in therapy for women, and in fact it has been reported that eight times as many women as men attempt suicide. What was especially surprising was that the typical woman who attempted suicide would be the woman we define as happy. She was white, married, living with her husband and two children, with a family at middle or upper income. The modal age was 35. It was surprising because I would have assumed that with greater options, there would be increased mental health. However, applying the Lewinian analysis to the intergroup relations just described helped me understand the situation and the dilemma. In Lewin's earlier information, he says the ground is everything and that an event is to be viewed from the perspective of a social group on the ground. It can be said that prior to the women's movement of the late 1960's, women might be defined as a social group tightly connected with rigid boundaries in the larger group of molds. Until very recently, women were in compact connected groups with rigid boundaries between women and men. They looked different, could be easily identified, were limited in access to occupations, and had very limited access to certain roles. While women may have been quite circumscribed in how they could act with men, they were at home in the "region with other women." This comfort and the group norms were expressed in the Ladies' Home Journal, McCall's, and other such magazines. The prime thrust of pressure would be on women as a group, from the outer world, and women would have their norms of acceptable behavior in dress, language, and occupations on the inside. With the women's movement expanded free space for locomotion, there was no longer the solid support of the traditional women or the strong "impassable" group boundary. Women became dispersed in many occupations and in many lifestyles. There the breakdown of being in the tight boundaries of the traditional conservative group mold. As Lewin defined it, there was increasing pressure and conflict on individual women as they sought to pass into occupations which had been denied them. Now, they could live any place alone or with men, they could buy houses, they could have their own credit. There is a conflict between being the traditional woman in the old confined region of her social group, and a woman today no longer within the confines of a concentrated social group. The result, as a Lewinian analysis would predict, is increased tension, depression and anxiety about individual women leaving the solid region. Once this was clarified, I then set about examining what the regions are in which an individual woman now exists and feels conflicted in. It was determined that one social group of her life has to do with her psycho-social development, (i.e., movement over

time through various regions of development). We assume that, based on
acculturation of that earlier era, she developed certain false assumptions which needed to be clarified. This can be thought of as her life
space, and that others were closed to her. This needed to be re-examin-
ed, given the access of free movement of the current situation.

A second "social group" we saw as important in a woman's life was
her family. We thought this was one of the most significant "grounds"
which influenced how she handles events in her life. Here, too, we
thought that the group and the boundary conditions needed to be re-
examined. We examined how, within the family social group, a husband
and wife might redefine the character of the relationship they decided
they would want. We thought there was a need for greater intimacy (close-
ness), for greater contact within the sub-regions (being supportive), and
for resolving conflicts (opposing forces).

The third hypothesis was that a woman's occupation, or studies outside her home, was also an important social group for her. In this region, she needed to examine what her space of free movement had been and
what she wanted it to be now. From the Lewinian analysis and the creation
of the three hypotheses we were able to develop a training intervention.
We were able to conduct programs with women between 30 to 50 for three
years. The intervention was a fifteen-week program with 15 women, and,
for the middle segments, their husbands. The evaluations and the follow-
up have indicated that the program is highly successful. Whereas most
of the women reported being depressed at least half the time prior to
the program, at the conclusion only 4 persons were depressed more than
half the time. There was an increase in the women's self-confidence
and self-competence. The Lewinian analysis was crucial in our understanding that the focus for the intervention had to be on the individual
woman. It also helped us understand that the group as a context (the
ground) would help her feel less isolated and overwhelmed.

The Network Program

A similar analysis was done in attempting to understand why some
middle-class blacks had such a high rate of divorce. Again, we used
the Lewinian formulation which helped us clarify that, in the early
times, blacks had limited occupational opportunities, were readily visible, and lived in their own Ghetto with tight boundaries. As middle-
class blacks have moved from the Ghetto, have educations which allow
them to work in many occupations, they too have left their support sys-

tem, and the pressure on them is to succeed where there are members and non-members (blacks and non-blacks) and where there are limited support systems.

In the "Network Program," which was developed for black middle-class families, we helped blacks reduce the conflict for them on whether to be in a black region or a white region. We focused on members of a middle-class group becoming supportive of each other; it was an alternative to being in a region where they felt like isolated individuals and families. We further focused on such boundaries as what do whites think of blacks, and how are blacks influenced by those descriptions (in Lewinian terms, understanding the definition of the group by the external environment and from the inside understanding through self-definition).

An eight-week program was designed, held weekly, for black couples. The evaluations of the program indicated that participants could be more comfortable with how being black (a part of that social group) was different from being white. They understaood how others' definitions of them were not helpful for their formulation of their own social groups and movement into occupations and geographic regions. Removed from their Ghetto, region, and support system they were building skills as individuals to cope as well as building a new support system of middle class blacks. While there would not be the tightness of the group in a Ghetto, nor the concreteness of the barrier, there would nevertheless be a new social group as a stronger force to deal with the white world than dealing with the conflicts only as individuals.

Coping with Unemployment

In a more recent project we have worked with a new phenomenon of middle-class unemployment. Again Lewinian principles were helpful in designing the program for middle-class unemployed.

We analyzed the problem from the perspective of a major group which is employed and a region within that group of unemployed. We then analyzed the effect of the large number of people, previously middle class and employed, being thrust into the region of being unemployed. This would affect how people perceive themselves within this unemployed social group, how the external environment relates to them and categorizes them, how social groups like their friends and former colleagues have contact with them. We also examined what was involved in crossing from the unemployed group into the majority group. The outcome was a special program created for middle-class unemployed and their spouses. It examined feelings of being part of an unemployed group, contacts they had with those employed, stereotypes from the external environment on them, and the impediments to moving outside the unemployed group. Again, the outcomes were excellent and the design helped participants deal with being unemployed.

SUMMARY

Lewin's principles have been a major guide in being able to analyze and understand conflicts and social problems. The idea that the ground is a vital factor in how an individual acts in a given event has helped us understand women, middle-class blacks, and middle-class unemployed. The paradox is that with greater free movement there is greater tension. This is due to conflict between movement into the new group, which is desired but not comfortable, and comfort in the old group, which is only partially desired. The old group was large, rules were well under-stood, and there was severe limitation by the rigid boundaries to move out of the group. In the new situation the boundaries are more easily passable, but there is no longer the solid cohesive group with its sup-ports. We even applied Lewinian principles in a reverse situation, in the unemployment one, where we thought of the problem as people coming from the major group being thrust into the "minority" group. The Lewinian constructs have been found to be very helpful in analyzing current prob-lems and understanding the intervention which needs to be made.

REFERENCES

Lewin, K. (1951). Cartwright, D. (Ed.), Field Theory in Social Science: Selected Theoretical Papers. New York: Harper & Row. (Field theory and experiment in social psychology, pp. 130-154.)

Lewin, K. (1948). Lewin, G.W. (Ed.), Resolving Social Conflicts: Se-lected Papers on Group Dynamics. New York: Harper & Row. (Psycho-social problems of a minority group, pp. 145-158.)

Marrow, A.J. (1969). The Practical Theorist: The Life and Work of Kurt Lewin. New York: Basic Books, Inc.

Application of Lewin's Life Space Concept to the Individual and Group-as-a-Whole Systems in Group Psychotherapy

Yvonne M. Agazarian

Philadelphia

This article began as a talk at the Lewin Conference at Temple University in the summer of 1984. The dynamics of the conference itself illustrated much of what I am going to cover in this article about the influence of the group-as-a-whole upon the individual, when that individual is performing a role at the group level. The audience had experienced two days of the conference at which they had met and listened to many Lewin theorists. The climate of the conference was one of enthusiasm and encouragement. It was to this audience that I presented the following ideas, and it is perhaps, sufficient to say that I talked for three hours without noticing the passage of time, to an audience that not only listened for three hours, but left the room and gathered in more people from the halls! For myself, WHO I was, and how I BEHAVED while talking to the group was more effectively explained as a function of my role in the conference group dynamics than it was by my individual dynamics.

Central to what I was presenting was the idea that it is not only possible, but probably essential to conceptualize group-as-a-whole as a system that is separate and discrete from the individuals that are its members. It's necessary to define group and individual systems at two different conceptual levels, similar in structure and function, (isomorphically and hierarchically related) and described by two different versions of the Lewinian definition of behavior. At the Individual System level, all behavior is defined as a function of the Individual in interaction with the Environment ($b = f [I,E]$), and at the group-as-a-whole system level all behavior is defined as a function of the group in interaction with the Environment ($b = f [G,E]$). These two definitions represents two different explanations of behavior of the SAME EVENT conceptualized at different levels of abstraction. This makes it possible to make two apparently contradictory statements, both of which are true, and both of which apply contemporaneously to the same group event: 1) the behavior in this event can be explained by understanding the individual dynamics in the group and without referring to the group dynamics; 2) the behavior in this event can be explained by understanding group dynamics and without referring to individual dynamics. As both of these statements are true, which explanation one uses depends more upon which explains most usefully what one has observed or experienced.

My goal in this paper is to describe the way that I conceptualize all groups and specifically how that applies to therapy groups. The intent is to discuss first the application of the Field Theory to group psychotherapy. The second part conceptualizes the development of a psychotherapy group, goal specific in Lewin's framework of the Life Space, with each developmental phase represented as region with a subgoal, and show how by applying a force field to what is happening in a group you have some way of knowing 1) what phase of development the group is in, defined by the behavioral field of force, and 2) which restraining forces you might want to weaken if you want the group to re-equilibriate.

I shall start by introducing you to the model that I use to conceptualize individual and group-as-a-whole, two discrete but isomorphically related systems, each one of which can be represented by a Life Space, behaviorally defined by its life space equation, (b = f [I,E]) and b = f [G,E]). (See Figure 1).

You will see that in Figure 1 there are four regions, two at the individual level: Person and Member; and two at the group level: group-role and group-as-a-whole. I will start by describing the two at the individual system level and defining them in terms of their life space.

INDIVIDUAL SYSTEM DYNAMICS: B=f (I,E)

When one thinks of the individual, specifically of the individual patient who is about to enter a psychotherapy group, it is important to be able to understand the person from two perspectives: the perspective of the inner person dynamics, and the perspective of the interpersonal dynamics. Let me therefore define two separate systems at this point (hierarchically and isomorphically related), each of which will have a different life space and a different behavioral equation that can be used to define two different and discrete dimensions of individual dynamics in a group. The first system we will call the system of the person, whose behavior is a function of the person in interaction with the inner person environment. The second system we will call the system of the member, which exists for the individual as a member of the group, and whose behavior is a function of the member in interpersonal interaction with the group environment.

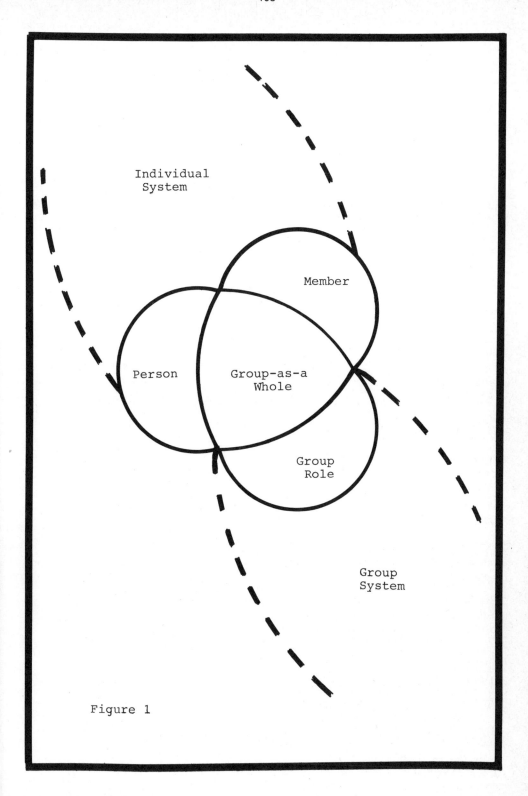

Figure 1

PERSON SYSTEM DYNAMICS: B = f (P,E)

When I think about the person's Life Space, I say that their behavior can be understood if you understand that person in interaction with their psychological environment as it applies to their inner person experience (at both conscious and unconscious levels). Thus the inner person experience is a function of their psychogenic history. Psychogenic history basically entails environmental factors, their genetic makeup, their home life, vicissitudes in development, the particular kinds of pressures from outside, and the particular kinds of pressures coming from inside. Was the child born with a lot of energy? Was the child more active than passive? Did the child have a strong temper that needed to be mastered? Was it a child who patterns easily to social requirements waking conveniently every morning no earlier than 7:30, drinking juice everyday at 11:00, going to bed regularly at 7:00 and sleeping all the way through the night? The easy patternability of children like this, elicits a social response which will be quite different from the child whose social responsiveness is more random and less predictable, who does not pattern easily, if at all, who seems to have a rhythm that isn't even co-ordinated with the moon. Four o'clock one day they'll be ready for bed and they'll sleep right through the night, go to sleep at one o'clock the next day and be awake again at three in the morning.

To sum up, if you understand this person with the particular biological predispositions and innate qualities and know the history of their developmental resolutions, you will have a good idea of the psychodynamic predispositions of this person which will govern their perceptions of the environment (in our case the therapy group). You will therefore, be able to begin to both predict and explain their behavior. This is the perspective from which psychoanalysts most often perceive group psychotherapy.

MEMBER SYSTEM DYNAMICS: b = f (M,E)

It is probably useful to be able to distinguish between the times when you are understanding the person in relationship to their developmental dynamics from the times when you are thinking about the person in terms of their interpersonal dynamics. From the member system perspective the individual's behavior is explained by observing the person's interpersonal behavior and understanding it in terms of the

particular pattern of socialized roles acquired by this person, which
express on the one hand their person level dynamics, and which reproduce on the other hand role interactions which are in line with the
individual's perceptions of the group environment.

These role interactions manifest the interpersonal social expectations that the individual has developed through previous group memberships: the original social interpersonal interaction between self and
mother; self and parents; self and family; self and school, church,
play and peer groups; class groups; fraternity or sorority groups; friend-
ship and work groups; etc. All of these both repeat in certain aspects, and modify in certain other aspects, our individual responses.
Thus our social responsiveness becomes modified in increasingly mature
and sophisticated ways and each group experience will provide another
life space experience, rather like adding another bead to a string.
However, this is also to say that in the current experience there is
contained the potential for re-experience and re-expression of any
earlier life-space experience, so that the current life-space can be
overlaid by earlier life-spaces, and our behavior in the current life-
space modified according to the behavior of previous life-spaces. In
psychotherapy we understand this process through the constructs of transference and regression, in which we are said to regress to earlier experiences and to transfer them, like an overlay, upon the present.

When you or I or anyone goes into a group, whether it is a therapy
group or a social, training or work group, what we proceed to do is to
train the group to treat us in a way that is familiar to us. The more
we can train the group to treat us in a way which is familiar to us,
the more comfortable we are with the illusion that we are not confronted
with anything new or different. We believe that we are protected from
our terror at being in a group and from our rage at having to share
time, space and attention with other individuals, or to experience our
need to be loved and accepted. All of these more primitive and regress-
ive responses are ALWAYS mobilized (albeit unconsciously) in group membership. The more unfamiliar or stressful the group experience, the
more strongly these responses are mobilized.

We can, therefore, expect members of any group to attempt to re-
create in the group previous member roles. They will only be partially
successful, however, in that some of the pre-set role behaviors will fit
in with the group norms and some of them will not. The member will
then experience group pressure to conform to the here-and-now group even
though the conformity demand is in conflict with the there-and-then
group. In a therapy group, this modification process is particularly

important in two ways. First, the social roles with which the patient enters the group will have, predictably, a large component of unrewarding, frustrating and socially maladaptive behaviors. Second, the goal of the group is to understand what the individual is doing that leads to the socially unrewarding experience. What is more, in a therapy group, the group goal is to bring into focus and mastery the primitive experiences that are stimulated by the process of group, and thus the resistance to these experiences are analyzed. The more these primitive experiences are brought closer to the threshold, the harder members attempt to train the group to treat them in the familiar, repetitive patterns, and the more likely members are to regress because we no longer have our more sophisticated defenses and what we try to reproduce at that point are the salient issues of our childhood. In the meantime, we are in a group of people where all the other members are doing the same thing. The interpersonal nature of group development permits members to find some other member (or members) whose role is perceived as compatible and reciprocal, and this is the basis for pairing; either cooperative pairing where the role relationships are complementary, or contending pairing, where the reciprocal role is perceived as threatening or frustrating. These interpersonal dynamics explain the group phenomena of pairing, flight and fight from the individual perspective. Thus the environment that the individual member is part of is the group environment of interpersonal relationships which can be very usefully explained at the individual level, as a function of the interpersonal attempts to reproduce patterns of behavior which defend against the primitive forces that are set off by a strange group.

The individual system perspective explains all group behavior in terms of interpersonal theory, without having to conceptualize the group-as-a-whole. However, there are some advantages to conceptualizing these dynamics from the group-as-a-whole perspective, without necessarily focusing on, or even being aware of, individual dynamics. It is to this that I address myself next.

GROUP DYNAMICS B = f (G,E)

In defining the individual system dynamics, I defined person as a necessary system to understanding member. I'm going to do the same thing with the group-as-a-whole. Just as, at the individual level, the inner person system dynamics manifest in interpersonal member behavior

in the group environment; so at the group level, the group-as-a-whole
system contains the group dynamics which are manifest in group-role
behavior in the group environment.

GROUP-AS-A-WHOLE SYSTEM DYNAMICS: $b = f \ (GW, \ E)$

In defining the system of the group-as-a-whole dynamically, it is
perfectly possible to explain all group behavior based on the genetics
of the group, whether it is predominantly dependent or counterdependent;
whether its energy is predominantly active and outgoing, or passive and
inward focused; how much group potential energy is bound in dependency,
how much in flight and fight, whether it is predominantly overpersonal
or counterpersonal; whether its nascent defenses are more primitive or
sophisticated, whether it has a lot of inherent resources or whether
its resources are limited, restricted or skewed. It is possible to identify the genetic makeup of a group in a way that is equivalent to the
thinking that we did about the person. Similarly, there are vissici-
tudes in every group's development. There are fixation points in every
group's development. There are patterns of behavior in every group's
development. Once you get to know a group, you can often predict with
some accuracy what the group is going to do under certain kinds of circumstances, but not WHO in the group will do it!
    The environment of the group-as-a-whole is the outside environment.
Certain influences come from the real world that exists as the environ-
ment--a new member joins or leaves, there is a vacation, there is a hol-
iday and the group doesn't meet, there are certain annual events like
Christmas and Easter and the Jewish holidays all of which have an impact on the group as a whole. There is the weather, there are snow-
storms and hurricanes and thunderstorms, there are natural and artificial disasters. All of these influences in the environment have an impact on the group. So, to understand group dynamics through the group-
as-a-whole life space allows us to define the behavior of the group as
a function of the group-as-a-whole in interaction with the environment.
In another sense, the individual system also serves as a source of
environmental input to the group system.

GROUP-ROLE SYSTEM DYNAMICS: $b = f(R,E)$

Just as member behavior at the individual level expresses the person dynamics, and just as it makes sense to think about the member behavior functioning to keep equilibrium in the person system; to give voice to, to express, to contain the conflicts inherent in the inner-person, so one can also think of group-role behavior as giving voice to, expressing or containing this equilibrium at the group level.

So, role is to the group-as-a-whole, as member is to person. Member behavior is a function of the person, as defined by the inner-person dynamics in interaction in the group environment. Perception of the environment is a function both of the transference overlay of the person's perceptions from previous group experience, and the modification that occurs from the interpersonal events in the group. Group-role behavior is a function of the group-as-a-whole defined by inner-group dynamics, in interaction with the group environment, which is in turn both a function of the group norms, the changes in the group dynamics that result from the input into the group from the environment outside the group, and from the individual member behavioral input.

It is important to understand the stimulus response nature of the input-output relationship between the individual and group systems. The individual system output serves as a group system input. Similarly, the group system output serves as an individual system input. Clarifying this concept, and learning what can be further understood when this particular interdependence between group and individual system levels, is a current theoretical focus for me. Anita Simon and I are currently working on analyzing data on this by using the SAVI observation system. We are still at the beginning of our research into this, but we have, so far, demonstrated that in at least one case the communication pattern in a group is a function of group dynamics, and that individual communication patterns changed in order to maintain the equilibrium of the group communication pattern, which sometimes entailed individuals communicating in ways that were significantly different from their usual style. When the relationship between the group and individual systems are brought more clearly into focus, it will become possible to demonstrate more clearly the operational relationship between the group-as-a-whole and individual systems. Sufficient for now is the fact that at the individual level, output from the group serves as input into the individual system from the environment. At the group level, output from the individual serves as input into the group system from the environment. Thus behavior is individual, in the group and also of the group.

Group role behavior serves the same equilibriating function for
the group-as-a-whole that member behavior serves for the person.

APPLICATIONS TO GROUP PSYCHOTHERAPY

Group therapists who know only the individual level of dynamics do
not have the conceptual tool that permits them to view group dynamics
as a separate and discrete, though related, phenomenon. Thus, their
understanding of group is confined to the individual level, and their
decisions to influence the behavior of the group must, of necessity, be
targeted through the individual. This can have a significant impact
upon not only the probable outcome of the individual issues that members
bring to group, but also, more seriously, impact upon the nature and
potential of the development of the group itself.

I will illustrate the therapeutic issues by using the role of the
scapegoat as an example. The scapegoat is an excellent illustration of
a member role, at the individual level, and of a group-role at the group
level. In this illustration, let us name the scapegoat Billy G. Billy
G. comes into the group and the group scapegoats him for behaving in ways
that the group does not like. After some work, a compromise is worked
out and Billy G.'s unacceptable behavior is modified by the group. In
the process of modifying Billy's behavior, the group adapts itself in
order to integrate Billy G. as a member. Examining the scapegoating
event from the individual perspective, you will often find that Billy
G.'s psychodynamic solution to inner-person disequilibrium was masochism;
that he was the family member who was consistently scapegoated, one has
a history of being the target of anger. Even though he may well claim
that it is one of the repeated experiences in his life that is most pain-
ful to him and that he would most like to change in therapy, he repro-
duces it in group and thus volunteers for the role. Interpreting to
Billy G., the therapist could attempt to help him understand, in terms
of his masochism, why he sets himself up this way. There is very good
potential for doing excellent therapy against the matrix of the group
at the person level, not only with Billy G., but, through resonance,
with others in the group. The therapist could also point out the dynamics of the reciprocal interpersonal member behavior. Those who attacked
Billy G. are probably repeating their family member roles in the group
and they also have the opportunity to gain insight into both their person and member dynamics. The individual system perspective, however,
does not tell the whole story.

At the individual level, Billy's member behavior of eliciting scape-goating, serves an equilibriating function for his person system. So from the group system perspective it can also be said that scapegoating is serving some equilibriating function for the group-as-a-whole and that Billy G.'s behavior is serving a group-role. This understanding brings with it some important implications for group dynamic development.

GROUP DEVELOPMENT AND THE GROUP-ROLE

A useful way of conceptualizing development, both at the individual level and at the group level, is to think of maturation as a function of discrimination and integration. One of the attractions of conceptua-lizing maturation in this way is its elegant correspondence to the deve-lopment of cell complexity through miosis which results in living beings. Just as the maturation of the cells in a living being is a function of the discrimination and integration of similarities and differences of structure and function, so is the maturation of a group. However, the process of maturation of the group inevitably arouses resistance to change at the individual level. The work of perceiving and integrat-ing differences must, by its very nature, arouse cognitive dissonance. One way to maintain the comfortable equilibrium of homogeneity, and avoid dealing with emerging differences, is to deny difference, to split off awareness, and to use a group member as the container through projec-tive identification (usually a member who volunteers for the role, as in the case of Billy G.). The group can then deal with that member as a deviant, and bring the not inconsiderable group pressure for con-formity to bear upon the deviant member. The group can maintain its norms unchanged if it brings the member into line, or excludes or ex-trudes him, in order to "get rid" of the difference that it would other-wise have to integrate. (Parenthetically, the same "containment" dyna-mic exists when a sub-group rather than a single group member performs this group role, as, for example, when disagreement in a group is con-tained in a silent sub-group who do not give voice to their disagree-ment, or when differences in group feeling are isolated by a split, as when the group functions at a level of intellectualized flight, with all feeling in the group denied and unavailable. The correspondence between these group dynamics, and the individual dynamics of denial, intellectualization and isolation are manifest.)

Thus, group role dynamics represent an important step in containing, for the group, differences that the group is not yet able to integrate and, consequently, maintain the group equilibrium. Scapegoating, in the early phases of group development, serves the function of containing differences that the group is not yet developmentally able to integrate. Scapegoating occurs developmentally when group flight is giving way to group fight. During the flight phase, members solved differences through homogeneous pairing. Members pair for power and control: power to protect against control by others, by the leader, by the group, by unconscious forces; or power to control others, the leader, the group, or unconscious forces. The fight phase introduces heterogeneity. Unlike people fight, and in the process of resolving the fights, members come to terms with differences. However, there are differences that the group is not able to integrate and the group solution is to project them into a deviant member who will contain them for the group. In the group communication pattern to the deviant, the group pressures the member to conform to the group norms, to become converted or to leave. In the process of integrating the scapegoat, the group comes to tolerate some of the differences that were intolerable, and these differences thus become available to the group as resources, which would otherwise have been split off and remained unavailable had the scapegoating been resolved through conversion or extrusion.

It can now be shown clearly what happens DYNAMICALLY to a group when the therapist works with scapegoating at the individual level. By targeting interventions at the individual level, no matter what the content may be, the therapist joins the communication pattern to the deviant. This is the solution of the "identified patient" in groups (and in families too) which maintains the group equilibrium by binding the underlying tensions in an acknowledged role which forms part of familiar role interaction functions.

What happens when a psychotherapy group successfully works through a scapegoating phase? First, the person who is the scapegoat usually makes significant therapeutic gains. Second, the group learns to tolerate differences that it would not be able to tolerate had it not worked through a peer level. Whenever a group is unable to come to terms with differences, the group inevitably limits its potential for development and its potential for functioning as a therapeutic environment for the individual. The basic dynamic of maintaining group-as-a-whole equilibrium through requiring a group-role system to contain, express or voice dynamics of group function that are still in the process of being mastered by the group is true for each developmental phase of the group. It is therefore important for group therapists to be able to deliberately facilitate the process of differentiation and integration, which is in the service of group maturation. Facilitating work at the individual level, therefore, is best done within the context of the group developmental needs which will both stimulate inner-person relevance and encourage the working through of resolutions rather than repetitions of member roles.

Part II: Practical Theory

Section B: <u>Education</u>

   To begin, <u>Steven Krupp and his associates</u> at Lincoln University
write: "Although Lewin made remarkable strides toward the conceptual
formalization of the social sciences, he was also able to poignantly
demonstrate the utility of social science knowledge in understanding
and solving real-life problems." It is the Lewinian action research
cycle (which organically combines research and practical decision-making) that these faculty in the Human Services program focus on. This
cycle is not only the organizing feature of the graduate training, it
is also the core content. In the article they are clear about what is
happening.
   It shouldn't be surprising that Lewin's influence shows itself in
the business, management, and administration programs of colleges and
universities in the United States. This is particularly evident in the
course offerings in organization behavior, organization development, and
group dynamics. <u>Gerald Biberman</u> describes concretely these courses,
from the standpoint of an insider--he is both a Lewinian and a Business
School faculty member. Then he goes on to survey Lewin's influence
on teaching approaches, and even the professional organizations that
business faculty belong to and the conferences they usually attend.
Biberman concludes that Lewin's influence in business schools in universities in the United States is <u>increasing</u>.
   <u>Emmy Pepitone</u> invites our attention to the "socialization" and
education of children at home and in school. Summarizing her own and
certain related research, employing a Lewinian focus on cooperation and
competition, she leads us to what may be surprising conclusions about
the behavior of some upper middle class and working class children. She
remarks: "Combining our empirical evidence with various psychodynamic
theories had several effects: for one thing it drove us to return to,
and consider more seriously again, the well-known Lewinian formula
about $B=f (P,E)$." She concludes with the beginnings of a scheme which
classifies different children according to patterns of material possessions received in relation to duties performed, "whose consequent mediating expectations are likely to differ, as well as their overt behavior
in interdependent situations requiring collaboration."
   After several years of working together, <u>Richard A. Schmuck</u> and
his colleague at the University of Oregon, Philip Runkel, decided that

if consultation in OD were to facilitate self-renewal at the grassroots level in public schools, it would have to break out of the mold of a traditional, hierarchical expert relationship. Schmuck's article describes their work of implementing, within school districts, participants as consultants to themselves. He concludes with considered speculation about how this participatory action-research could happen <u>within a school</u>, involving the on-site administrator ("...it is not impossible...") faculty ("To start with, there are some obvious ways..."), classified personnel ("Every school participant who is affected by administrative decisions should have a right to participate in those decisions"), students ("It may sound crazy at first, but ..."), and parents ("...it is not unreasonable to consider that even they can be brought into consultative functions for the school").

Action Research as a Guiding Principle in an Educational Curriculum: The Lincoln University Master's Program in Human Services

Steven Krupp, Robert F. DeHaan, Szabi Ishtai-Zee, Effie Bastas, Karen Castlebaum, and Evelyn Jackson

Lincoln University, Pennsylvania

Kurt Lewin is the social scientist who most exemplifies the funda-mental orientation of the program in graduate Human Services at Lincoln University. Although Lewin made remarkable strides toward the conceptual formalization of the social sciences, he was also able to poignantly de-monstrate the utility of social science knowledge in understanding and solving real-life social problems (Lewin, 1948, 1951).

The Action Research Cycle

In his assessment of organizational and social problem solving, Lewin observed that there is too often a gap between research and decision mak-ing. The action research model is based on the assumption that social change efforts are enhanced through systematic data collection around some perceived problem or goal.

The Lincoln University Master's Program has evolved during its existence of seven years to place social problem solving through this action research process at the core of the educational curriculum.

The final year of study is designed to have students spend that whole time on a major change project which unfolds through the three major phases of program planning, program implementation and program evaluation. The educational curriculum revolves around this central pro-ject and each of the units of study in Community Planning, Program Ad-ministration, and Organizational Development and Planned Change feeds into the project as does each of the specific courses.

Specifically, each student works through an action research cycle which involves each of the seven following steps.

1. Problem Definition

    Students begin by identifying a felt need in their community or organization. They conduct a review of literature to supplement their own observations and assumptions about the problem. This step is completed when they have formulated a working problem statement which may be modified as they move through the process.

2. <u>Data Collection - Needs Assessment</u>

Each student conducts a needs assessment to investigate and substantiate the problem statement. This generally consists of a minimum of three data collection sources and methods:

a. existing data from agency records or social indicators relevant to the problem are reviewed;

b. key informants who have special information or expertise concerning the problem are interviewed or surveyed; and

c. a target sample survey is conducted with staff, clients or community members who experience the problem directly.

3. <u>Data Analysis, Feedback, and Recommendations</u>

Needs Assessment data is analyzed and interpreted including an assessment of alternative program options based on the findings. The information is fedback to the appropriate systems and persons involved and the process culminating with a recommendation for program development and change.

4. <u>Action Planning</u>

An action plan is formulated which systematically lays out project goals, objectives, steps, resources, and time frames for implementation.

5. <u>Implementation</u>

The project is implemented as designed or modified as necessary to conform with constraints and realities encountered during the intervention.

6. <u>Data Collection - Monitoring</u>

Student projects are monitored on a formative basis as the program is being implemented. If the program reaches a conclusion it is summatively evaluated. Evaluation is based on the efficiency, effectiveness, and impact of the projects which are implemented. Program records, participant self report data, staff and expert sources are all employed to assess the project. When feasible before and after comparisons are made.

7. <u>Problem Redefinition and Program Reformulation</u>

During all phases of implementation, data is collected systematically to assess the change project. This data is utilized to refine the understanding of the problem and modify the direction of the change project to better ameliorate the problem.

Throughout this action research cycle, students are utilizing systematic data collection techniques to enhance the quality of their action and intervention. The problem definition and reformulation is at the crux of the process. The literature review supplements the student's own conception of the problem. The needs assessment allows students to substantiate their analysis of the problem and to solicit options for addressing the problem. The action planning provides them a structure, format, and management system for seeing their project from design through implementation. The evaluation is directed toward data collection which will enable students to increase the effectiveness of their change effort. The data collection is intended to be relevant; easy to collect, analyze, and utilize; and designed toward enhancing the problem solving capacity of the project, rather then meeting strict research requirements.

Some students are able to form action research groups within the agency or community setting where they are implementing the project. Not all students have this opportunity. However, every student is part of a field group which serves as a support group and consists of student/professionals from diverse human service fields. Each student throughout his or her course of study works with this group and uses it as a sounding board for input, integration, and analysis of the evolving change projects. For the purpose of the Masters Program this group serves as an action research support group which is integral to the development of the planned change approach. The following case illustration describes a project which has been carried out utilizing the action research process employed in the Lincoln University Master's Program.

Action Research in the Development of a Church-Sponsored Credit Union

The pastor of the Antioch Baptist Church of North Hills, Pennsylvania, became aware that some of the members had difficulty in meeting their financial obligations. Because he believed that the establishment of a credit union would be beneficial to all of the members of the church, and especially to those persons who were experiencing financial difficulties, the pastor engaged the change-agent to establish a credit union.

Action Research Process

In establishing the credit union, the change-agent employed the
Action Research approach to research and decision-making (Cunningham,
1976).

1. Problem Definition

    Some of the members of the Antioch Baptist Church are unemploy-
    ed or underemployed, have reduced income, or are retired on
    a fixed pension; therefore, they have difficulty in managing
    their financial resources.

2. Data Collection--Needs Assessment

    After the literature was researched, particularly the subject
    areas of money and credit, unemployment and underemployment,
    inflation, retirement, volunteerism, religion, and credit
    unions, a needs assessment was designed and conducted to deter-
    mine the extent and scope of the problem as well as the need
    for and interest in a credit union.

    Two surveys were distributed, one each to sample group members
    of the church and members of credit unions. Board directors
    of four church-sponsored credit unions were interviewed.

3. Feedback of Data

    The findings of the data collected confirmed the problem defi-
    nition. All age groups were affected and the problem was
    widespread.

4. Action Planning

    The pastor, board of deacons, and the change-agent developed
    several alternative solutions to the problem. The concept of
    Lewin's force-field analysis was applied to each of the alter-
    natives to determine the most feasible alternative. For each
    possible alternative, both the driving and restraining forces
    were given consideration. (See Figure 1 for an example of
    how one of the options of opening up a Thrift Shop was analyz-
    ed using this model.) The establishment of a credit union was
    chosen as the sanctioned project because of the dignity and
    respect afforded each member, its feasibility of operation,
    resources for implementation, ease of establishment, and
    lasting effects to be expected.

    A sponsoring committee was formed and several specific goals
    were developed. The primary goal was to teach the members
    of the credit union to better manage their financial resources
    through borrowing privileges. Secondary goals were also devel-

Figure 1 Force-Field Analysis of the Alternative Solution of Opening a Thrift Shop

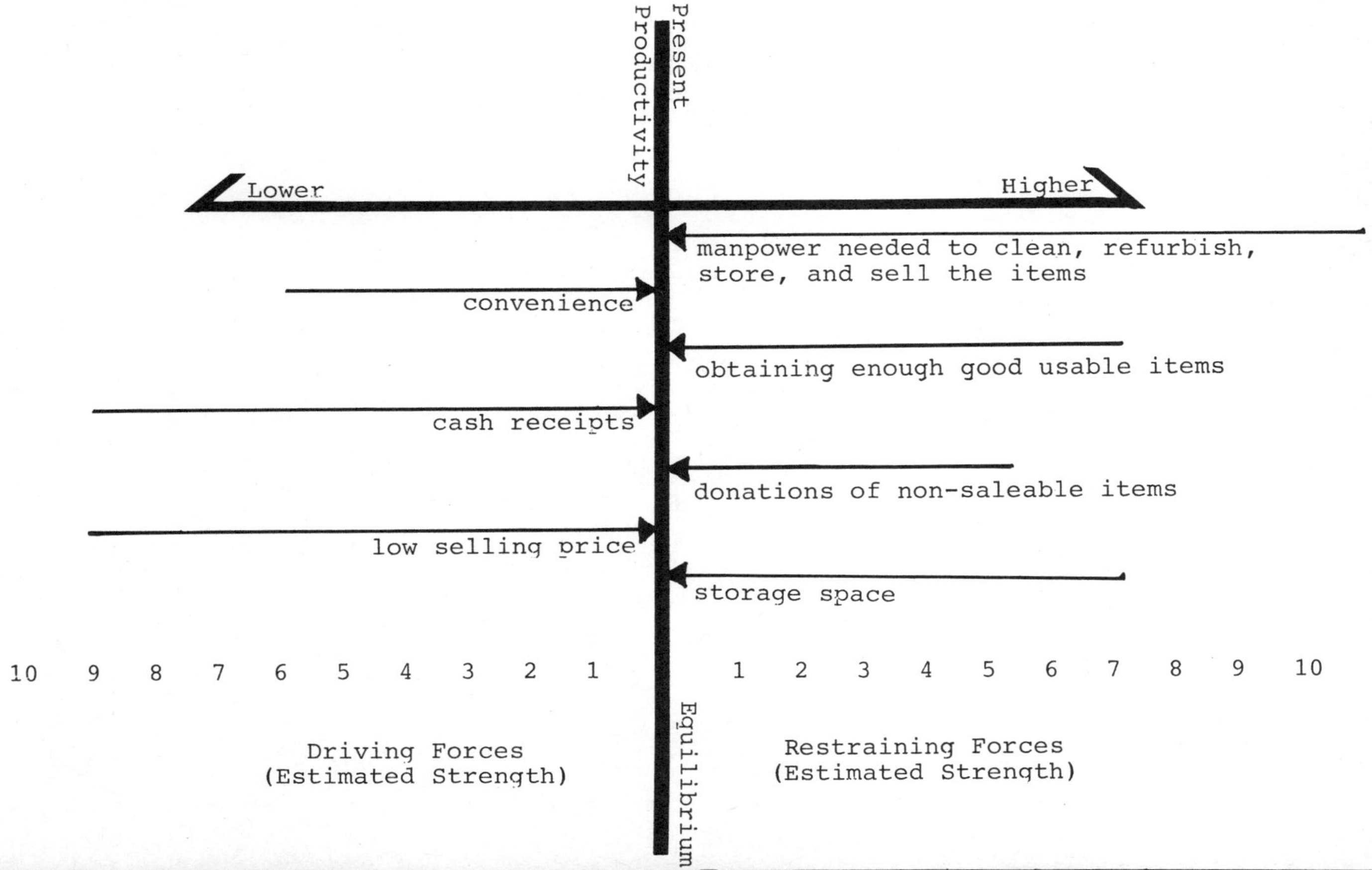

Higher

Lower

Present
Productivity

Equilibrium

manpower needed to clean, refurbish, store, and sell the items

obtaining enough good usable items

donations of non-saleable items

storage space

1 2 3 4 5 6 7 8 9 10

Restraining Forces
(Estimated Strength)

convenience

cash receipts

low selling price

1 2 3 4 5 6 7 8 9 10

Driving Forces
(Estimated Strength)

oped, all of which were realistic, performance-oriented, and observable.

To accomplish the project goals, six action plans were developed. The available resources were determined and responsibility for each strategy of the action plans was delegated. Time frames for achieving the strategies were determined.

5. Implementation

Because many members of the church were not familiar with the functions of a credit union, Lewin's theory of the normative-reeducative process was used during the promotion of the credit union. Lewin's three dimensions to effective reeducation--cognitive and perceptual structures, values and valences, and motoric action--involve changes in the self and the working through of self-supported resistance to such changes (Bennis, Benne, Chin, & Corey, 1976).

6. Data Collection - Monitoring

The credit union is still in the implementation stage. However, the action plans were formatively evaluated by the change-agent and the sponsoring committee. Surveys were conducted with enrollees in the credit union, the pastor and deacons, and the sponsoring committee. The findings indicated that progress was made on each of the action plans and the goals of the program. However, the findings also indicated that the marketing and promotion plans needed to be strengthened.

7. Program Refinement

As a result of the evaluation, several new strategies were developed to achieve the stated objectives. After implementation, these strategies will be evaluated and, if necessary, new strategies will be developed to meet new objectives. Progress is continuing to be made and it is anticipated that the credit union will open for business in about one month. Successful achievement of the project goals may lead to increased membership in the church, increased offerings, pledges, and tithes to the church; improved power base of the church and of the community; and the development of other cooperatives, such as a grocery store, because of the skills and knowledge gained in developing and operating a credit union.

REFERENCES

Bennis, Benne, Chin & Corey (1976). The planning of change. New York: Holt, Rinehart and Winston.

Cunningham, B. (1976). Action research: Toward a procedural model, Human Relations, Volume 29, Number 3, pp. 215-238.

Houle, C. (1980). Continuing education and the professions. San Francisco: Jossey Bass Publishers.

Lewin, K. (1943A). The special case of Germany. Public Opinion Quarterly, Winter, pp. 555-566.

Lewin, K. (1943B). Cultural reconstruction. The Journal of Abnormal and Social Psychology, Volume XXXCII, pp. 166-183.

Lewin, K. (1948). Resolving social conflict. New York: Harper Brothers.

Lewin, K. (1951). Field theory and the social sciences. New York: Harper & Row Publishers.

Zaltman, J., Duncan, R. (1977). Strategies of planned change. New York: John Wiley & Sons, Inc.

Kurt Lewin's Influence on Business Education

Gerald Biberman

The University of Scranton

Kurt Lewin's theoretical influence is very much in evidence in the curriculum and teaching practices of a great many business and administration programs of colleges and universities throughout the United States. This is particularly evident in course offerings in organization behavior, organization development and group dynamics. This paper will examine the nature of the Lewinian influence in terms of curriculum and course content. It will also look at teaching approaches and methodologies used in these courses, and organizations to which university management faculty influenced by Lewin belong.

BUSINESS SCHOOL CURRICULUM

Many colleges and universities in the United States and throughout the world have very large and active academic programs in business, administration, management or related areas. Most of these programs have a core sequence of courses which all of their students are required to take. One such course appearing in many curricula is called Organization Behavior or a similar title such as Managerial Behavior, Organization Psychology or Management.

Organization behavior is a fairly new field of study in business schools. Doctoral programs in organization behavior have only been in existence for the past 20 years or so, and continue to be small in number (although increasing steadily). Researchers and faculty of organization behavior courses typically have backgrounds in industrial/organizational psychology, applied social psychology and applied sociology, as well as in business administration and management, and in specialties within these larger areas including group dynamics, organization communication and organization development (Kelly, 1980; Gibson, Ivancevich and Donnelly, 1982).

The field of organization behavior is frequently conceptualized as having two major focuses - micro and macro. The micro focus is concerned mainly with individual and personal behavior and with group dynamics in organizations, and often has an applied orientation. The macro focus is concerned more with theoretical aspects of organization theory and design (i.e., with the organization as a whole) and with how the organization relates to its environment. Kurt Lewin's influence is particularly prevalent in the micro area, as evidenced in the action research and survey focus of some organization behavior research and the emphasis on group process and organization development in the organization behavior curriculum.

Course outlines and textbooks in introductory organization behavior usually cover topics involving research methodology, perception, leadership, motivation, interpersonal behavior, communication, group dynamics, decision making, stress, organization development and organization theory. The extent and nature of coverage of Lewin's contributions to applied social sciences within organization behavior courses varies with the particular textbooks used and the background and preferences of the instructor (Dean and Schwindt, 1981).

Lewin's name is often mentioned in connection with descriptions of the change process (unfreezing-change-refreezing) and its use in organization development. Most texts and courses also discuss the use of survey research methodology and action research (although they may not mention Lewin per se) within the context of organization development. Survey research is used as a research technique in organization behavior, although the use of self-report instruments (such as surveys) has in recent years been criticized and is declining in favor of more "objective" behavioral measures. Most organization behavior texts have one or more chapters on group dynamics, in which the influence of Lewin's students is apparent. These chapters typically discuss group process and ways of observing it in a group, stages of group development, and group training methodologies such as sensitivity training and team building. While T groups are not often specifically mentioned, they form the historical antecedent of these other group methodologies (Back, 1973), as well as the historical basis for much of the current research on group process and development (Bradford, Gibb and Benne, 1964; Benne, Bradford, Gibb and Lippitt, 1975). In addition, several schools offer courses in group dynamics or development in which part of the course involves the use of T groups (Biberman, 1979). Many organization behavior texts and courses also include a discussion of decision making, in the context of which force field analysis is sometimes mentioned.

We can see, then, that Lewin's theories and those of his students play an important role in organization behavior courses, and that they play an even bigger role in business school course offerings in the more

specific areas of group dynamics and organization development, wherein
the theories are elaborated on in more detail.

Another major Lewinian influence is felt in the business schools
in terms of the approach many management and organization behavior faculty use to teach organization behavior and management courses.

LEWINIAN INFLUENCE ON TEACHING APPROACHES

There are a number of approaches currently being used by management
faculty to teach organization behavior and related courses. Many faculty use lecture and discussion, with an emphasis on theory and research
in organization behavior. Other faculty prefer using mainly cases.
Still other faculty prefer to use an approach which has been called the
"experiential" approach to teaching. Each approach is useful for accomplishing certain teaching objectives. Many faculty use a combination
of these approaches throughout a course. The approach which has been
most influenced by Lewin, and even more so by Lewin's students, is the
experiential approach.

The experiential approach involves the use of surveys and exercises
to engage the student as an actual participant in a learning experience.
The underlying theory behind the use of "experiential exercises" is
that the student will learn by having an experience and then analyzing
(or processing) what he/she has learned from the experience (Kolb,
1979a). This philosophy and approach to learning, with its emphasis on
generating and learning from data regarding one's own behavior in an
experiential setting, can be traced back to the action research and
particularly "laboratory" approach to learning which formed the theo-
retial basis for T group training and the laboratories which were developed at National Training Laboratories (now called NTL) by Lewin's students (Back, 1973; Bradford, Gibb, and Benne, 1964; Kolb, 1979a). Indeed, many of the classroom exercises used by organization behavior
teachers were first developed by staff members at National Training
Laboratories sessions or by NTL members. Several NTL members teach
courses in organization behavior, organization development and group
dynamics in business school settings. In addition, the T group as originally conceived of by Lewin (as having a group dynamics and research
oriented focus) now seems to be conducted in this "purist" sense only
in university settings, including business school course settings
(Biberman, 1979).

Textbooks in organization behavior reflect these various teaching approaches. Some textbooks use mostly cases (e.g., Schlesinger, Eccles and Gabarro, 1983). Others use mostly experiential exercises (cf. Kolb, 1979b). Many use a combination of approaches which include experiential exercises (cf. Schermerhorn, Hunt and Osborn, 1982; Gibson, Ivancevich and Donnelly, 1982; Cohen, Fink, Gadon, and Willits, 1980). The Lewinian approach to learning by generating data about one's own behavior and then processing it has thus become increasingly prevalent in texts for business school course such as organization behavior, group dynamics and organization development.

Experiential exercises used in organization behavior courses include such "classic" exercises as "Lost on the Moon" (The NASA exercise) and the bomb shelter exercise, and involve such teaching techniques as using fish bowls, brainstorming and role playing. Most exercises involve the use of small groups. Some instructors devise their own exerices or modify and adapt exercises from published sources such as the University Associates series (Jones and Pffeiffer, 1969-1984; Pffeiffer and Jones, 1969-1984). Most of these exercises can be historically traced back to exercises developed in conjunction with the laboratories conducted by National Training Laboratories and other organizations which used laboratory training approaches. Lewin's influence, and especially that of his students, is thus very much alive in recent trends in teaching behavioral courses in business schools.

PROFESSIONAL ORGANIZATIONS AND CONFERENCES

Faculty who teach organization behavior and other behavioral courses may belong to several professional organizations, each of which involves different academic or scholarly interests.

A major organization to which most behavioral faculty belong is the Academy of Management. The Academy has several divisions. Divisions which may be of interest to faculty with a Lewinian applied social science philosophy include the Management Education and Development, Management Consultant, Organization Behavior (the largest division in terms of membership), Organization Development and Social Issues Divisions. The Academy holds a national meeting each year in August, publishes two journals, and has a placement service. There are also five related Regional Academy divisions which also hold yearly meetings (Academy of Management, 1983).

Many organization behavior teachers also belong to the American Psychological Association and its related divisions (particularly the industrial/organization psychology division), and to the American Institute for Decision Sciences.

Organizations which have more of a historical or theoretical connection to Lewinian philosophy and theory to which some organization behavior faculty belong include the OD Network, OD Institute and NTL Institute.

An organization of business school faculty which is concerned with teaching approaches to organization behavior and which shows strong philosophical ties to the work of Lewin's students is the Organization Behavior Teaching Society. The Society holds an Organization Behavior Teaching Conference each year whose focus is on sharing strategies, exercises and teaching designs. They also publish a quarterly journal called Exchange. The executive director of the Society is David Bradford at Stanford University. Faculty who are actively involved in the Society tend to have an experiential focus. Several members of the OBTC have historical ties with NTL either as members or as program participants.

THE LEWINIAN TRADITION CONTINUES

The theories and learning philosophy of Lewin and his students are thus very much alive and becoming increasingly influential in the curriculum, courses, and teaching styles of business schools and universities. Organization behavior and related areas in particular are becoming strong vehicles for continuing research and theory building in the ideas and areas started by Lewin and his students, and for continued development of teaching strategies, designs and techniques involving experiential learning and the "laboratory" approach to learning. Many job opportunities exist in business schools throughout the country and world for researchers and scholars trained in applied social sciences (such as organization development, applied psychology and sociology, group dynamics and the newly emerging organization behavior). Organization behavior and business schools may thus become a leading force in the perpetuation and advancement of Lewinian concepts, theory and philosophy.

REFERENCES

Academy of Management (1983). The Academy of management handbook. Baltimore, Md.: Author.

Back, K.W. (1973). Beyond words: The story of sensitivity training and the encounter movement. Baltimore, Md.: Penguin Books.

Benne, K.D., Bradford, L.P., Gibb, J.R., & Lippitt, R.D. (Eds.) (1975). The laboratory method of changing and learning: Theory and application. Palo Alto, Cal.: Science and Behavior Books.

Biberman, G. (1979). Trainer behavior in a T-group setting: A survey of current practice. Small Group Behavior. Vol., 10, No. 4, p. 501-522.

Bradford, L.P., Gibb, J.R. & Benne, K.D. (Eds.) (1964). T-group theory and laboratory method. New York: Wiley.

Cohen, A.R., Fink, S.J., Gadon, H. & Willits, R.D. (1980). Effective behavior in organizations: Learning from the interplay of cases, concepts, and student experiences (Rev. Ed.). Homewood, Ill.: Richard D. Irwin.

Dean, J.W. & Schwindt, R. (Eds.) (1981). Business administration reading lists and course outlines: Vol. 10. Organizational behavior. Durham, N.C.: Eno River Press.

Gibson, J.L., Ivancevich, J.M. & Donnelly, J.H. (1982). Organizations: Behavior, structure, processes (4th Ed.). Plano, Texas: Business Publications, Inc.

Jones, J.E. & Pffeiffer, J.W. (Eds.) (1969-1984). The annual handbook for group facilitators. La Jolla, Cal.: University Associates.

Kelly, J. (1980). Organizational behavior: Its data, first principles, and applications (3rd Ed.). Homewood, Ill.: Richard D. Irwin.

Kolb, D.A., Rubin, I.M. & McIntyre, J.M. (1979a). Introduction: Thematic trends in organizational psychology. In D.A. Kolb, I.M. Rubin & J.M. McIntyre (Eds.), Organizational psychology: A book of readings (3rd Ed.). Englewood Cliffs, N.J.: Prentice Hall.

Kolb, D.A., Rubin, I.M. & McIntyre, J.B. (1979b). Organizational psychology: An experiential approach (3rd Ed.). Englewood Cliffs, N.J.: Prentice Hall.

Pffeiffer, J.W. & Jones, J.E. (Eds.) (1969-1984). A handbook of structured experiences for human relations training. La Jolla, Cal.: University Associates.

Schermerhorn, J.R., Jr., Hunt, J.G. & Osborn, R.N. (1982). Managing organizational behavior. New York: Wiley.

Schlesinger, L.A., Eccles, R.G. & Gabarro, J.J. (1983). Managing behavior in organizations: Text, cases, readings. New York: McGraw Hill.

Children in Cooperation and Competition: The role of Entitlement and Deservedness*

Emmy A. Pepitone

Bryn Mawr College

My research started as a propaedeutic attempt as a social psychologist in a developmentally and clinically oriented department to counteract graduate students' focus on the individual psyche by wanting to
demonstrate some social effects children may have on each other. The
method evolved proved surprisingly reliable and versatile, and hence
remained in its basic features almost unaltered. Most of the time,
children are studied within the familiar setting of their elementary
schools. In a spare classroom, different social fields are produced
through instructions that create various degrees of competitive or
cooperative conditions in which groups of children are placed. The
basic controlled procedure consists of engaging several children--usually
like-sexed triads--in a task which involves construction of a flat block
design on a round table top (the "Pep-board"). The task varies from
exact specification of a model to copy to a wholly unstructured request
that the child make anything s/he wishes. Depending on the particular
variable being studied, children are asked either to work together to
make one product (role-related cooperation) or to work on their own
product on the same table (coaction), or explicitly instructed to "see
which one of you can make the best X" (competitive coaction). Polaroid
photographs are taken of the products and later used for scoring. Observers record children's interpersonal behaviors into precoded categories.

In my studies to date (Pepitone, 1980; Pepitone, in press), one of
the most significant persistent findings is that children from suburban
Upper Middle Class backgrounds (whose comfortable life style might be
assumed to dispose them toward greater generosity to needy others) were
precisely the ones in whom competition over needed materials was most
prevalent. These findings in and of themselves are not surprising;
there are a few studies using game-theoretical methodologies that suggest (although experimental control could not always be rigorously
executed) that UMC children, both in the United States and other cultures, engage generally in more self-maximizing than do rural and less

---

*A companion article describing the historical and theoretical context
  of this work is in the Research section.

economically privileged children (e.g., Kagan and Madsen, 1972; Shapira and Lomranz, 1972). Further, most of these studies suffer from the game-theoretical limitations of exclusive focus on choice behavior. Our research involving the total K-5th grade population of two elementary schools--one located in suburban Philadelphia with predominantly professional familial background (the UMC sample), the other a working class sample (WC children) in North Philadelphia--permitted examination both of children's performance and behaviors. Here, matters looked much more complex: In a competitive coaction situation, at every level, K-5, UMC children's performance exceeded that of WC children. In role-related cooperative conditions, both samples performed about equally until the end of second grade; thereafter WC children outperformed UMC children significantly at every grade level. Furthermore, WC children's amount of helping behavior was shown to exceed that of UMC children dramatically and significantly.

Most attempts at interpreting these results focus in one way or another on parental socialization practices. One of the most convincing functional interpretations (Kohn, 1963) argues that UMC parents begin to train their children early to develop initiative and independence in preparation for the positions of power and authority for which they are slated in the future. By contrast, so the argument continues, WC children will move into positions where they must take orders from authority figures and collaborate with their coworkers; hence, obedience, submission, reliance on each other for help are desirable traits to develop in working class children.

What caught our attention, however, was the particular quality of self-orientation among many of the UMC children. Records note over and over again, children pulling the box containing blocks toward themselves, attaining sole possession, digging both hands in and thus effectively preventing others from having access to the blocks. When competition was heightened in another study by creating material scarcity such that there were fewer blocks than needed to permit each child to complete the task, again there were a number of children who quite openly hoarded the blocks, frequently taking more than actually needed, often hiding them in their pockets or under the PEP board; frequently, other coactors, literally not more than a few inches away, were wholly ignored. This was not mere self-maximizing, but rather a general oblivion to the very presence of others. If others were seen at all, they were seen primarily as obstacles in one's path, or as comparison figures by which to measure one's own progress. Of course, when coactors were equally self-oriented, fights broke out, with aggressive behaviors ranging from playful accusations of unfairness, mild verbal invectives to overt physical combat--especially boys. If coactors objected to having blocks snatched from their own pile of blocks, these children tended to look up innocently, objecting: "but I _need_ them to finish my work"--as if there were no question that these needs must be taken care of--in fact that they deserved to be taken care of, and that it was their right to amass these blocks for themselves.

These were consistent results in a number of small studies. In a somewhat different variant, spatial conflict was created by asking second graders to make a long train, with the experimenter knowing that sooner or later trains would have to come into collision with each other. Again, we noted children's ingenious ways of barrelling their way through and around the other's train and continue, intent on bypassing, but wholly oblivious of the others' need for free movement as well. It may be argued that these children were simply fulfilling the task requirements: having been asked to compete, they acted within that spirit. There are two important pieces of evidence that contradict this interpretation: in a control condition, identical except for the fact that explicit competitive instructions were omitted, results were no different. Children had been given the option of making one long train together, yet none of them availed themselves of this option. In fact, several actively objected when another child attempted to "hitch" her train to that of another. Further, when this study was replicated in a three-room schoolhouse in a small village in rural Vermont whose parent population ranged from teacher to carpenter downward, we saw even 6 year olds asking each other to move their wagons a bit. To our amazement, room for the other to pass was made, often by dismantling one or more of their own wagons to accommodate the other. This rural, poorer counterpart more readily shared what was available, accommodated their partners and collaborated easily, with several groups providing elaborations involving railroad tracks, roundhouses, etc.

In the same study children were also requested to state their favorite wishes (after Dembo, 1960). Among the many findings, one of the most interesting was the magnitude of material wishes. For the rural children, a special category of "modest" wishes had to be created on one pole--e.g., "a paper dolly"; "a box of pencils"--wishes which were almost completely absent in the suburban sample. In the latter sample we had to create a category on the opposite extreme of "excessive," defined as a collectivity of objects, e.g., "all the toys at F.A.O. Schwartz"; "to have a tree that grows cars so that we could pick one whenever I wanted." My favorite example is that of a seven year old son of a cardiologist who cited his wish as: "all the Nobel prizes in the world." Coders experienced no difficulty agreeing that this wish should be categorized as excessive, but engaged in quite a discussion as to whether it was imaginary or realistic. The young boy had to think hard when asked whether his wish would come true. He shook his head sadly from side to side, then brightened up and asserted: "Well, maybe ONE Nobel prize at least." The number of children wishing for a million dollars, diamonds and other luxury items was considerable.

The phenomenon is clear. Clinical professionals have been pointing to a variety of self-oriented syndromes referred to as the "Narcissistic Personality" (Akhtar & Thomson, 1982), or its breeding ground, the "Culture of Narcissism" (Lasch, 1978; Sampson, 1977). Here, the expectation is one of instant gratification. The connection is also made with material affluence, as described in great detail by Coles (1977, pp. 361-412): "...they grow up surrounded by possessions, animate as well as inanimate. They have learned to look after them, and to depend upon them for support... the quantitative difference in their material acquisitions prompts a qualitative psychological difference: an enhanced expectation of what life has to offer...." Parents are described as often constituting strong normative role models, with "...continuous and strong emphasis put on the self,...its display, its possibilities, its cultivation and development, even the repeated use of the word... these privileged ones are children who live in homes with many mirrors. They have mirrors in their rooms, larger mirrors in adjoining bathrooms. When they were three or four, they were taught to use them...."

Some of the children of the affluent, proudly fulfill parental expectations: "I've got lots of chores. We're not spoiled here! I have to clean out the stables and brush the horses carefully before we go riding. I have to pick up my room." However, in many of the case histories, Coles also identifies a predominant attitude of passivity. He exemplifies this attitude of entitlement aptly as a child "seem(ing) to be sitting on a throne of sorts--expecting things to happen, wondering with annoyance why they don't...reassuring himself that they will, or if they haven't shrugging his shoulders and waiting for the next event..."

Combining our empirical evidence with various psychodynamic theories had several effects: for one thing, it drove us to return to, and consider more seriously again, the well-known Lewinian formula about B = f (P,E). At a time when members of division 8 of APA insist on identifying themselves as either "Personality" psychologists, or social psychologists, it seems essential to re-emphasize the inherent connection between the Person and his/her life space.

Secondly, the function of material objects in our lives became exceedingly important in our theoretical considerations. We are in good company here; after all, William James spoke about the "material self" as one of the important aspects of the person; so did Cooley; to say nothing of Thorston Veblen's writing about the consuming habits that make up personalities of the "leisure classes." And more recently, an intriguing study of The meaning of things by Czikszentmihalji & Rochberg-Halton (1981) asserts as their working hypothesis that "the things that surround us are inseparable from who we are. The material objects we use are not just tools we can pick up and discard at our convenience; they constitute the framework of experience that gives order to our otherwise shapeless selves..." It seems that the very persons who should be most aware of the material world that must be incorporated as an integral part of a person's life space--our fellow social psychologists-- are strangely and singularly nonresponsive to this dimension. While psychologists have developed elaborate theories about "object relations" with other people, there are no theories, and certainly no theories that have been put to experimental test, about effects of relations with material objects.

Our own conceptual framework is beginning to link children's self-oriented behavior to their accustomed familial environment. What surrounds us may be looked at as an extension of ourselves. Thus, who we are becomes at least in part defined by ourselves as well as by others by what we have. This may be particularly true for young children, since it is possible to form strong attachments to possessions in their concrete form without mediation of abstract thinking that is beyond the capacity of the young child. The environment in which young children grow up is their world--the only world they as yet have come to know intimately. Familiar objects with which parents surround their children become their possessions. Possessions, becoming part of oneself, enlarge the self; thus, possession of objects may become linked to self-importance, or power. If so, sheer quantity of objects one possesses may become related to feelings of personal omnipotence, legitimizing and increasing needs for further possessions. Thus, part of the self-concept is constituted by the different expectations built up by the child with regard to what s/he will receive; taken for granted, it comes to be "what one 'deserves'." The concepts of personal deserving and entitlement are central intervening variables in our attempt to link material context of the home surroundings on the one hand, and children's self-oriented behaviors that involve objects in interpersonal contexts on the other hand.

In closing, we outline some major features of the theory which we have begun to examine empirically. The cornerstone is the assumption that children's self-oriented behaviors are reflections of their experiences within the familial context. More specifically, the combined levels of what a child receives over time within the material context of the family[1] and his/her own responsibilities within the household forms part of the self-image of what s/he may rightfully expect to attain. These expectations in turn determine children's behavior. One may conceive of classifying different children with different patterns of material possessions received in relation to duties performed, whose consequent mediating expectations are likely to differ, as well as their overt behavior in interdependent situations that require collaboration. The beginnings of such a classificatory scheme are outlined below.

1. Highly "Entitled" Children

These are children who are given a great deal, unconditionally, with minimal demands made on them to contribute to the household. They may be expected to develop an inflated sense of their entitlement. It should be noted here that the term "entitlement" is not used in the intergenerational contextual theoretical sense of being rightfully owed, that is a justifiable demand for "righting" of an experienced "wrong." In fact, in that theoretical context, those who are given much without giving in return are considered objectively "indebted." We have chosen the term entitlement because it seems appropriately descriptive of children who are given much and phenomenally feel that they have a right to expect this flow of material goods to continue. In cooperative conditions, their behaviors may be expected to be primarily self-oriented, manifested either in aggressive, domineering, or in passive resistance such as refusals to collaborate; in either case, the group's progress will be obstructed by entitled children.

2. "Deserving" Children

These are children who, like the entitled children, are given a great deal but are also responsible contributors to the functioning of

---

[1] This, of course, is not to deny effects of the nonmaterial socializing environment in which children develop. More, although not nearly enough, is known about effects of parental affective giving and demanding on children's entitlement and indebtedness, as postulated for instance in contextual intergenerational theories. It is suggested here merely to isolate generally neglected aspects of the physical environment. The hope is to determine main effects of both the material and nonmaterial contexts of children's growth, and ultimately, to incorporate both in theories around their interaction.

the household. They may be expected to develop a strong sense of their deservedness. This term overlaps with its usage by Lerner (Lerner, Miller & Holmes, 1976) in the sense that it includes the aspect of "merited" receiving. It differs in that Lerner ties recognition of need for postponement of immediate gratification to emergence of children's sense of justice; no such derivation is made here. Deserving children are children who earn what they receive. Feeling justly treated, and indeed being so treated objectively, these children may be expected to have a strong and positive self-concept of their value and role in the family, and confidence in their own ability to contribute. In inter-dependent situations, they may be expected to take the initiative in leadership, assuming active group- and task-roles that move the group to successful task completion.

3. "Dutiful" Children

These are children who do not receive a great deal of material pos-sessions, but who contribute to the household, often substantially. They lack the self-assurance gained from living in affluent surroundings. Their expectations are likely to reflect norms of their comparison group. If their contact is largely with peers in similar material circumstances, they are likely to be satisfied and accepting of their state (should they attend school in heterogeneously composed classrooms with more pri-vileged children, signs of feelings of "relative deprivation" may emerge). Dutiful children may be expected to be highly attuned to each other; since there are no strong self-orientations that may interfere with collaboration, they are likely to prefer to work together. In the presence of either Entitled or Deserving children, they are likely to play subordinate helping roles.

How will children who differ in degree of entitlement and deserved-ness behave when unable to obtain what they want or need? Since our focus is on consequences of material affluence available to children, it is most appropriate that their behavior be studied in situations where the available supply of resources is insufficient to satisfy all demands for it--i.e. in experimentally created conditions of scarcity. Scarcity of resources around the globe affects today untold numbers of peoples and hence, of course, is a social problem worthy of study in its own right. However, the human response to scarcity is of great theo-retical interest in that it has the inherent potential for allowing a variety of solutions to situations where demands exceed available re-sources. Attempted solutions may range from competitive self-maximizing at the expense of others, to sharing and apportioning resources according to several distribution practices based on principles involving different degrees of fairness in giving to self and others.

Thus we return to the next phase in our study of children in competitive and cooperative situations. The basic design contains two parts: 1. administration of a questionnaire ascertaining their familial material context; 2. children are required to reproduce a model design under severe conditions of scarcity, such that--unbeknownst to them--the only viable solution is that of abandoning attempts at individual solution. Whether, when, and how children will turn a competitive coaction solution into one of role-related cooperation, and how they will proceed working together I hope to be able to report in the near future.

REFERENCES

Akhtar, S. & A. Thompson, Jr. (1982). Overview: Narcissistic personality disorder. _American Journal of Psychiatry_, 139, 1.

Coles, R. (1977). Privileged ones: The well-off and the rich in America. Vol. 5, _Children of crisis_. Boston: Little, Brown.

Czikszentmihali, M. & E. Rochberg-Halton. (1981). _The meaning of things: Domestic symbols and the self_. New York: Cambridge University Press.

Dembo, T. (1960). A theoretical and experimental inquiry into concrete values and value systems. In B. Kaplan & S. Wapner (Eds.), _Perspectives in Psychological Theory_. (Essays in honor of H. Werner). New York: International University Press, p. 78-115.

Kagan, S. & Madsen, D.C. (1972). Experimental analyses of cooperation and competition of Anglo-American children and Mexican children. _Developmental Psychology_, 6, p. 49-59.

Kohn, M.L. (1969). _Class and conformity--a study of values_. Homewood, Ill.: Dorsey Press.

Lasch, C. (1978). _The culture of narcissism: American life in an age of diminishing expectations_. New York: W.W. Norton.

Lerner, M.J., Miller, D.T. & Holmes, J.G. (1976). Deserving and the emergence of forms of justice. In L. Berkowitz and E. Walster (Eds.), _Advances in experimental social psychology. Equity theory: Toward a general theory of social interaction_. New York: Academic Press, 9:133-162.

Pepitone, E.A. (1980). _Children in cooperation and competition: Toward a developmental social psychology_. Lexington, Ma.: D.C. Heath & Company.

Shapira, A. & Lomranz, J. (1981). Cooperative and competitive behavior of rural Arab children in Israel. _Journal of Cross-cultural Psychology_, 12, 1, 3-20.

Participants as Consultants to Themselves

Richard A. Schmuck

University of Oregon

> "...I keep picturing all these little kids playing some
> game in this big field of rye and all. Thousands of
> little kids, and nobody's around--nobody big, I mean--
> except me. And I'm standing on the edge of some crazy
> cliff. What I have to do, I have to catch everybody
> if they start to go over the cliff--I mean if they're
> running and they don't look where they're going and I
> have to come out from somewhere and catch them. That's
> all I'd do all day. I'd just be the catcher in the
> rye..."
>
> Spoken to Phoebe by Holden Caulfield,
> in J.D. Salinger's The catcher in the rye.

After several years of working together, Phil Runkel (my colleague)
and I surmised that if consultation in OD was to facilitate self renewal
at the grassroots level in schools, then it must necessarily break out
of the mold of a traditional, hierarchical expert relationship, and
move to reduce the inevitable social distance that arises between the
consultants and the school's participants. In the novel, Salinger makes
Holden Caulfield believeable as a "catcher in the rye" because Holden
poses no social threat to the fictitious children whom he promises to
guide as they run through the potentially dangerous fields. We looked
toward peer consultation as our metaphor and as a solution to the problem
of social distance between consultants and participants.

Peer Cadres of OD Consultants

We decided on a strategy for disseminating OD in which practicing
educators themselves would take on the formal and legitimate functions
of the OD consultant in relation to one another. Such peer consultation
could be structured through horizontal interactions among organizational
cousins (those who hold jobs within the same school district, but who
are not members of the same interdependent task unit). Thus, in contrast to placing normative emphasis on expertise, peer consultation could

gain legitimacy through norms in support of collegial responsibility
and peer helpfulness. OD cadres made up of peer-colleagues would offer
an alternative to the traditional professional-client helping relationship.

We have established peer cadres of OD specialists within three
school districts and consultants elsewhere have by now created five other
cadres. Members entering these OD cadres are regular district personnel
such as teachers, principals, counselors, curriculum specialists, and
assistant superintendents, each performing only part-time in the role
of OD specialist while carrying out full-time teaching, administrative,
or coordinating responsibilities. The in-district specialists use their
understandings and skills as facilitators to help their peers clarify
communication, assess progress toward educational goals, cope with interdependence and conflict in productive ways, systematically solve
problems, reach out to use relevant resources and make decisions collaboratively. A detailed account of cadre functions and activities can
be found in Schmuck, (1978).

Typically cadre members are divided into small teams to provide OD
consultation. The specialists usually choose the team to which they
wish to belong using criteria such as willingness to work closely with
the others on the team, belief that a balanced team with regard to district jobs should be created, and significant interest in the particular
tasks to be performed. They form new intervention teams after completing
their designs with the client groups and when new clients are identified.

Considerable emphasis is placed on building strong temporary teams
for delivering the consultation. By understanding and supporting one
another, the OD specialists can more validly diagnose the organizational
problems of their clients and design more effective interactions. Moreover, cadre members who feel comfortable working together learn from one
another during the team planning and consultations. No specialist is
allowed to participate as a member of an intervention team that is providing consultation in his or her "family group."

Thus a cadre member who teaches in a particular school is not
supposed to join the team that is working with his or her staff. This
limitation was thought by us to be important for several reasons: (1)
As a member of the client group, the OD specialist could be directly
involved in any problem or plan of action for change designed during
the intervention and therefore would have to be free to devote full
energies and attention to that task; (2) cadre members who do participate
as clients in training events could give constructive feedback to cadre
members who are acting as their consultants; (3) the use of OD specialist

who work in other schools sets a useful example of interschool cooperation; and (4) the failure of specialists to participate as clients might
be perceived as a lack of faith in what the consultation is intended to
accomplish.

BEYOND CONSULTATION FROM THE OUTSIDE

Although the peer cadre for a school district has been a highly
effective structure for delivering OD consultation to local schools on
a regular basis,--indeed it has been the most important invention of our
Oregon Program--I am now puzzling over how we might take another creative
leap in conceptualizing and acting to facilitate self renewal in schools.
I wish to explore ways in which OD techniques and the procedures of
continuous problem solving could become institutionalized in schools,
making only minimal, if any, external assistance necessary. I feel
challenged to conceive of ways in which the participants themselves--
the on-site administrators, teachers, and students--might become "con-
sultants-to-themselves" so that continuous diagnosis, problem solving,
and planned change are initiated and maintained from within the school.
My motivation to think this way grows out of a view of the moral basis
of OD which sees all participants being responsible for the effectiveness and well being of one another, making unnecessary the protective
presence of a Holden Caulfield.

The Moral Basis of OD

A moral norm shared by many OD consultants calls for the techniques
of democratic participation to be given away to "the people." As such,
OD takes its place next to the host of self-help technologies that are
sweeping the globe. Thus, OD consultants strive to present the theory
and technology of goal-setting, problem solving, and decision making
to organizational participants at all levels and statuses of a client
organization. At its best, OD offers concepts and procedures for actualizing democracy in the workplace--where the concern is not only for an
enhanced quality of life, but also for system-wide achievement and
productivity.

With regard to OD in schools, this moral norm would call for the
OD process to include not only administrators and teachers but also

students, parents, classified personnel, and perhaps other citizens
who have a stake in schooling. To paraphrase Robert Dahl's (1961)
"Principle of Affected Interests:" "Every school participant who is
affected by the decisions of a school administration should have the
right to participate in those decisions." In practice, of course, the
"democracy of OD" in schools hardly ever goes far enough. It is typically only the administrators and teachers who are involved.

Still, of the different forms of educational consultancy, OD is
the only one that has some chance of actualizing democratic norms, structures, and procedures in the school. Specialized technical assistance
merely fills a temporary gap or satisfies a particular need, but offers
no fundamental change in the democracy of the school. Curriculum specialists typically strive to change the knowledge and skills of individuals, but offer little that would bring about new, more democratic norms
or procedures. Indeed, even much of the process consultation in schools
is focused on helping individuals to grow rather than establishing more
supportive interdependencies among them. But, even though, in theory,
OD can raise the level of system democracy, in practice OD faces the
possibility of losing its democratic soul by including only the elite
members of a school in the process and by structuring unproductive dependency (counterdependency) into the hierarchical relationships between
inside participants and outside consultants.

Participants As Consultants

At first glance, the concept of participants acting as consultants
to themselves seems peculiar. By definition, consultants are neutral
outsiders invited into an organization on a temporary basis to help re-
form and reorganize the current situation. At the same time, however,
when the institutionalization of a structure for self-renewal is the
goal, it turns out that outsiders must eventually transfer their primary functions--those of diagnosing, observing, monitoring, and coach-
ing--to the insiders. And, as I have already cited, OD consultants use
designs that are geared to ease their departure and to educate the participants in OD norms and skills. So, for example, in many OD designs,
it is routine for the participants to act as observers and for them
subsequently to give feedback to their colleagues about what they have
observed. Moreover, it has been effective for educators within a district to participate as members of a cadre of OD consultants through
which regular and continuous collegial consultation in organization

development is made available. Now, let us go a step further in the direction of defining some of the participants themselves as internal consultants for self renewal within their own schools.

First and foremost is the principal who should strive to initiate and support the norms, structures, and procedures needed for organizational problem solving. Although principals cannot easily remove themselves from the flow of school life, they can start the conditions necessary for communication, goal-setting, problem solving and decision making. For example, to facilitate collaborative decision making, the principal should practice such communication skills as paraphrasing (making sure that there is understanding of the others' messages), behavior description (describing behavior objectively without impugning motives), descriptions of own feelings (describing to others how the principal is feeling directly and succinctly), impression checking (describing how another appears to be feeling to verify or to disconform the perception); and "gate keeping" (seeing that others have a chance to contribute).

Also, the principal should stimulate interest in goal setting and in systematic planning on how to reach the goals. The STP model for problem solving can be employed in which the S is the situation (current state of affairs), the T is the target (ideal goal state to pursue), and the P is a plan of action to move from the S to the T. The principal can help staff members to explore the nature of the S in depth by encouraging discussions about the facilitating factors and the restraining factors that are keeping the S in quasi-equilibrium. Innovative group techniques can be initiated for enhancing the staff's acceptance of self analysis and self renewal. One technique, for example is the fishbowl procedure during which a group of observers sit around a group that is carrying out problem solving. The outsiders have been provided with particular categories to guide their observation. A variation of the fishbowl involves a group formation in which two or three empty chairs are left in the inside group so that colleagues in the outside group might occasionally enter the inside to give feedback on the problem solving.

It is not impossible for the principal to step out of the authority position, at least temporarily, to act as a consultant to the staff. In one of our projects, the principal of a high school did just that, and for an entire academic year while on sabbatical leave and studying for a doctorate, he served as an organizational consultant to his own staff and study body (Flynn, 1971). Data from questionnaires answered by all the staff members indicated the principal was able to step out of his role and be effective as a consultant with the majority of his staff. Thirty-four of 58 staff members placed him in the role of OD consultant throughout the intervention year; 14 saw him in a half-way position; and 10 saw him still in the role of principal throughout the consultation. Compared to those last 10, the 34 who saw him in the consultant role thought that he was more competent, more facilitating, more open, and more willing to let the faculty member find out for themselves rather than pushing for what he wanted to do. Those who saw him in the principal role throughout the year had difficulty in viewing him as helpful. The evaluation also showed that the staff improved its communication, that participation in group meetings and initiation of influence attempts became more widespread among the staff, and that the staff was clarifying and developing a new, more participative decision-making structure by the end of the school year.

Second, teachers, counselors, and resource persons might act as OD consultants within their own schools. There are the obvious ways, already discussed in relation to the principal, such as participating as observers and coaches in fishbowl arrangements, acting as convener or recorder during meetings, and using the communication skills listed above in giving and receiving feedback with colleagues. They can also form into "helping pairs" to facilitate one another's professional growth, both as classroom teachers and as staff members, observe each other, give each other feedback, and generally support one another through personal change.

In relation to OD for the entire school, they can serve as members of a school-wide renewal committee to collect data on the system effectiveness of the school and to arrange for feedback to the staff so that collaborative problem solving might be stimulated. A few of the members of the renewal committee might also act as trainers in the STP problem solving model to their colleagues, especially since that model is easily communicated and has been instrumented. The consultative role of the teachers then is to guide their colleagues through an already instrumented training design.

Intergroup consultation within the school is also a useful model as for example when one team of teachers observes another in the style of a fishbowl. The team on the inside works on a real problem, while the outside group observes and comments on the processes of the inside group. Later, the two groups can change their inside and outside positions and reverse roles. Again, in this context, already instrumented observation systems can be employed by the outsiders. Also, such designs for consultation might be enhanced if members of one team have already been paired with members of the other team as in the "helping pair" arrangement.

It is not unreasonable to consider that even parents can be brought into consultative functions for the school. As an arm of the school-wide renewal committee, for example, they can collect questionnaire and interview data from other parents and citizens in the community; they can analyze those data and put them into tables and figures; and with the collaboration of the principal and teachers they could present the data to the staff. Moreover, parents can be brought into staff and team problem solving to add their thoughts to the general reservoir of ideas obtained during brainstorming. And there could be instances in which parents would be helpful consultants to "helping pairs" as, for example, when a pair is wrestling with ways of increasing the involvement of particular parents in their children's education.

Finally, and perhaps most importantly, students offer an untapped resource as consultants to their own schools. At first, that concept sounds crazy, but its craziness grows out of a view of students as the clients or as the products of the school. Consider students as organizational participants who at least theoretically could participate in some aspects of school-wide diagnosis and planning, educational problem solving, and staff decision making. Indeed, the consequences of failing to consider students as organizational participants could be one of the major contributors to low student motivation and to high student alienation. Teachers and administrators can become so preoccupied with their own management efforts that they lose touch with the students. For their part, students can feel "put down," even oppressed, by imposed rules and become alienated when their ideas and energies have not been used.

Perhaps the most straightforward procedure for helping students to act as organizational participants, involves strategic change in the social studies curriculum. A course has been developed by Arends, et al., Understanding School Life Through Organizational Psychology (1977) to help students understand the dynamics of the school as a formal social organization, to delineate their roles as potential organizational participants, and to present the students with the skills required to design and participate in a school wide improvement program.

In conclusion, I have come to believe that school participants including the students can successfully act as OD consultants to themselves, and that they can be effective in initiating a self-renewing school, without the need for large amounts of outside consultative help. Perhaps the concept of "participants as consultants to themselves" is no more radical or outrageous than "being conscious of the impact of your own behavior" and of "being aware collectively of how the system is operating." It is after all the function of an organizational _mirror_ that the disinterested consultant offers. And once the participants can look at themselves in the mirror, it is possible for them to manage changes in their own systems. Self-renewal, we might say, is simply self-reflection accompanied by concerted, collaborative action to right the wrongs that are discovered during the self-reflection. Why can't the participants themselves learn to hold up an organizational mirror together?

This metaphor of organizational participants erecting an organizational mirror of their own directly confronts the metaphor of the "catcher in the rye." Holden's fantasy goes well beyond the mirror in terms of the depth of intervention. Holden himself intends to intervene acting as a savior to restrain physically those children who get too close to the dangerous edge. He takes himself out of the role of member, placing himself above the children in a style not dissimilar from an organizational consultant in relation to the client organization.

Even though Holden Caulfield's image relates to little children, still it is protective, adolescent, paternalistic, and even condescending. While its romanticism is deeply touching, it nevertheless proffers the ill winds of dependency and custodianship. I worry that organizational consultants, like Holden, might share in a similar tragic flaw as they symbolically descend upon a school with a savior's intent. Somehow the way to grassroots, self-help, democracy in schools does not lie there; it must involve brand new ways of viewing participants with a responsibility to act as OD consultants to themselves. When everyone has access to the vantage point of the "catcher" and takes on shared responsibility for the well-being of one another, then the need for a catcher in the rye withers away.

REFERENCES

Arends, R. et al. (1977). _Understanding school life through organizational psychology_. Washington, D.C.: American Psychological Association.

Dahl, R.A. (1961). _Who Governs_? New Haven, Connecticut: Yale University Press.

Flynn, P., Schmuck, R., Arends, J., & Francisco, R. (1979). Transform-
ing the school's capacity for problem solving. Eugene, Oregon:
Center for Educational Policy and Management.

Salinger, J.D. (1951). The catcher in the rye. Boston: Little, Brown,
and Company, pps. 224-225.

Schmuck, R. (1978). Peer consultation for school improvement. In
Cooper, Gary and Alderfer, Clayton (Eds.), Advances in Experiential
Social Processes. New York: John Wiley.

Schmuck, R. & Runkel, P. (1970). Organizational training for a school
faculty. Eugene, Oregon: Center for Educational Policy and Management.

Schmuck, R., Murray, D., Smith, M.A., Schwartz, M. & Runkel, M. (1975).
Consultation for innovative schools: OD for multiunit structures.
Eugene, Oregon: Center for Educational Policy and Management.

Schmuck, R., Runkel, P., Arends, J., & Arends, R. (1977). The second
handbook of organizational development in schools. Palo Alto,
California: Mayfield Publishing Company.

Part II: Practical Theory

Section C: <u>Organizational and Human Resources Development</u>

<u>Steven L. Krupp</u> addresses a subject that has been of considerable current interest: What Quality Circles are and how they are used in human resources development programs. His specific aim is to describe properly this combination of concepts and techniques that is at the forefront of a human resource(s) development movement which has spread throughout business, health care and government organizations. Underlying this aim is another: To show how Lewin's work had an enormous impact on the formulation of and development of the ideas and practice of Quality Circles. "It is precisely this synthesis of human relations principles and the scientific method of research and statistical control which distinguishes Quality Circles from other approaches to team building or problem solving which may seem similar," Krupp says. "Lewin originally pioneered the incorporation of applied research methodology to practical problem solving through the formulation of action research. The fact that the Quality Circle evolves from this rich tradition in the behavioral sciences, and that it is based on a total systems concept, helps to explain its impressive success. Furthermore, Quality Circles are the only approach to organizational development which clearly and consistently documents its impact on productivity and bottom line business concerns as well as human relations and people building."

The next article pursues this same basic theme of the contribution of Kurt Lewin to human resources development, in the setting of a University residence hall. <u>Jean H. Woods and Irene G. Casper</u> describe an actual project carried out by The Residential Life Office at Temple University. The goals of the project were (1) to involve residence students in actively creating a positive living environment, and (2) to train undergraduate and graduate students in a method of planned intervention and action research skills. There were some positive results and some unanswered questions at the end, Woods and Casper say.

In a refreshing interlude between more complex considerations, <u>Mel Silberman</u> addresses a very concrete matter: How to teach force field analysis. This Lewinian technique, force field analysis, is often used at critical points in action research and other group problem solving. It is a valuable practical skill for persons and groups in organizational life. Silberman's final illustration is a business example.

This same notion of force field analysis is featured in the next article, by <u>Jay M. Yanoff</u> and <u>William E. Bryan</u>. Using general Lewinian theory and particularly the force field analysis technique, they describe in detail how they went about reshaping a medical education program to meet emerging health care needs. Noting that institutional change is difficult particularly in medical schools, they are confident about their success in using Lewinian principles as a conceptual base for planning, developing and implementing an institutional planning process within such a setting. Their model, they assert, is applicable to other such institutions.

In the last article, <u>Edmund Amidon</u> and <u>Tim Doris</u> describe in human detail their action research work with a tense and troubled department, from the beginning of their intervention to the end, when they were "no longer needed and out of a job."

The Quality Circle Phenomenon

Steven Krupp

Lincoln University, Pennsylvania

The importance of Human Resource Development Programs, which involve all levels of the work force in goal setting and problem solving, is achieving growing recognition throughout corporate American. Thirty-three percent of companies with over 500 employees and over half of New York Stock Exchange companies have introduced such employee involvement programs. In a study conducted by the New York Stock Exchange, Office of Economic Research in 1982, entitled People and Productivity: A Challenge to Corporate America, it was documented that such programs were initiated with the expectation of cutting costs (58%), improving worker attitudes (46%), and increasing productivity (38%). For over 50% of companies surveyed, this reflected a change in managerial philosophy. The same study found that 82% of companies considered employee involvement programs to be a promising new approach and not a passing fad. The sound business rationale which underlies this phenomena is evident when the outcome findings, reported by the companies who used such approaches, are reviewed. According to their own standards and measures, the companies report improvements in attitude and morale (67%), cost containment (56%), productivity (55%), quality (54%), service (53%) and quality of working life (48%).

Quality circles are at the forefront of this movement which has spread throughout business, health care and government organizations. The rate at which quality circles have spread in this country is phenomenal. Zemke (1980) has described this as the fastest growing productivity improvement strategy in existence and Cole (1983) estimated that circles were at 6,200 sites.

Although quality circles have had enormous popularity and success throughout diverse organizations, it is an approach which continues to be misunderstood and poorly applied in many cases. The quality circle movement has been experiencing the growing pains associated with its accelerated expansion and too often quality circles are not fully integrated into the organizational system or culture.

This paper examines quality circles from a new perspective. The theoretical basis for quality circles has been largely attributed to

Maslow (1954), McGregor (1960), and Herzberg (1966) in terms of motivational principles. The emphasis on statistical quality control has been associated with the work of Demming (1967), Juran (1976), and Ishikawa (1972). Dewar (1980) has been at the forefront of articulating the concept and methodology in this country. An examination of quality circles in light of Lewin's work and legacy can serve to put this approach in a broader historical and theoretical context. It will bring a focus to the essence of the quality circle approach and why it works when properly implemented. This has great practical significance because many organizations implement quality circle for poorly defined reasons and without appreciating that this should be a systematic approach to organization development.

Many practioners utilizing quality circles have a limited view of the broad body of knowledge which supports and could guide their efforts. Quality circles are successful, when properly implemented, precisely because the approach utilizes the best behavioral science principles concerning motivation, group process, systematic problem solving, and a systems approach to planned organization development.

Lewin had an enormous impact on the formulation and development of these concepts. Illustrating how the quality circle approach emanates from this tradition may provide behavioral scientists and organizational development practioners, who have been skeptical of quality circles, an enlarged perspective from which to view this methodology.

THE ESSENCE OF QUALITY CIRCLES

Definition

    According to James and Elkins (1983), the quality circle:
* Is a group of three to twelve employees who volunteer to participate
* Is trained in problem solving techniques
* Is led by the unit supervisor
* Is assisted by a facilitator
* Meets regularly on company time
* Identifies, analyzes, and solves work-related problems
* Recommends solutions to management

*   Implements the solutions

*   Evaluates the resulting impact

The basic purpose of a circle is to identify, analyze, and solve problems in the immediate work area. The focus is on problems which prevent the unit from doing a better job. Generally, efforts are geared to increasing efficiency, reducing errors, better productivity, improving quality of service or production and enhancing communication. Circles meetings are not gripe sessions nor is there discussion of personalities, personnel issues, grievances or anything outside the task responsibility or domain of circle members.

Philosophy

The basic tenets which underlie the approach come from the human relations school of management:

1.   People take pride and perform better when they have input;
2.   Participation yields better results;
3.   The most creative thing you can do is to recognize and use the creative talent of others.

Structure

The quality circle problem solving teams are formed and installed as a system which is consistent with the existing organization structure or hierarchy. The circle members represent the frontline employee level; the circle leader is generally the unit supervisor; the facilitator, who coordinates circle activities and links the circles to top management, is at the mid-management level; while the steering committee which oversees all circle operations is staffed by top management.

The important point is that the quality circle program is conceived as a total system and should be fully integrated into the organization. It is not an isolated activity run at the department level. Planning, goal setting and policy guidelines all come from top management, and to be successful the quality circle program must have strong management and union support. The facilitator or coordinator manages the overall circle activities and results are formally and systematically communicated to the appropriate management persons through the vehicle of the management presentation. Through the active participation in the management presentation and the steering committee, management involvement is built into the system.

Theoretical Basis

Maslow's Motivational Theory has been helpful in explaining how quality circles meet the belonging, esteem, and self actualization needs of circle members, while McGregor's Theory Y reflects the assumptions which underlie the managerial philosophy associated with quality circles (Dewar, 1980). Herzberg's (1966) contribution, concerning the importance of providing opportunities for achievement and recognition for workers, gets at the heart of why the approach has so much potency. Through providing workers the opportunity to identify and solve problems as an autonomous group, and to measure their impact and contribution in concrete terms, the quality circle creates an ideal setting for achievement. The recognition component is thoughtfully and ingeniously incorporated into the whole process. This occurs primarily through the management presentation where the circle ceremoniously presents its recommendations and accomplishments to management. In this way, circle achievements are linked to and recognized by the organizational hierarchy.

Demming (1967) and Juran (1976), who originally brought statistical quality control techniques to Japan, essentially follow from the tradition of Frederick Taylor (1911) by incorporating statistical methods to insure management control. They emphasized quality control as a bottom line goal and based on their teaching this became a national preoccupation and value in Japan. This laid the foundation for the development of Quality Circles by the Japanese Union of Scientists and Engineers (JUSE) under the leadership of Ishikawa (1972) who synthesized various theories and techniques into the actual Quality Circle approach as we know it.

Quality Circle Benefits

It is precisely this synthesis of human relations principles and the scientific method of research and statistical control which distinguishes Quality Circles from other approaches to team building or problem solving which may seem similar. Lewin originally pioneered the incorporation of applied research methodology to practical problem solving through the formulation of action research (French and Bell, 1978). The fact that the Quality Circle evolves from this rich tradition in the behavioral sciences, and that it is based on a total systems concept, helps to explain the impressive success of this approach.

Quality Circles are the only approach to organizational development which clearly and consistently documents its impact on productivity and bottom line business concerns as well as human relations and people building.

Why It Works

As a means of summarizing this section and presenting the framework for the remainder of the paper, four fundamental reasons why Quality Circles work, which all reflect the Lewinian heritage, are presented:

1. Quality Circles incorporate the best human relations principles of motivation;
2. Quality Circles incorporate the best of group dynamics theory and practice;
3. Quality Circles incorporate a systematic action research approach to problem solving; and
4. Quality Circles incorporate a systems perspective on planned organization development and change.

THE LEWINIAN CONTRIBUTION TO QUALITY CIRCLES

Changes in a system, when they are reality oriented, take the form of problem solving. A system...must develop and institutionalize its own problem solving structures and processes. These structures and processes must be tuned both to human problems of relationship and morale and to technical problems of meeting the systems task requirements, set by goals of production...The problem solving structures and processes of a human system must be developed to deal with a range of socio-technical difficulties, converting them into problems and organizing the relevant processes of data collection, planning, invention, and tryout of solutions, evaluation and feedback of results, replanning, and so forth, which are required for the solution of the problems.

The human parts of the system must learn to function collaboratively in their processes of problem identification and solution, and the system must develop institutionalized supports and mechanisms for maintaining and improving their processes. Actually, the model in these approaches is a cooperative, action research model. The model was suggested by Lewin...(Benne, Bennis, Chin and Corey, 1976).

This statement epitomizes the Lewinian approach and sets forth the basic premise for Quality Circles. It speaks to the four reasons why Quality Circles work, but with particular emphasis on the action research model of planned systems change, which will be the focus of the remainder of this paper.

Action Research

Central to the work of Quality Circles is a systematic problem solving sequence and process which, although not generally labeled as such, parallels action research.

Of the varieties of action research, discussed by Chein, Cook, Hardings (1948), participative action research most closely approximates the Quality Circle. Those who are to take action are involved in the entire research and data collection process from the onset.

The value of action research, as a paradigm for Quality Circle organizational problem solving, is that it focuses attention on key aspects of the process in terms of what needs to happen at each phase, rather than on specific techniques which might be employed. This over-emphasis on techniques, instead of the process of problem solving, was identified as the single biggest problem impeding a majority of circles by the research of Everett and Davis (1984).

1. Problem Selection and Definition

This phase involves generating possible problems in the immediate work area, selecting one and defining it clearly. The emphasis here is on problem definition. The step is not completed until a clear statement of the problem has been written down which everyone agrees with and understands.

2. Data Collection and Problem Analysis

This phase flows from the previous one. The secret to data collecting and problem analysis is to have a clear statement of the problem which will suggest what information is required to fully investigate it. Emphasis should be placed on collecting information which has practical rather than statistical significance. Data should be collected from several sources and vantage points to allow for a convergent analysis.

3. Solution Review and Selection

Once data has been analyzed, to verify the problem, the circle begins to consider possible remedies. The important thing here is not to
get locked into any one solution before many have been considered.
Brainstorming, cause and effect analysis, solution analysis or any other
method which will serve the purpose should be employed. Equally important is the formulation of criteria for an acceptable solution based on
the preceding analysis of the problem and its cause. Lewin's (1951)
force-field analysis can be a useful addition to the Quality Circle
practioner through its focus on the various forces which may impact the
successful implementation of a given solution.

4. Action Planning

Once a solution has been selected and tested for its likely effectiveness, a plan for implementation must be formulated. It is incumbent
upon the Quality Circle to provide in its presentation to management a
careful assessment of what will be involved in carrying out its proposed
solution. This will enable management to accurately gauge the costs and
benefits of a given solution.

5. Recommendation and Implementation

The crux of this phase, and something which distinguishes the
Quality Circle approach, is the Management Presentation. Here the circle
puts together all its work in an organized, systematic, formal presentation to the key decision makers relative to the proposal.

This provides management with the information needed to make an
intelligent decision about the proposed action. Upon approval, and with
input from management, the circle commences its implementation of the
plan. The management presentation serves to practically and symbolically
link all circle activities and accomplishments to the upper escelons of
the organization. It embodies the systems perspective of integrating
the Quality Circle into the larger organizational field. Furthermore,
it provides recognition at the management level for circle achievements.

6. Monitoring and Evaluation

Evaluation of the impact of circle efforts is essential to the problem solving process. It lends credibility to the circle efforts by
documenting, in objective concrete terms, what has been accomplished.
As Lewin advised, it is only through such assessment that the circle
knows whether it has moved in the right direction and whether the problem
has been ameliorated. The studies which had been conducted at the problem analysis stage can be continued and replicated after the solution
has been implemented for before and after outcome comprovisions. The fact

that circle members conduct the research study themselves, has invaluable benefits on the esprit de corps of the Quality Circle.

7.   Problem and Solution Reformulation

In action research, action is always supported by and interwoven with data collection and analysis. This results in an on-going process where there is a continual upgrading of the quality of problem resolution. Reformation of the problem and its solution is the hub around which action research problem solving revolves. It is the seventh but also the central step in the entire process. This also epitomizes the cyclical nature of problem solving. For a Quality Circle group the cycle moves from problem definition to solution to evaluation in the course of one problem solving sequence, and the circle initiates the process again as it continues around to its next problem.

A SYSTEMS APPROACH TO PLANNED CHANGE

Quality Circles embody a systems perspective which reflects the Lewinian tradition in two major ways:

1.   The importance of the entire organizational system or field.
2.   The importance of a planned change approach to organizational development.

The importance of incorporating the entire organizational field is manifested in the Quality Circle structure which is set up to parallel the existing organizational heirarchy. All elements of the organizational field are included if the Quality Circle program is properly installed. The steering committee is composed of key segments of the management horizontal plane as well as other relevant participants such as union representatives. The Quality Circle coordinator or facilitator serves as the linking pin between vertical levels of the Quality Circle system. The circles within a given system are each involved in distinct problems in their separate locations. They are led by circle leaders, usually the unit supervisor. The facilitator coordinates, connects, and serves as a liaison between the circles laterally and between the circles and other levels within the organizational vertical hierarchy. The facilitator helps guide the steering committee which is responsible for overseeing the entire Quality Circle operation. The steering committee develops a Quality Circle policy, formulates an implementation plan, sets goals, determines areas for pilot circles, evaluates the program, and supervises its expansion or modification as indicated. Communication of Quality Circle efforts throughout the organization through a newsletter or other formats is important to indicate that circle activities are fully integrated into organizational life.

When implemented as a planned change approach to organization development, Quality Circles embody a systems perspective. Action research, which has been proposed as a framework for problem solving on the small group level for Quality Circles, is also the appropriate model for introducing the Quality Circle program within an organizational system (Quill, 1984). Careful statement of the problem or reason behind introducing a Quality Circle program; data collection to assess need, readiness, and appropriateness; action planning; setting up a pilot program; evaluation of impact; and on-going refinement are essential when initiating a Quality Circle system. In other words, action must be supported by data, careful planning must precede action, and all action should be evaluated through follow-up data collection.

This indispensible model of planned change is based on Lewin's observation that all systems must go through a basic change process of unfreezing, moving and refreezing (Schein, 1970). Those installing Quality Circle programs should do so with a careful appreciation of the forces which may come into play and with a plan to counteract the inevitable resistance they will face.

It is essential to anticipate the impact on the total system especially as more practioners are espousing the goal of restructuring the organization and changing its culture through Quality Circles.

Metz (1981) has focused on the need for management to appreciate the implications of Quality Circles on the culture and management philosophy of an organization. He stresses that organizational readiness must be assessed and a determination must be made about whether circles are appropriate and where they should be considered.

This concern with diagnosing readiness rarely receives adequate attention by those using Quality Circles. From the Lewinian perspective this is basic to any carefully considered approach to change. It should be considered as one element in the overall plan which an organization develops for Quality Circles. If the principles of action research are applied to implementation on a systems level, Quality Circles have the greatest likelihood of success. This means forming an action research group or steering committee to guide the effort. This group would assume the typical functions such as selecting a facilitator, developing a policy and selecting areas for implementation on a pilot basis. However, it would go further by applying the action research model as previously elucidated. Emphasis would be placed on problem definition, diagnostic data collection, careful action planning, pilot implementation, evaluation and further refinement based on on-going data collection. It is important to emphasize that Quality Circles should be started initially on a pilot basis. Only after successful evaluation of a small pilot program should it be expanded and fully implemented within the system.

LEADING EDGE

It has been interesting to observe the growth of Quality Circles in this country. Quality Circles initially had something of a provincial quality. For many whose backgrounds were in production or engineering, this was a first exposure to the human relations approach to management. Nonetheless, the movement has mushroomed and successfully incorporated and extended the best principles of human relations, group dynamics, problem solving and planned change. Quality Circles have been enormously successful for this reason.

As the Quality Circle movement continues to evolve, the "leading edge" seems to be moving further toward incorporating a total systems perspective to planned organizational development. There is a focus on going beyond Quality Circles (Berry and Spurlock, 1984); and making circles an integral part of the management process (Donovan, 1984).

While it is imperative that practioners look beyond, it might be equally instructive to look behind Quality Circles at the foundation and heritage upon which this approach rests. The concepts and strategies for planned organization change, problem solving, and action research, which are a part of the legacy of Kurt Lewin, represent a gold mine for the Quality Circle practioner. Through examining some of the specific Lewinian contributions, this paper has suggested an important source for the continued evolution, expansion and refinement of the Quality Circle concept.

REFERENCES

Benne, K.D. (1978). The process of re-education: An assessment of Kurt Lewin's views. In W.G. Bennis, K.D. Benne, R. Chin, and K.E. Corey (Eds.), The Planning of Change. New York: Holt, Rinehart and Winston.

Berry, P.A. and Spurlock, G.P. (1984). Beyond Quality Circles: Proctor and Gamble and people involvement, International Association of Quality Circles Annual Conference Transactions.

Chein, I., Cook, S. and Hardy, J. (1948). The field of action research. American Psychologist. February.

Cole, R.E. (1983). A Japanese management import comes full circle. Wall Street Journal. February 22.

Demming, W.E. (August, 1967). What happened in Japan? Industrial Quality Control.

Dewar, D.L. (1980). The Quality Circle Guide to Participation Management. Englewood Cliffs, New Jersey: Prentice Hall.

Donovan, J.M. (1984). Making Quality Circles an integral part of the management process. International Association of Quality Circle Annual Conference Transactions.

Everett, M. and Davis, W. (1984). Integrative improvement process - An advanced problem solving method. International Association of Quality Circles Annual Conference Transactions.

French, W.L. and Bell, C.H. (1978). Organizational Development. Englewood Cliffs, N.J.: Prentice Hall.

Herzburg, F. (1966). Work and the Nature of Man. New York: World Publishing.

Ishikawa, K. (1972). Japan Quality Control Circles. JUSE. Tokyo.

James, R.G. and Elkins, A.J. (1983). How to Train and Lead a Quality Circle. La Jolla: University Associates.

Juran, J.M. (1976). The Q C Circle Phenomena. Industrial Quality Control, 23.

Lewin, K. (1951). Field Theory and the Social Sciences. New York: Harper & Row.

Lewin, K. (1946). Action research and minority problems. Journal of Social Issues, 2 No. 4.

Marrow, A.J. The Practical Theorist: The Life and Work of Kurt Lewin.

Maslow, A.H. (1954). Motivation and Personality. New York: Harper and Row.

McGregor, D. (1960). The Human Side of Enterprise. New York: McGraw Hill.

Metz, E.J. (1981). Diagnosing readiness. The Quality Circle Journal. November.

Mroczkowski, T. (1984). Sustaining and evolving a Q C program - A developmental perspective. International Association of Quality Circles Annual Conference Transactions.

New York Stock Exchange Office of Economic Research (1982). People and productivity: A challenge to corporate America.

Quill, J.H. and Ridgy, J.M. (1984). A cross-cultural approach to the design of Quality Circle systems. International Association of Quality Circles Annual Conference Transactions.

Schein, E. (1970). Professional Education. New York: McGraw Hill.

Taylor, F.W. (1911). The Principles of Scientific Management. New York: Harper & Brothers.

Zemke, R. (1980). Quality Circles - Can they work in the United States, Journal of Applied Management, Sept./Oct.

Using Graduate Students as Consultants to Teach Action Research to Residence Hall Staff

Jean H. Woods and Irene G. Casper

Temple University

Introduction

Residence hall life can be impersonal and devoid of a community atmosphere particularly in a large university. Students living in the residence halls have little in common except their pursuit of education. Concerted efforts need to be made to enhance the residential living situation so that it becomes a significant part of the students learning environment outside of the classroom.

In considering the best approach to meeting this goal, members of the Residential Life Office at Temple University in cooperation with faculty and students in the College of Education, Department of Psycho-educational Processes, implemented a program intended to enhance the quality of life in the residence halls.

The theoretical basis of the program was the theoretical framework of action research developed by Kurt Lewin. Since a conference honoring Dr. Lewin's contributions to social psychology was planned for the spring 1984, it was felt that this would be an appropriate time to investigate the efficacy of the action research model for enhancing the residence hall environment.

The goals of the project were to:

1. Involve resident or hall students in actively creating a positive living environment, and
2. Train underscore{undergraduate} and underscore{graduate} students in a method of planned intervention and action research skills.

Theoretical Rationale

Kurt Lewin was foremost a theorist who advocated practical applications of empirical research results. He suggested that action based research was a "tool for social improvement" (Benne, et al, 1975, p. 4). Lewin believed that social psychology, through the use of relevant theory and research applied to social practice, could provide information and understanding of societal problems.

He believed that knowledge is advanced and problems are solved through close cooperation between the researcher and the practitioner (Johnson & Johnson, 1982, p. 14). "Practitioners keep theorists in contact with social reality and theorists provide practitioners with a deeper understanding of the social problems that confront them" (Johnson & Johnson, p. 15).

According to Sanford, the theme of Lewin's advocacy for action research is "in order to gain insight into a process one must create a change and then observe its variable effects and new dynamics" (Reason & Rowan, 1981, p. 173). The notion of action research supports the premise that social change can occur through planned action and subsequent study of its results (Evered, 1977, p. 10). Action research within the organizational structure is applied research which integrates together scientific methodology with the consultative process.

Action research necessitates the active involvement of the client and assumes client competency, meaning that the client has the ability to assess and change the situation (Margulies & Raia, 1968, p. 2). The client examines his own system and identifies the problems, then formulates plans for solving those problems. The steps of action research involve the clients in problem identification, solution and evaluation. The action research process is as applicable in organizational change as it is in change planned for groups or individuals. Its findings lead to improvements in the operations of systems studied (Casper, 1984) by creating data that can be incorporated and which results in social change.

Thus, considering these theoretical underpinnings of applied research, the action research project in the residence halls at Temple University had two major foci:

1. A learning project through which graduate students would serve as consultants, teaching undergraduate students (in this case resident assistants) action research skills for application to improve the quality of life on their floors.

2. A research component: A process of data collection, the purpose of which was to study the effects of action research on the environment of the living areas, specifically looking for changes in attitudes, amount of damage reported and changes in resident assistant evaluations ratings by residents.

The Research Question

The overall research question was whether or not undergraduate student resident assistants could be taught action research principles so that they would implement them to change the quality of residential living. Specifically the research questions were:

a. Are attitudes more positive about resident hall living?

b. Is there an improvement in programs planned for residence hall students, including educational programs?

c. Is there less damage to the living areas reported?

In order to evaluate the effectiveness of the project, this research was implemented comparing "experimental" residence hall floors (resident assistants had a consultant) with "control" floors (resident assistants did not have a consultant) (Casper, 1984).

There were two project staff teams. The team concerned with the action research aspect of the project consisted of four graduate students who served as consultants to six undergraduate resident assistants and the steering committee of the Tri-Dorm Senate. The other team consisted of the staff of the residential life department. They collected and analyzed the research data using the University Resident Environmental Scale (URES), damage reports, resident assistant evaluations, and program reports to determine the effectiveness of the project.

The graduate student's consultant role had two major functions: (1) to use an action research process model as a process consultant, and (2) to teach the resident assistants how to use an action research approach: (a) to enhance a sense of community on their floor or (b) in their work with the student senate. The consultants met regularly with these students (Casper, 1984).

During the year resident assistants and the senate implemented various activities which reflected the use of action research processes.

The Consultant Model in Action

The Consultant Role

The action research model which consultants encouraged resident assistants (RAs) to use involved the following steps:

1. Problem identification (identifying the gaps between what is and what ought to be, supported by data)

2.   Needs assessment/Data collection

3.   Action (planning and carrying out steps that will improve
     things)

4.   Evaluation (feedback of the data/how did it work, what is
     needed next)

5.   Redefinition of the situation, problem.

After an initial orientation meeting with the project team, the
consultants' task was to establish a relationship with the RA consultee.
The issues involved in establishing that relationship were similar to
those experienced by any consultant entering an unknown system: assessment of the system, definition of the boundaries, assessment of problem
areas and the consultees' energy and committment to solving the problems.
The difference was that instead of the consultant formulating the plans
for intervention, the RA was encouraged to use an action research model
by assuming responsibility for assessing the needs of their floor and
exploring relevant solutions.

The issues which concerned the consultants initially and throughout
the project was role definition. How the role was translated by the
consultant, influenced how the RA utilized the action research concepts
on their floors. There was a hesitancy on the part of the consultants
to use the terms "research" or "data" with the RAs. Since the RAs had
had experience with many research projects throughout their academic
careers, the consultants were fearful that use of the terms would foster
resistance to the process.

The consultants were themselves learning the action research process
and the consultant role at the same time that they were trying to teach
it to the RAs. It was often confusing. However, gradually, the consultants internalized the process and patterns of change became more
evident.

The Resident Assistants' Role

The RAs were anxious to participate in this project and had formulated goals for their floors which seemed consistent with the overall
goal of the project.

Some of the RAs had prior experience in the residence hall system
and were aware of the responsibilities involved. They were anxious to
improve some of the problems which they had previously encountered.
The primary goal as they defined it was to develop a cohesive community
where residents could feel free to socialize, study and solve problems.

A sub-issue was to encourage the residents to take some responsibility for the kind of programs offered on the floors and to develop a system for enforcing floor rules through peer pressure. Another issue for them which proved to be very important throughout the project was their relationship with the Residential Life Administration and a need to try to find a way to change it.

For those RAs who were new to the system, the issues were more concerned with role definition. Their overall goal was to become socialized into the role without appearing to be the "heavy", the authority figure.

The Process

Each consultant was involved with either two resident assistants or the Tri-Dorm Senate. Consultants met biweekly throughout the year with other project team members to review the process and biweekly with the RAs. One concept continually stressed was helping the RA client conduct a needs assessment. The RAs were never clear about the needs assessment as a formal step or expectation. However, for some of them, the assessment of the needs appeared to be almost an automatic process or way of thinking for them.

Usually the discussions with the consultant and RAs began with discussion of their problems with the system before they moved to the issues of the residents. The meetings helped RAs gather new information about their fellow residents. Consequently, RAs began to include issues of concern to the residents in their program plans for the floor. One RA circulated a questionnaire to gather information about the residents which would be helpful to them.

It must be noted that the steps of the action research as previously outlined (see section entitled The Consultant Role), were not formally distinguishable, however in retrospect, one can observe elements of data collection, needs assessment, planning for change and evaluation of the effects as an integral part of what happened during this year. The activities in which the RAs involved themselves and their residents were: Movie nights, CPR training, rock climbing; visits to Chinatown, museums, and other historical sites, as well as combining efforts with "control" floors resident assistants to plan more extensive programs.

The Formal Research Process and Results

The data for the research was obtained by administering the University Resident Environmental Scale (URES) to members of the entire resident hall community. The URES is a general survey of living conditions which tests the social climate of the floors. The scale was administered twice during the project year, once during the fall semester and once during the spring semester. In addition, supervisory evaluations which evaluated the skill level, discipline, and ability of the resident assistant within the community were analyzed. Finally, the amount of damage on experimental floors was compared to the damage assessment on control floors.

The results of the initial findings for the fall semester, were fed back to the residents and the resident assistants at the beginning of the spring semester. Interviews were also conducted with the consultants, senate executive committee members and resident hall staff.

Data Analysis

A multiple analysis of variance was performed on the data obtained from the URES and revealed no significant difference for any of the ten items measures. The items assessed were: involvement, emotional support, independence, traditional social orientation, competition, academic achievement, intellectuality, order and organization, student influence and innovation.

The supervisory evaluations were scaled for the items included on a Likert-type scale of one to five to determine if there were differences in the performance of the resident assistants on the experimental floors as compared to the performance of those on the non-experimental floors. Preliminary analysis suggests again that there is no significant difference in performance. (However, there is evidence of approaching significance.)

There was a lower amount of damage reported for those floors with consultants, than those floors without.

Further Results

Retrospective analyses of the process of action research with the RAs reveals some positive changes occuring on the experimental floors. RAs became more secure during the year, and while initially they were concerned with problems being presented to them, later in the year they would report what measures they took to solve the problems. They began to feel a sense of their own power in being able to take charge. Additionally, the RAs began to realize that the problems they perceived with the administration were part of the job and that they could conserve energy by not resisting the process. RAs became more astute in identifying issues, they were able to allow residents to become involved with planning and assuming responsibility for following rules. The residents assistants seemed to be particularly pleased with the atmosphere generated on their floors and were anxious to expand these feelings to other non-experimental floors. They included some of the RAs from "control" floors in their program plans. Residents also seemed pleased with the atmosphere on the floors. On one floor a resident prepared a bulletin board which summarized the involvement of the students during the entire year.

Summary

There appears to have been some positive results from the project as far as the individual resident assistants were concerned in their attitude and approach to their jobs. Each RA developed a close relationship with their consultant and one must question whether the charisma attached to that relationship alone initiated the changes, or whether the RAs indeed learned the action research process. One would need to observe these RAs in other situations where the action research process is appropriate and observe whether they can apply the principles without a consultant.

There are some unanswered questions. For example can the effectiveness of action research be evaluated empirically during the process of the action. It may be premature to expect to measure change while that change is occuring. Perhaps, action researchers should record data that is necessary for more formal analysis.

Other problems encountered during this process for the consultants was their very limited knowledge of the action research process prior to the beginning of the project. It is suggested that with this model, the consultant should have a thorough understanding of the process and their role in the process. The process can then be implemented more smoothly.

One part of the action research process not fully utilized was the feedback loop. Generally, resident assistants resisted feeding back data which they had generated to their client system--students living on the floors. They felt that such information was not wanted or might "stir things up." Rather they used the data in formulating plans and activities for their floor.

Feedback of data from the traditional research process was limited to mid semester feedback. Resident assistants on each floor were given data about the URES; however, at the time of the completion of the action part of the project (the consultants meeting with resident assistants), the data was incomplete and neither the RA or consultant received feedback from this data due to the ending of the project and academic year.

REFERENCES

Benne, K.O., Bradford, L.P., Gibb, J.R., Lippitt, R.O. (1975). The laboratory method of changing and learning. Palo Alto: Science and Behavioral Books, Inc.

Casper, I.G. (1984). "Teaching resident assistants action research." Project summary.

Evered, R. (1977). "An exploration of Kurt Lewin's contribution to social sciences." Unpublished paper prepared for the Kurt Lewin Memorial Conference and Workshop. Bethel, Maine, July 1-4.

Johnson, D.W. & Johnson, F.P. (1982). Joining together: Group theory and group skills. Englewood Cliffs: Prentice Hall, Inc.

Margulies, N. & Raia, A.P. (1968). "Action research and the consultation process." C53 Con SKII 7/11/68.

Sanford, N. (1981). "A model for action research." In Reason, P., and Rowan, J. (Eds.), Human inquiry: A sourcebook of new paradigm research. Chichester: John Wiley and Sons, pp. 173-181.

Teaching Force Field Analysis: A Suggested Training Design

Mel Silberman

Temple University

In my experience, force field analysis is often misunderstood. And when it is understood and even highly praised, it is seldom actually used by groups or individuals on any sustained basis.

What a pity this "current state of affairs"! Indeed, it lends itself to its own force field analysis. What are the forces which block understanding and/or utilization of force field analysis?

As I diagnose the problem, I find that people often confuse force field analysis with the old decision making process of listing pros and cons of a given course of action as a way to decide whether to undertake it. Moreover, they are confused by some of the terminology in force field analysis as well as its diagrams of restraining and helpful forces. To make matters worse, many perceive, from the training they receive, that force field analysis is a tedious process and so few want to do it more than once. Finally, the highly rational quality of force field analysis often discourages individuals and groups that have problems for irrational reasons.

Despite these obstacles, I believe that force field analysis is a valuable problem solving tool that deserves to be taught well and encouraged. With this thought in mind, I'd like to suggest a training design for teaching force field analysis that I have found successful (although I can't make any claims as to real changes in the future behavior of participants).

I.   Introduction

Participants are invited to write down a personal and/or work related problem they are currently experiencing. They are told that a suitable problem is one in which they have been pursuing or thinking about pursuing a goal (e.g. stopping smoking; obtaining more business) but have thus far not attained.

Next, they are introduced to the term "force field analysis" and told that it is a tool for obtaining unattained goals such as those they have just listed. By contrast, it is not a tool to make a decision (e.g. should I quit my job?)

A request is then made for a few participants to share with the group one of the problems they have selected. The trainer either verifies that the problem chosen will "work well" with force field analysis or helps to modify the problem statement so that it does.

II. Lecturette

The trainer discusses with the groups some common patterns people use when they have trouble obtaining desired goals. One way these patterns can be described is to utilize the following list:

Procrastination--not dealing with the problem and perhaps even denying it.

Fretting--continually stewing about the problem but taking no clear directions with it.

Brainstorming--generating many solutions to the problem but not commiting oneself to implementing any of them.

Repeating--utilizing basically the same solution over and over again even though it fails to produce change.

III. Dyadic Discussion

Participants are invited to pair off and share with each other those patterns which they use most frequently. It is suggested that the participants especially consider the patterns used with the problems each has identified in I (above).

IV. Lecturette

The trainer emphasizes that force field analysis is an effective way to counteract procrastination, fretting, excessive brainstorming or repeating. It is a useful tool because it provides a focused framework for solving problems and builds in social support for implementation.

The trainer proceeds to identify three basic principles in force field analysis: 1) getting clear what is happening now with the problem; 2) identifying some of the obstacles which prevent goal attainment; and 3) selecting a concrete place to begin solving the problem.

V. Demonstration

Participants are given form A (follows). This form streamlines the
process of forced field analysis by eliminating the identification of
helping forces. It also uses simple language.

Next, the participants listen to a pre-recorded case demonstration
in which an interviewer asks probing questions to help a "client" identify responses to each of the five steps on the form. Form B shows the
results of an interview with a client who distributes watches.

VI. Dyadic Activity

Participants are asked to pair off with their partner from III.
Each is instructed to interview the other as per the case demonstration.
The problem selected for each interview is one previously identified by
the participant.

VII. Ending

Participants are invited to share their reactions to and questions
about the previous activity. The trainer may discover that some participants were plagued by a problem which was not sufficiently concrete.
Some resistance to the limits placed by the process (e.g.--selecting only
one obstacle) may be anticipated and deflected with assurances that problem resolution begins with specific first steps which are actually implemented. The trainer should also encourage participants to announce pub-
licly those action steps they intend to undertake and suggest that one's
partner be used as support during the process.

FORM A

I.   The Situation As It Is Now: _____

_____

II. The Situation As I Want It To Be: _____

_____

III. What will keep the situation from changing?

_____   _____

_____   _____

_____   _____

_____   _____

_____   _____

IV. Your top priority obstacle: _____

_____

V.   Possible Action Steps: Resources Needed:

_____   _____

_____   _____

_____   _____

_____   _____

_____   _____

_____   _____

_____   _____

_____   _____

FORM B

I.   The Situation As It Is Now: Over 25% of our accounts complained that they did not receive their Xmas order in sufficient time.

II.   The Situation As I Want It To Be: In the future, our accounts should receive their Xmas order by November 10th.

III.   What will keep the situation from changing?

Delivery delays	My own disorganization
Our drivers don't want to work overtime	
Orders from our accounts are late	

IV.   Your top priority obstacle: Orders from accounts are late.

V.   Possible Action Steps:

Possible Action Steps:	Resources Needed:
Survey accounts re: their obstacles	Ask Ass't. to develop survey
Establish discount for early orders	Get fiscal projections
Establish discount for order date	Meet with shipping
Involve more people in taking orders	Meet with secretaries

Utilizing Lewinian Principles for an Institutional Planning Process Within a Medical School

Jay M. Yanoff and William E. Bryan

University of Medicine and Dentistry of New Jersey

Perspective On Change

The health field is undergoing dramatic changes in the 1980's. A variety of forces are operating to influence new directions for the delivery of health care. The changing structure of health care financing is altering the needs of the hospitals and the relationship of physicians to their hospitals. Physician behavior is key to this changing environment as they hold positions of control in the delivery system. Thus, the education of physicians and how they are taught to practice is a key component in reshaping the delivery of health care toward quality care that is cost effective.

The reshaping of a medical education program to meet the emerging needs of health care requires a conceptual framework that is comprehensive in design and dynamic in process. The description of the change that is underway, was described in the first paragraph of this paper with such underlined words as field, forces, new directions, structure, needs, relationships, behavior and environment. These words are the concepts and processes of Kurt Lewin that he used to understand human behavior and has become known as field theory.

Lewin developed a constructive method to view human behavior according to its relationships. This method used the concepts of life space, field forces and tension systems to present a wholistic and dynamic view of human behavior. A person or a group of persons operate in a life space that includes everything that exists for them at that moment. The life space is structured into regions or spheres that have varying power (valence) to influence behavior at a given moment. We behave in this life space and change its structure through the forces that are operating. These forces are viewed as vectors with direction, magnitude and point of origin, with resultant changes in behavior. Lewin describes five types of forces. There are driving forces which push toward or away from current behavior and lead to movement. There are restraining forces that are actually obstacles for barriers to movement. Induced

forces represent the wishes of others in our life space. The impersonal
forces represent social norms. Finally, there are personal forces which
represent one's own needs. These opposing forces set up tension systems
within the life space and function to cause action to reduce tension and
to achieve equilibrium. Thus, change can be produced by increasing the
tension in some region and forcing movement with greater tension or by
decreasing the tension in some region and achieving equilibrium by tension reduction. The former leads to dissatisfaction whereas the latter
approach achieves some satisfaction with the change.

The authors used this field theory of Kurt Lewin to construct a
planning model which provided the structure to begin to reshape a medical school program and at the same time would better meet the emerging
needs of the health care industry.

A Planning Model

The Planning Model was organized into two distinct phases using
the concepts of Lewin. Stage I was the conceptual stage and emphasized
an analysis of the health field in general and developed the "whole" to
present the context for the "part" which is the medical education component of the health field. The analysis of the whole identified five
general need areas in the health field.

We proceeded from this analysis of the whole to place the part in
context. A mission statement of the medical school was reviewed in terms
of the analysis of the field and was changed slightly. A comprehensive
review of the commitments of the school was then conducted to place the
medical school in the context of the health field. Ten commitments were
identified and agreed upon by the faculty that would become the general
goals and objectives for the school as it tried to reshape itself in a
changing environment.

Thus, Stage I of the planning process focused on the conceptual
whole that is an underlying concept of Lewin's Theory. We then proceeded
to Stage II which is the Action Planning Stage to analyze the field that
is operating and to induce positive change in the medical school programs.

Forces Operating In A Medical School Environment

Medical schools are complex institutions and have tended to be resistant to change. They look to tradition and the past as justification for their future. Consistent with Lewinian field theory, there are driving and restraining forces operating in the health field that are pushing for and resisting significant change.

Major driving forces have combined to establish the need for significant change in the planning, organization, financing, and curriculum of medical schools:

(1) The need for cost containment in medical care is a major political and economic issue that is forcing change. Over 10% of the Gross National Product (GNP) of the United States ($322.4 billion) is presently spent on health care. The cost of health care has increased so greatly in this country that it is now one of our greatest social and economic problems.

(2) Manpower studies are predicting both an oversupply of specialty physicians and a maldistribution by geographic area. Such data have direct implications for medical school enrollments and medical practice areas. Even with a projected oversupply, some areas of the country and some groups of people remain unserved or underserved. The need to plan for these changes is obvious.

(3) The new prospective payment system known as DRG's (Diagnosis Related Groups) has changed the way medical costs are reimbursed. The DRG system has changed the system from a cost basis to set payment for a specific diagnosis. Such changes mean that different physician behaviors are needed. The medical school needs to educate a different professional for an emerging era.

(4) Competition among physicians for patients is increasing. The Wall Street Journal notes, "More doctors are finding that they must become savvy businessmen if they want to get more patients--or keep the ones they have." The impact of this new competition places new pressures on practitioners, students, medical schools, hospitals, etc.

(5) Medical schools must become more attentive to institutional planning in a time of shrinking resources.

(6) Medical educators are questioning the content of what medical schools teach. The Council on Medical Education of the American Medical Association reported in its document, Future Di-

rections for Medical Education (June 15, 1982), thirty-five
(35) broad recommendations for changes in medical education
in the United States. This effort is very much needed since
the last major effort for change in medical education occurred
as a result of the Flexner Report in 1910, over seventy years
ago. Medical schools will need new institutional planning
skills to carry out the challenge to change.

These are but six of the driving forces operating that indicate
the need for change. There are major questions as to whether medical
schools will change in response to these needs. Many institutions have
become more entrenched, have used justification methods to continue doing
the same behaviors, have developed counter-arguments, and have ignored
the need to change. These behaviors will not suffice if medical schools
are going to realistically prepare medical students to face the problems
of the year 2,000.

The restraining forces that are operating as barriers to change are
many. Some are typical to any change, while others are specific to the
medical field.

(1) Institutions tend to perpetuate themselves. There is a fear
     of the new and unknown, and there are inherent risks in any
     change.

(2) There is a bit of selfish resistance by an ever present "old
     guard." Many physicians, administrators, etc. have made their
     careers and fortunes based upon the old rules of the game. New
     rules to an old game (driving forces) are forcing reactions.

(3) There is a criticism of the new, external forces (especially
     government) which have begun to place new pressures on former-
     ly independent communities. Medical schools, hospitals, physi-
     cians, etc. were not used to being examined with scrutiny and
     made to be accountable as they are today.

(4) There are many "old buddy systems" in existence. Referral
     patterns, allegiances, networks, etc. have been established.
     The driving forces are putting pressures on such systems.

(5) Another common resistance is the demand that others change
     while keeping ourselves the same. Questions like "Who will
     cut back costs?", "Which medical schools are willing to reduce
     enrollment?", "Who will develop curricula for physicians in
     the year 2000?" are referred to others.

(6) Because the forces are so great and are generally seen as ex-
     ternal to the institution, it is difficult to develop owner-
     ship. There is a blaming of others for present day problems.

(7) Change is always difficult. In the medical community it is
     even more so. Physicians have been trained to be problem
     solvers with answers. They are not trained in the elongated
     processes of change, and they tend to be impatient with the
     energy, work, and evaluation that are needed for planning, con-
     flict management, management by objectives, etc.

As noted, all change is difficult and complex. We found that Kurt
Lewin's Force Field Analysis provided a conceptual framework for problem-
solving and for implementing planned change. Lewin demonstrated that
resistance increases if change is pushed or mandated. However, if resistance is reduced and diminished, change and growth are possible.
Medical schools are complex organizations. As noted, they need to change.
However, because there are so many self interests, careers, academic and
research positions, and economic issues involved, medical schools are
very resistant to change.

The Planning Process

     The authors planned, developed and implemented a successful institu-
tional planning process that is causing productive change within the
UMDNJ-School of Osteopathic Medicine. This model is responsive to the
issues raised above and to reducing the resistances for change within a
school. The primary strategy of the planning process is to decrease
tension and to use positive and willing forces to initiate planning to
cause needed change in a medical school. The planning process has the
following objectives:
     1. To initiate institutional planning to produce positive and
         significant change in a short time.
     2. To begin the planning process from the middle of the organiza-
         tion with the Department Chairperson to maximize participation
         and then to extend it to the entire organization.
     3. To identify individual and common concerns by groups of Chair-
         persons, Deans, etc. in 15 areas of activity.
     4. To validate individual and group input to determine needs and
         recommendations as a basis for a school plan.
     5. To develop, write, implement and evaluate an annual school plan
         to effect positive change in a medical school through a dyna-
         mic process.
These objectives are implemented through a process with several
distinctive characteristics:

(1) Medical schools have rarely participated in a constructive, institutional planning process designed for real change; it is often a perfunctory process to justify a status quo. Our model was developed as a constructive process that would lead to significant and positive change.

(2) If a medical school attempts an institutional planning process, it is usually facilitated by outside consultants who can be used as scapegoats to keep things as they are rather than organizing an internal process within the institution which grapples with real problems. This process was facilitated internally, defined the roles of the internal consultants, and dealt with the institution's real problems.

(3) Institutional planning is sometimes designed to be a long process with outcomes being extensive reports which leave confusion, committees that are dysfunctional, etc. All of these outcomes are additional blocks, hurdles or delays to the realistic changes needed in the organization. Our process was designed to reduce resistances to change, to produce immediate action, and to have impact upon the organization.

(4) If the institutional planning is completed, rarely is there monitoring of resultant changes. This process included an internal evaluation and monitoring system to assess the relative changes as a result of the process. These data were then used to reduce resisting forces for development of in-service training, skills development, outside consultant help, etc.

(5) In most institutions, the change process is begun at the top or the bottom of the organization and is rarely successful. Our process used change from the middle of the organization with Departmental Chairpersons which provided a new, dynamic model and then extended the process to the Dean's level and within departments.

The following outline describes the model for institutional planning with the expected outcomes. The model outline uses the Department Chairpersons as an example as the same outline was used with all groups.

Discussion

Kurt Lewin's Force Field Analysis views behavior (or attitudes) at a given moment not as a static "thing," but as the resultant of a number

STEP	PROCESSES	OUTCOMES
1. Needs Assessments/ Concerns	Structured interview by Bryan and Yanoff with each department chair	List of strengths and issues common to all departments and specific to individual departments.
2. Present document of common findings/ individual issues	Bryan/Yanoff, etc. compile information and draft document	Document of group findings.
3. Plan strategy with each Chair for individual issues.	For individual issues, determine appropriate strategy to resolve problems; i.e., training, outside/inside consultants, workshops.	Chairperson controls change process/problem solving through the department with outside assistance.
4. Plan strategy with all Chairs for common issues.	Chairs all work together to resolve common issues; Bryan/ Yanoff, etc. assist with skills training, outside/inside expert, consultants, workshops.	Resolution of common problems.
5. Training	Programs set up for Chairs, faculty, etc. through faculty development program; issues to be addressed would be determined from above.	Training related to departmental needs.
6. Evaluation	Assessment of degree to which problems identified are resolved, training improving skills of individuals.	Assess process of institutional planning with Department Chairpersons.

of opposing or conflicting forces. The dynamic equilibrium is thrown
out of balance if there is a change in the kind or strength of forces
operating in any given direction. It is obvious that the medical community is being thrown into a major imbalance by many, significant, new
driving forces. Lewin contends that when such an imbalance is created,
movement or change tends to occur until the forces are re-equilibrated.
Physicians, hospitals, medical schools, government, insurance companies,
etc. are all in the process of re-equilibrating. The authors entered
a medical school while such a process is occurring. There are two change
strategies that are possible if one uses Lewin's Force Field Analysis:

> (a) Increase either the number or intensity of the driving/pushing
> forces.

> (b) Remove or decrease the intensity of the restraining forces.

While medical institutions have been aggressive in the past, it would
appear that Strategy A would be more amenable to their control and therefore more tempting. Its drawbacks are enormous since they tend to increase tension, instability and brittleness in the institution. The
long range goals are better met by removing the restraining forces.
Likewise, when the driving forces are external to the institution, movement toward consensual validation will occur when there is a reduction
of "flight behavior" and an increase in "problem-solving and decision-
making."

We were able to focus upon the reduction of the restraining forces
in the following ways:

> (1) All individuals were presented with and agreed to the planning
> process.

> (2) All forces were identified through individual interviews.

> (3) Data were returned to individuals for validation.

> (4) Agreements were made by the group of what it wanted to do with
> the data.

> (5) Action oriented task forces were formed to solve specific,
> mutually agreed upon problems.

> (6) Staff supported the participants in order for them to "own the
> process."

> (7) Chairpersons used the same process in which they participated
> to do planning in their own departments.

As noted previously, institutional change is difficult particularly
in medical schools. Using Lewinian principles as a conceptual base, we
were able to plan, develop and implement an institutional planning process within a medical school. Such a model is applicable to other such
institutions.

Organizational Processes in a University Department: A Report of an Action Research and Organizational Development Project

Edmund Amidon and Tim Doris

Temple University

Introduction

This report describes the study of a department in an urban university, during their annual faculty Retreat.

First, however, we would like to make a statement regarding the use of interventions in organizations. Social scientists believe that interventions, for their own sake, serve little if any good for the development of a group. Such interventions succeed only to have an immediate, not long lasting effect. Interventions that are based on data that is gathered from the group will have a more far reaching effect for the group's development. Data that are collected from the organization is the basis for deciding the following questions:

1) What changes are appropriate for the organizations to make?
2) Are the goals of the interventions aligned with the desired change?
3) How will such interventions be evaluated?
4) How can interventions with organizations be integrated into the normal processes of the group?

"Action Research" is a process that focuses on the collection of data that indicate and assess group members' views of their reality and provide an image of the group's collective reality. Action research is also a method of focusing the group so that its members can use the information it generates for the achievement of its own goals. What results, then, is a process that comes from within the group to affect its own behavior.

Operating under the belief that the more data collected, the clearer the perception of the group's reality, it was the role of the "moderators" to begin with an assessment of the group. For the purposes of this report the process shall be termed a needs assessment.

Needs Assessment

A needs assessment contains both a formal documentation of responses and an examination of what appears to be common threads among responses.

The first step in the data collection was to listen to the Chairperson and Dean describe the problems and issues facing the Department, as they saw them. This description occurred in the first meeting. What was highlighted in this conversation was the ongoing accredition process, the decision-making process, curriculum, promotion, and departmental conflict.

The Department had made a decision to create its own intervention, but fearing conflict, felt the need for a consultant function. The next step of the needs assessment was to begin meeting with the various parties concerned with the Department. Those meetings were in the form of formal interviews that the consultants conducted. The groups that were interviewed included full time faculty, adjunct faculty, students, support staff, the alumni, the Dean of the college, and a sampling of professional architects in the community. The interview process was conducted by the use of a form developed for the Department. Specific results of the interviews are summarized by issues.

PERCEPTIONS OF THE DEPARTMENT

The reactions to the question "What do you think that fellow professionals think about the department" can be viewed as one indication of how the respondent feels about the Department. In order to present the data in a "graphic" way each respondent's answer was rated on a nine point scale (1 representing a low opinion of the Department and 9 a high opinion of the Department). To provide greater "reliability" and certainty in the judgments that were made a colleague was asked to join the consultants as a third rater. The ratings of the three groups: (1) Full time faculty; (2) Adjunct faculty and (3) Students, alumni, secretary and Dean, were calculated. Although these are small groups, still the trend is clear. The more involved group--full time faculty--has the most positive reaction while the least involved group--e.g. the students et al--has the least positive reaction. The adjunct faculty reacts more positively than the students et al group and less than full time faculty.

The conclusion regarding these outcomes certainly suggests the need to try to increase involvement of all groups in the activities of the

Department. Thus a direction for the retreat was suggested. That is, after presenting the data, to follow up with activities for the Department that increase the potential for involvement.

RETREAT FOCUS

Perhaps the data that were immediately most useful were the responses to the question "What do you want to happen at the retreat?

What do you do at such a retreat or off-campus work session? Clearly the answer is that problems are worked on that are most often mentioned by Department members. Almost every respondent made some mention of the Departmental conflict. Sometimes it was brought up as a fear: "I hope we don't have a destructive fight." Others said it would be good to get it out in the open. A few suggested that the consultants needed sympathy, good luck, and all the help they could get. Our conclusion was that the conflict was a big item for everyone, and it had to be addressed early in the two day meeting. Also, other issues were important. Specifically, the Department felt strongly about the need to learn to make decisions, work together as a group, and provide a mechanism for getting a new Chairperson, when the present Chairperson's term was up. If the conflict had not been such a focus for everyone, perhaps those other issues mentioned would have been even more prominent. As it was, a number of other issues for the retreat were mentioned, though not with great frequency.

DECISION MAKING

The question "How are decisions made?" brought out responses that showed they weren't made in a wholly satisfactory manner. Most respondents suggested that the Chairperson made the decisions, but the Department really needed a way that more people could be involved in decisions. The major responses were: "We need more whole Department input to decisions," and "The chairperson makes decisions because we can't make them as a group."

POSITIVE REACTIONS TO THE DEPARTMENT

Answers to the question "What do you like best about your Department?" were concerned with the human issues, the students, student-facu-
lty relations, freedom, flexibility, camraderie, diversity and intimacy
in the Department. Little emphasis was placed on facilities, space, or
the curriculum.

NEGATIVE REACTIONS TO THE DEPARTMENT

The positive reaction to the Department emphasized the human side
of its resources. The least liked aspects of the Department were also
reacted to in terms of interpersonal resources: Group and organizational
relations, conflict, ability to work together, and making decisions. In
a sense, it seems that the people were making the Department either attractive or unattractive.

IDEAL ORGANIZATION

The last of the central questions was "What would the Department be
like if it was the way you wanted it to be?" Answers to this question
seemed to support the conclusions made from previous questions. The
number one ingredient was peace or lack of conflict. Again it appears
that dealing with conflict becomes a number one goal for a large number
of Department members. Other items seem to support the theme of eliminating the conflict. An important point mentioned was the necessity for
open meetings with listening and mutual respect in developing a decision-
making structure. The generalization here seems to be that there are
some essentials to reducing conflict: Respect, mutual listening in open
meetings, and the development of an operational decision-making procedure.

The other main theme in the "ideal department" was to bring in more
talented adjuncts who are diverse and creative. In a sense there seems
to be a suggestion here to increase the number, diversity, and involvement of the adjunct faculty.

There were a number of other suggestions that had to do with program, leadership, students and autonomy for the Department. The answers

to the questions, when analyzed, suggested a basis for the Retreat days to follow.

General Trends in Data

Patterns seemed to emerge from the data that provided a clear picture of the organization and its issues.

One of these patterns was suggested by an earlier analysis. If the three groups of full time faculty, adjunct faculty, and students et al., are examined it seems that there are some important differences. First, students appear to be most concerned with increasing the number and diversity of adjunct faculty. They also most often voiced the need to bring in famous, well known, talented faculty.

Second, adjuncts seemed to be concerned with the status, security, and rewards for adjunct faculty. In some ways they suggested that they felt used, exploited and underpaid. Third, permanent faculty wanted the adjunct faculty to become more involved in the Department and its activities.

This illustrates a trend in our data and also a principle of social organization. Perceptions of organizations depend on the position that one occupies within the structure. Although this finding verifies what is already known about organizations, it is often difficult to verify for any specific issue without systematic data collection and a feedback process.

Another implication of the interviews seems to be the need for awareness of the varying perceptions of the different groups within the organization. For example the students were apparently most concerned with communication with other groups--mainly the faculty. It may be they perceived themselves as being less involved in the exercise of power and decision making. The faculty was most concerned with program, curriculum, and student relationships. They saw these areas as their job, and felt invested in working for their improvement.

The adjunct faculty appeared mostly concerned about status, rewards, and security.

Retreat Plan

When the Department Chairperson and the Dean first contacted the consultants, no particular plan for a Retreat was apparent. The collection of data pinpointed two related issues. (1) Nearly everyone was upset about the interpersonal conflict. (2) The Department had difficulty working as a unit on problems all groups must learn to solve in order to be effective, satisfy members, and ultimately survive.

Based on the data collection, a detailed plan for the Retreat was developed. In essence it had three steps.

1. The first step was to report to the group what they said they wanted to do at the Retreat.

2. The second step was to orient the group to the Retreat by presenting feedback of data collected in the interviews.

3. Then, to provide sessions to work on skills indicated by the interviews.

The Retreat and Reactions to it

Thus far we have focused on two basic topics, data collection and retreat design. It is important to note that whenever a design is implemented there must be an ongoing process of reality testing. Through checking the group's reaction (in this case, three feedback exercises within the retreat) the consultants could review their own perception of the process and also make alterations in the design to meet the needs of the group.

Now we will examine the flow of the Retreat and the reactions of the members to the design. We also will include our own reactions and perceptions of the process.

Tuesday Evening

The Tuesday evening section of the Retreat was designed first to present the data collected on what the group wanted from the Retreat, and secondly, to begin to build the group's cohesion in order to work on the issues at hand. Following the data presentation the group was given their first task. That task was to "talk in groups of two or three, with people you don't spend much time with, about the information presented." At this point the formal presentation ended. The members proceeded to break into smaller groups and began talking about issues presented. As time went on the general topics of discussion changed from the Departmental issues to outside topics. The consultants' reaction was that the individuals were talking with each other, they were becoming acquainted with their group in a new surrounding, and were focusing on, at least at some level, the issues that were facing them at the Retreat. It was the intent of the consultants to not begin the Retreat with highly structured activities or to force the participants into areas that would produce more tension than what everyone was experiencing.

Wednesday Morning

Wednesday began with a review of data collected. Following this review the Retreat members were asked to participate in an exercise of prioritizing various issues that were facing the Department. What was evidenced in this exercise was that the group had difficulty accomplishing the task due to 1) lack of proper communication patterns, 2) extreme diversity of interests among members, 3) investment in protecting individual interests within the realm of Departmental issues.

The prioritizing activity served a two-fold purpose. The first purpose was to examine the group's decision-making process and the second was to illustrate the mechanics of the group's interaction style. The group needed another way of looking at their own behavior. It was also clear that the group needed a format for getting through impasses in the decision-making process. Information gathered from the interviews indicated that the members had many strengths and were willing to work on issues. What seemed appropriate was to provide tools to build a framework for decision-making.

The one major impasse to making decisions was the conflict in the Department. It was the consultants' feeling that the task was not accomplished because of the underlying conflict. A structured feedback activity was designed to begin to develop a format for airing conflict.

The feedback piece seemed to provide a way to start, letting the conflict emerge in a controlled manner. What appeared to us when we monitored the small groups was that the clarity of what was being stated was increasing. Tension was also mounting and issues were coming to the surface.

Wednesday Afternoon

Following lunch, more structure was added by providing the data on conflict within the Department, a short lecture on pieces involved in conflict resolution processes, and the use of a sociograph.

If one word could describe the Wednesday afternoon session it would be "tension." The session grew at one point, prior to the break, to an almost unbearable tension. Everyone in the room felt the pressure. Someone was even chewing on his hand. What happened allowed the conflict to be clear and in the open. Since this had not been done in the past, the pressure of the conflict had to be great. What seemed to be happening was that a litany of issues kept flying back and forth. Initially this created the high level of tension. Then the group realized that this behavior was not serving any purpose and came to another impasse. The level of tension remained high but the group realized that there had to be some reasonable resolution. Then there was a break. When the group reconvened it knew that it had to do something. What resulted was a social contract.

The session was clearly the most tense time of the Retreat. It was also the time of greatest accomplishment of the Retreat. There were no more semi-secret battles. The group was aware of itself and its behavior. The group also adapted a new norm in the process. That norm was openness. A general feeling of hope seemed to pervade the group. That is, the conflict problem, if not resolved, was dealt with sufficiently to release energy to examine other issues facing the Department.

Wednesday Evening

When the group reconvened, it was clear that people were nearing exhaustion from the work they had done earlier. In this state, the members still were willing to work. People were obviously more positive. The task of Wednesday night was the same, in process, as the failed Wednesday morning session. Yet the material was more complex and the issues were greater in number. The group completed its task in record time and successes began to occur. The group was obviously involved. We, the consultants, were surprised at the willingness and energy of the group to work.

Thursday

    Thursday had been designed to utilize the methods of decision-making and feedback in order to develop a package to return with to the Department. Our other agenda item was to turn the group back to its own control. Or, to give the group back to itself.

    Our observation of the group's behavior was that they felt they no longer needed consultants. It was clear that the group felt it wanted to work on its own issues. Initially the consultants felt rejected and a little uncomfortable. The group seemed to be taking control much faster than what was anticipated by the consultants. After we processed this between ourselves we interpreted this behavior as the highest form of flattery we could receive. It appeared that we accomplished our task of working ourselves out of a job.

    The final piece of this section is the feedback we received during the Retreat process. Feedback had been collected at three intervals during the Retreat. The first was Wednesday before lunch, the second was Wednesday evening, and the third was at the Retreat's completion. The feedback allowed us to monitor the progress of the design, the participants' reaction to the design, and any needs of the group that should have been addressed in the design. The following is a tabulation of the three feedback pieces that were gathered.

First Evaluation (before lunch Wednesday)

1.   How do you feel about what happened so far?

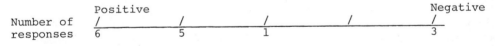

Positive   Negative

Number of responses: 6   5   1   3

2.   What would you like to have in the program?

    4 Intensity-ventilation of hostility
    3 Feedback for Retreat members from members
    1 Discussion and definition of problems
    1 Focus on goals, priorities, and beliefs
    3 Focus on decision-making
    1 Curriculum discussion without Dean

3.   What did you like best?

    1 The trust that seemed present
    8 Feedback activities
    1 The open types of discussion
    1 Not sure
    1 Focus on the Department, relating session to interview data

Some examples of various responses to the first questions:

Positive

1. "Liked the emphasis on the positive."
2. "Opened my eyes to lack of decision-making."
3. "Good start, letting-down hair."
4. "Interesting introduction to basic concepts."

Negative

1. "So far not enough structured interaction."
2. "Up until now it looked like you didn't know what you were doing--everything was vague except your dominating personality."

Mixed

1. "I feel a shaky momentum--some insight too soon for evaluation."

Neutral

1. "It's been polite--but how can we cope with the conflict."

Second Evaluation (Wednesday)

1. What is your reaction to what we have done so far?

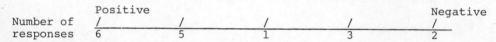

	Positive				Negative
Number of responses	/ 6	/ 5	/ 1	/ 3	/ 2

Some examples from reactions at various points on the scale:

Positive

1. "It was an extraordinary accomplishment."
2. "Excellent progress. Have already exceeded my expectations."
3. "Group is opening up. Your ideas are clear and logical."
4. "I feel positive now, more so than I ever have."

Moderately Positive

1. "Good beginning but am concerned about efforts in working on the social contract."
2. "A real hair letting down. Air is clearer, I see hope."
3. "Exhausting, informative, development of a better structure for dealing."

Negative

1. "Tramatic confrontation, still need Chairperson of strength."
2. "Afternoon session needed to be stopped."

Final Evaluation

Four questions in the final evaluation.

1.   What do you feel was accomplished at the Retreat?

```
              Positive                                      Negative
Number of     /           /           /          /          /
responses     12          2           1
```

   Positive

   1.   "We worked together demonstrating it's possible."
   2.   "Dissolving the list of what we don't like."
   3.   "Helps establish common ground among faculty."
   4.   "Unity, still being your own person."
   5.   "A decision-making process came into place."
   6.   "A new spirit of cooperation."
   7.   "Integration of students in decision-making process."
   8.   "Peaceful coexistence of conflicting interests."
   9.   "Tools for having a decision process in the future have been developed."

2.   What was your greatest learning?

   1.   "Ability of members to play various roles."
   2.   "I have been encouraged to take on more responsibility."
   3.   "Able to see more clearly overt and hidden agenda."
   4.   "Able to recognize other attitudes and give more respect to others."
   5.   "Learned to be open to the flow of the group."
   6.   "See need for more organization in myself."
   7.   "See myself and colleagues from a different point of view."
   8.   "New steps in group manipulation techniques. No group is incorrigible."
   9.   "More aware of dynamics of this particular group."
   10. "Feedback process has changed my attitude about others."

3.   How have you changed as a result of the process?

   1.   "I stood for principle even on the witness stand."
   2.   "I could have neat discussions with others not my closest friends."
   3.   "Learned new spirit of cooperation."
   4.   "Impossible circumstances need not be impossible."
   5.   "Aware of vulnerability of groups."
   6.   "Aware that people worked together."
   7.   "I saw things differently."

4.   Rate Retreat on nine point scale:

```
Poor                        Uncertain                      Good
/       /       /       /       /       /       /       /       /
```

Final Feedback from the Consultants to the Group

Since the members of the Department were working on their problems without consultants' participation, we, the consultants removed ourselves from the environment and discussed how to summarize the process.

Three issues were decided on as the focus for the last session. First, continuing the intervention or follow-up activities. Follow-up was defined as continuing the process that had been started. This included periodic data collection and another meeting so that the Department members could discuss the feedback and their progress.

Second, we gave the department some feedback regarding the Retreat and raised questions about some remaining issues and observations.

1. How do you know when you succeed?
2. Are there non-negotiable issues?
3. How do you monitor the social contract?
4. Can you expand and experiment with your roles?
5. Can you continue to be as good as you were at the Retreat?
6. How can you all participate in enforcing your rules?
7. How can you integrate, communicate with, include and involve students in Department processes?
8. What modifications of adjunct roles and status do you want?
9. How and when to select a new chairperson?
10. How can you change your image?
11. How can a group of academics find happiness in an ugly building?
12. How can you develop a procedure for continual studying, monitoring, and modifying the program and curriculum?
13. How can you make all Department members feel part of and involved in Department processes?
14. How can you keep your energy-momentum alive?
15. Which of your innovations, used at the Retreat, do you want to continue (Ranking--time keeping--data collection--process observation--etc.)?
16. How can you accomplish follow-up?
17. What part of the facilitators' roles can be taken over by Department members?
18. How can you learn to fight without making the group paranoid, schizoid, or psychopathic?

Third, we provided some feedback and made some comments about their observations.

Some Reflections by the Consultants

We observed the following, in conclusion:

1.   The members of the Department seemed involved and also to be
     enjoying their work, particularly when working on their own
     agenda Thursday afternoon.

2.   The group worked hard and members felt success in the use of
     a number of tools, feedback, guidelines, a social contract,
     and decision-making procedures.

3.   Members acted like applied social scientists when they exchang-
     ed feedback and process comments at the last session.

4.   The members talked and listened to each other.

5.   People confronted one another.

6.   Some affirmations that were used by the consultants and work-
     shop members were:

     a.   "Above all else I want to see things differently."

     b.   "Forgiveness ends the dream of conflict here."

     c.   "There is another way of looking at this."

     d.   "I am never upset for the reason I think."

     e.   "My mind is no longer preoccupied with thoughts of the
          past."

These affirmative statements that were used throughout are useful
in solving any interpersonal conflict. It is our hope that they will
continue to serve us all.

Part II: Practical Theory

Section D: <u>Community psychology and community action</u>

In searching for theoretical roots in their profession, some environmental psychologists are drawn to Kurt Lewin. In his field theory they have found a notation system for conceptualizing the environment and methodologies for the analysis of behavior. <u>Leanne Rivlin</u>, <u>Maxine Wolfe</u> and <u>Matt Kaplan</u> cite this and another reason of their own: "One of the main reasons that we are interested in revitalizing the Lewinian action research framework," they say, "is the value we attach to the connection it made between increased citizen involvement in identifying social, environmental, political, and economic problems, and subsequently people's increased motivation to take action and to be in control of their lives."

The next article, by <u>Jeannette Turner</u>, is fully devoted to reporting an action research project carried out by some students and faculty at Temple University with members of the Hunting Park Community Action Council in the North Philadelphia area. The University group was motivated by a desire to collaborate with the surrounding community using the action research scheme so familiar to them in their training and consulting work with other kinds of organizations.

This action research (reported by Turner in the previous article) generated another project. A graduate class in Temple University became interested in collaborating with the Hunting Park Community group in an effort to restore and preserve the park which had been for many years a center of community life. <u>Stephanie Reynolds</u> describes the planning, data collection, analysis and feedback phases that the Temple class went through. Though incomplete at the time of this report, the project represents some work in the Lewinian action research tradition, particularly the systematic data gathering phase. This article and the one preceding it are practical companions.

From an entirely different and more dramatic setting, <u>David Bargal</u> and <u>Tsiyona Peled</u> report still another project characterized by the conceptualizations and motivations of the Lewinian tradition. They carefully present seven theoretical guidelines underlying interventions in this kind of encounter. Then an analytic framework and operational implications are developed, ending with a consideration of the chronic problem of transferability of encounter effects to real life situations. Using

this framework, the micro-level intervention programs in Arab-Jewish relations in Israel during recent years are evaluated. Their limitations
are described, and four levels for macro-level interventions are proposed
beginning with "Pupils of all levels of the educational systems."

Environmental Psychology and Action Research: Lewin's Legacy

Leanne Rivlin, Maxine Wolfe and Matt Kaplan

City University of New York

Environmental psychology developed out of research that began in the late 1950s and 60s, focusing on the impact of the physical environment, an area that had been largely neglected by social scientists. Much of this work came out of a period of building, of expansion, a time of questioning and environmental activism. Some social scientists found that designers and planners also were raising questions about the people/environment interrelationship and a number of disciplines embarked on a collaboration that has persisted into the present. Despite its name, environmental psychology has drawn on a wide range of social sciences, including anthropology, sociology, economics, geography, political science and history--as well as the design and planning specialities--architecture, landscape architecture, urban design and urban planning.

In searching for theoretical roots in their own profession, environmental psychologists were drawn to the work of Kurt Lewin. Many already had been influenced by him. Lewin's field theory (Lewin, 1936; 1951) contained a notation system for conceptualizing the environment and methodologies for the analysis of behavior and experience. The environment, albeit the psychological environment, was a central feature and although Lewin did not focus on its physical parameters, his concept of life space encompassed more than social and cultural features. In addition, his involvement in action research provided a guideline for some researchers who wanted to do more than look at people in their physical settings. Action research is a methodology for empowering people to have control over their situations. However, the "action" and "citizens participation" components of the original action research framework, as conceptualized by Lewin and his associates, have been minimized by contemporary social scientists.

From our review of the literature describing modern "action research" projects covering a variety of environmental and social issues, we have found that the human "subjects" rarely conceptualize, carry out, evaluate or determine how to use the research according to their needs (see for example the research descriptions offered by Cunningham, 1983; Light and Smith, 1970; Stone, 1980; and Weisman, 1983). In addition to the neglect of the participatory aspects of the Lewinian action research model, the social activist implications which were evident in the early Community Self-Survey work (e.g., see Wormser, 1949) have been downplayed by researchers who have gravitated toward work that is more passive, non-threatening to the social order, and dominated by professionals.

One of the main reasons why we are interested in revitalizing the Lewinian action research framework is the value we attach to the connection it made between increased citizen involvement in identifying social, environmental, political, and economic problems, and subsequently people's increased motivation to take action and to be in control of their lives. We feel committed to re-establishing this connection because we see it as an important component in the quest to create environmental development processes and products that are less alienating, more satisfying for current and future users, and more consistent with societal democratic ideals.

The participatory research approach, based on the belief that research should be liberating in intent and participatory in process, also finds support in the work of Paulo Friere and his colleagues (see Freire, 1970; Hall, 1976). It is interesting to note that Lewin and Freire, having come from such different backgrounds and having different goals, arrived at similar formulations about the roles they wanted research to play in human and societal development. Lewin argued for the legitimacy of a "community self survey" approach and socially conscious action as a part of "social research" (Lewin, 1946; 1947). He arrived at this position through his diligent efforts to understand how people in "developed" countries understand, experience, and act in relation to societal problems. Freire's initial concern was with the dire need to stimulate action to eradicate poverty conditions in developing countries. He focused on the role of people's awareness—of how their own conditions are related to other people and larger social issues—for promoting social change that meets people's needs. Despite differences, both argued that human and societal change must evolve from human learning, involvement and action in societal development processes.

Since there are schools of action research which are not participatory, we will use the phrase "participatory action research" to describe the form that we are advocating. Some useful accounts of participatory action research projects do exist (e.g., Adeney, 1971; Baldassari, Lehman and Wolfe, 1984; Burns, 1978; Mackay, 1978; Mies, 1980; and Mtuma, 1982), but such accounts are few in number and scattered. Two examples of research which reflect our efforts aimed at stimulating people-oriented and people-empowered environmental research and improvement will illustrate our meaning.

The Red Room Study

For over six years beginning with its opening, we studied a state children's residential psychiatric hospital, a place designed for 192 children and adolescents. The program for the facility required that it be a single building with educational, recreational, administrative and residential facilities and services, all contained under one roof. The building consisted of eight residential "pods" or houses with three apartments in each one. Long corridors led to a school, a gym, dining rooms, recreational spaces, administrative offices and therapy rooms. Furnishings were selected for their durability rather than aesthetics and both staff and residents described its appearance in quite negative terms. The staff's expressed need to surveil was revealed in the clustering of patients in public areas. In our interviews with residents they voiced their desire to "get away," a place where they could be alone or with another person. In fact, some told us that they would deliberately get into trouble so as to be placed in the "Quiet Room," a small room where so-called "out-of-control patients" were secluded. When the administration decided that the one Quiet Room in each house was insufficient, that three were needed, a single room in each apartment was converted for this purpose. We asked to plan a new arrangement for the former Quiet Room and were permitted to have residents of the adolescent units work with us. We were told that patients could be involved in the planning but not the actual physical work. We had to be satisfied with a series of planning and design discussions with two separate groups, one male and one female.

The result was two colorful and attractive rooms (one in the male adolescent unit, the other in the female one) with rules for their use and care set by the residents themselves. The final design was a clear contrast to the bland color scheme and furnishings throughout the hospital. Also, the democratic decision-making process was in stark contrast to the decision-making processes we had previously encountered.

Our follow-up study revealed that the rooms were used in the intended ways, as private places for one or two persons. The rules were respected and maintenance was excellent (in contrast to many other public areas in the hospital). The participatory research approach effected a number of changes both physical and attitudinal. First, it helped to ensure a change that met the needs of users. Moreover, the participatory process demonstrated to a skeptical staff and administration of the hospital the ability of the residents to work reasonably and effectively despite the psychiatric labels that had been applied to them. Residents had clear images of their needs and the kinds of changes that would make their life in the institution more tolerable.

The participatory action component of our research, where we prompted resident participation in the development of what came to be called the "Red Room," revealed a great deal about how institutionalized life affects the ways children think, act and learn. Furthermore, as residents took advantage of this opportunity to effect an environmental change, we were able to observe the dynamics underlying the institution's environmental and programmatic development. We were able to examine the constructive tensions introduced into the power structure of the institution by the participatory environmental change project.

The Youth Video Project

This project began as a response to the problem of rampant vandalism in a new, New York City playground and its surrounding area. The playground leader of the site was doubtful as to the value of the traditional approaches to vandalism, building higher fences or getting guard dogs, but was enthusiastic about trying an alternative that would promote community interest and involvement in running the playground. Due to problems obtaining funds to conduct this project, it has not progressed beyond the initial efforts to obtain a core of youth participants. Although this project is in its very early stages, it is useful to describe the plan because it illustrates several points about the participatory action research approach.

The essence of the Youth Video Project is a working group of local teenagers who will conceptualize, document (via video), and intervene in local vandalism and related recreational problems in the area. The plan is to approach teens in local schools and youth groups who want to get involved in any of the facets of this project, i.e., script writing, filming, organizing presentations to the community, and organizing action groups (which are hopefully multigenerational) working to solve identified problems. The researcher's role is to initiate the organization of the video group, train youth in research techniques and in the use of video, and consult the group (and spin-off groups) in their efforts to communicate their findings to other community residents and prompt community-based action on the basis of research results.

There have been indications that this project will be of interest to local teenagers and will ultimately be perceived as a youth-directed project. Even before we initiated our outreach effort, students in a teenage-run newspaper in a local high school heard about the project and, showing great interest in its progress and a desire to get involved, requested an interview with the research coordinator. We see this as a good sign because according to the participatory action research model, a sense of local "ownership" of the project is an important component for generating subsequent action based on the findings.

The research intervention of facilitating a youth-created video film and stimulating subsequent youth-prompted community action aimed at solving identified problems will undoubtedly uncover many aspects of teen life in the area that are relevant to the vandalism problem. For instance, we have noted a total absence of local outdoor recreational resources for teen use. Although this is acknowledged by youth worker professionals as a problem, its connection to vandalism and other local problems generally has not been made and this is not a priority issue as far as policy-makers are concerned. An action research approach is appropriate here because it goes beyond a mere identification of local problems and prompts community residents and policy-makers to ask questions, look for answers and take action. This research approach differs from many academically-oriented spheres of inquiry which falsely assume that providing evidence of human and neighborhood needs will automatically lead to citizen, organizational and political change.

From these examples and others we have reviewed, it is clear that there is a real need and a great potential for applying participating action research to many environmental development problems. But there also are some serious problems. Most participatory action research projects go through "crisis periods," points of extreme tension with the possibility that the entire project might fail. In addition to the stress involved, professionals often have much to lose if the project runs into difficulties. Another burden is the unpredictability of project stages which may make it difficult to raise funds from agencies and foundations which expect to be told all the details of the research process prior to the onset of the work.

The stress and isolation of the participatory action research process limits the amount of information exchange among persons involved in this area. Many participants do not write up the results of their work, failing to share their experiences with others. Some have no interest in publishing while others have great difficulties in locating interested outlets. Informal communication and support among participatory action researchers, where it exists, is the primary link across projects. Since project participants often are absorbed and involved in their own localities, there are serious constraints on the information exchange process and the generalizability of the experiences.

Despite these problems, it is clear that Lewin's work has left an important direction for environmental research to pursue. Lewinian field theory and his action research model provide guidelines for the study and improvement of environments, a legacy that is likely to persist.

REFERENCES

Adeney, M. (1971). Community action: Four examples. London: The Runnymede Trust.

Baldassari, C., Lehman, S., & Wolfe, M. (1984). Imaging and creating alternative environments with children. In T. David & C. Weinstein (Eds.), Spaces for children. New York: Plenum.

Barker, R.G. (1968). Ecological psychology. Stanford, CA: Stanford University Press.

Barker, R.G. (1963). The stream of behavior. New York: Appleton.

Burns, R. (1978). Beyond statistics. In M.C.J. Elton, W.A. Lucas, & D.W. Conrath (Eds.), Evaluating new telecommunication services. New York: Plenum.

Cunningham, J.B. (1983). Gathering data in a changing organization: Human Relations, 36(5), 403-420.

Friere, P. (1970). Pedagogy of the oppressed. New York: The Seabury Press.

Hall, B.L. (1976). Creating knowledge: Breaking the monopoly. Toronto, Ontario: Participatory Research Group, Working Paper #1.

Ittelson, W.H., Rivlin, L.G., & Proshansky, H.H. (1970). The use of behavioral maps in environmental psychology. In Proshansky, Ittelson & Rivlin (Eds.), Environmental psychology: Man and his physical setting. New York: Holt, Rinehart, & Winston.

Lewin, K. (1951). Field theory in social science. New York: Harper & Row.

Lewin, K. (1947). Frontiers in group dynamics: Channels of group life: Social planning and action research. Human Relations, 1, 143-153.

Lewin, K. (1946). Action research and minority problems. Journal of Social Issues, 2, 34-46.

Lewin, K. (1936). Principles of topological and vector psychology. New York: McGraw-Hill.

Light, R.J., & Smith, P.V. (1970). Choosing a future: Strategies for designing and evaluating new programs. Harvard Educational Review, 40, 1-28.

Mackay, A. (1978). Expectations of a local project. In R. Lees & G. Smith (Eds.), Action research in community development. London: Routledge & Keegan Paul.

Mies, M. (1980). Towards a methodology for feminist research. In G. Rowles & R. Duelli-Klein (Eds.), Theories of women's studies. Berkley, CA: University of California.

Mtuma, E.K. (1982). Appropriate technology for grain storage at Bwakera China Village. In Y. Kassam & K. Mustafa (Eds.), Participatory research: An emerging alternative methodology in social science research. Khampur, New Delhi: Society for Participatory Research in Asia.

Proshansky, H.M., Ittelson, W.H., & Rivlin, L.G. (1970). The influence of the physical environment on behavior: Some basic assumptions. In Proshansky, Ittelson & Rivlin (Eds.), Environmental psychology: Man and his physical setting. New York: Holt, Rinehart & Winston.

Stone, F.A. (1980). Action research: A qualitative approach to educational studies. Multicultural Research Guide #5, The I.N. Third World Education Center, University of Connecticut.

Weisman, G. (1983). Environmental programming and action research. Environment and Behavior, 15(3), 381-408.

Wormser, M.H. (1949). The Northtown self survey: A case study. Journal of Social Issues, 5, 5-20.

Community Action Research in North Philadelphia

Jeannette Turner

Temple University

INTRODUCTION TO ACTION RESEARCH

In conjunction with the First International Kurt Lewin Conference, held at Temple University, the Department of Psychoeducational Processes (PEP), under the direction of volunteer faculty members and students, initiated an action research project involving other graduate students in PEP and a local community organization. After some negotiations, the Hunting Park Action Council (in the North Philadelphia area), agreed to participate in a project called C.A.R.P. (Community Action Research Project). The project would demonstrate Lewinian action research theory and practice. The following is a rationale and a report of the events that transpired.

THEORETICAL BACKGROUND OF ACTION RESEARCH

Kurt Lewin was very concerned about the condition of democracy in the United States. Having witnessed and experienced oppression as a Jew in Nazi Germany, he was particularly sensitive to the needs of Blacks and other minority groups in the United States. Furthermore, Lewin firmly believed that science must be applied for the benefit of society and in his last years established institutes and programs to apply the scientific method to such ills of society as prejudice and discrimination (Marrow, 1969). It was during his establishment of the Commission on Community Interrelations (CCI) in 1945 that his concept of action research took form. Lewin defined action research in these terms:

> The research needed for social practice can best be
> characterized as research for social management or
> social engineering. It is a type of action-research,
> a comparative research on the conditions and effects
> of various forms of social action and research lead-
> ing to social action. Research that produces nothing
> but books will not suffice (Lewin, 1948, p. 203).

The CCI, under Lewin, in a search for solutions to racial and religious prejudice, named four varieties of action research as methodology:

1. Diagnostic. The staff of CCI would step in, diagnose the pro-
    lem, and make recommendations.
2. Participant. Residents of the area affected would be involved
    from the beginning. They would take self-surveys and partici-
    pate in a diagnosis of problems.
3. Empirical. Accurate records of similar groups would be kept.
    (This method led to the development of principles of groups.)
4. Experimental. This variety called for a controlled study of
    various techniques in identical social situations. (Marrow,
    1969, p. 198).

Action research, therefore, started out in an effort to provide measur-
able standards for social research and at the same time to effect solutions to social problems. Lewin believed in a close identification with
the community he tried to help, as well as in advancing the cause of
science.

LATER DEVELOPMENTS OF ACTION RESEARCH

Gordon and Ronald Lippitt have defined action research as a four-
step process, cyclic and continuous. They use a quote from French and
Bell which describes action research as:

> The process of systematically collecting research data about
> an ongoing system relative to some objective, goal, or need
> of that system; feeding these data back into the system
> based both on the data and on hypotheses; and evaluating the
> results of actions by collecting more data (G. Lippitt and
> R. Lippitt, 1978, p. 87).

The four-step process described by the Lippitts includes:

1. Data Collection--questionnaires, surveys, observation.
2. Feedback of data to the client as soon as possible.
3. Action Planning--which would include the participation of all
    persons involved, in a supportive climate and in a way rele-
    vant to client goals.
4. Action should have standards to measure progress, continually
    referring to data and changing direction if needed (G. Lippitt
    and R. Lippitt, 1978, p. 89).

THE HUNTING PARK ACTION COUNCIL AND PEP TEAM

In the Fall before the Lewin Conference, graduate students were
recruited to form a PEP Consultation Team for C.A.R.P. About 15 members
of the Hunting Park Action Council joined the team. (This council is a
grass-roots community organization located in a predominantly Black
neighborhood of North Philadelphia. Hunting Park is adjacent to Temple's
Broad Street campus and has "inner city" problems related to drug traffic,
health care, and youth.)

First and Second Meetings

The whole PEP team met with the H.P.A. Council for the first time
at the Hunting Park Community Center. After a collaborative brainstorming session, four major concerns appeared to have the greatest priority
for the Council; (1) Leadership training for Council members; (2) Motivation for themselves and others in the community to participate; (3)
Communication skills within the Council; and (4) Cultural and language
barriers. (Hunting Park, largely a Black community also contained His-
panic as well as White residents. Few members were able to converse in
Spanish.) We agreed to meet weekly to address these issues.

Data Collection

The team got together immediately after each meeting to discuss the
H.P. group's dynamics and to plan the next meeting. Data, in the form of
"feedback" sheets which had been distributed to Council members after
the meeting, were reviewed by the team. The feedback sheet had six items.
1. Productivity (How productive did you find the meeting to be?)
   Rate 1 to 7.
2. Cohesiveness (How cohesive or close were members?) Rate 1 to
   7.
3. Personal Satisfaction (How much personal satisfaction did you
   get?) Rate 1 to 7.
4. Tension (How much tension did you feel during the meeting?)
   Rate 1 to 7.
5. What did you like best?
6. What did you like least?

After discussing the data and group's dynamics, the PEP team felt that realistically our help to the Council would be to conduct ten sessions addressing organizational needs of H.P.A.C. The main difficulty of H.P.A.C. seemed to be an interpersonal conflict, a lack of effective leadership, and poor communication. Since the Council members had also diagnosed their own problems in this way, we would offer a program of training, including skills that would address interpersonal needs as well as organizational ones. We decided upon goal setting, decision-making, problem-solving, assertiveness training, leadership styles, and communication skills as topics. Later we added conflict resolution and cohesiveness. These skills were presented over a ten week period using a combination of didactic and experiential methods. Handouts were given for the Council members to take home for study. Training leadership was shared by six graduate students and one faculty during the sessions.

A Summary of the subsequent meetings

Third meeting. This session involved a fish-bowl design and centered around goal-setting for the Council's 10 weeks. Feedback from the meeting was as follows:

(1) Productive = 6.0 (Average of 11 participants); (2) Cohesive = 7.0; (3) Personally satisfying = 6.0; (4) Tension = 3.0; (5) What I liked best: "positive attitude," "people friendly," "talked openly about problems," "information about what we need--," "leadership"; (6) What I liked least: "uncertain about goals," "tension," "trouble participating," "I have problems speaking out and I wish someone would help me."

Fourth meeting. (A session on refining goals using a fish-bowl design):

(1) Productive = 6.5; (2) Cohesive = 6.3; (3) Personally satisfying = 6.3; (4) Tension = 2.0; (5) What I liked best: "cooperative mood of the group," "the way the group got along," "learning my faults," "truthfulness of the group", "goal-oriented," "getting to know what we want," "group involvement," "positive attitude," "seeing people give feedback without getting into arguments," "cohesiveness," "group dynamics;" (6) What I liked least: "would like to see more directions," "the time frame to critique," "the way the group gets along," "never coming to an agreement," "present objectives not identified," "giving negative feedback," "more ex-

planations," "two or three people talking at same time," "subject not clear."

Fifth meeting. (A session on Assertiveness Training)
(1) Productive = 6.7; (2) Cohesive = 6.6; (3) Personally satisfying = 6.5; (4) Tension = 1.5; (5) What I liked best: "Andrea," "Jeannette and Theresa role play," "importance of assertiveness," "insight into leadership qualities," "interaction of community and Temple groups;" (6) What I liked least: "nothing," "people raise hands before talking," "not enough time," "coffee break."

Sixth meeting. (A session on Assertiveness and Leadership Skills Training)
(1) Productive = 6.7; (2) Cohesive = 5.7; (3) Personally satisfying = 6.4; (4) Tension = 2.4; (5) What I liked best: "the whole evening," "everything," "group interaction," "interaction II," "play acting," "speakers;" (6) What I liked least: "the way a particular subject was brought up by one of the group members--community solving problems," "nothing" (3); "people still don't raise their hands before they talk how to reach the community," "coffee break," "explain what leadership training is about and for what purposes," "lack of identification with Action Council," "reorganization of H.P. Action Council--how to do it?".
At this meeting, there was conflict between members regarding goals for the Council.

Seventh meeting. (Session on Communication and Listening Skills)
(1) Productivity = 6.8; (2) Cohesive = 5.5; (3) Personally satisfying = 5.7; (4) Tension = 2.8; (5) What I liked best: "nothing," "everything," "was the group of three that we formed and how nice it was talking to a person that would listen to your problems without ignoring you," "speakers," "play-acting," "the topic," "commaderie," "listening;" (6) What I liked least: "nothing," "not getting to the issue."

Eighth meeting. (A session on Leadership Styles)
(1) Productivity = 6.8; (2) Cohesive = 6.4; (3) Personally satisfying = 6.1; (4) Tension = 3.0; (5) What I liked best: "nothing," "everything," "listening without being ignored," "speakers," "play-acting;" (6) What I liked least: "nothing," "not getting to the issues."

Final meetings

There was a two-week lapse because of the Spring holidays and because of political participation of many H.P.A.C. members in elections.
In the interim, the PEP team met to review what had happened and to plan
future meetings. It was suggested that the H.P.A. Council plan the next
meeting--the content of training.

At this following meeting we had a session on conflict using a
conflict exercise from Group Magic by Amidon, et al (1976). Strong
feelings emerged and members became more aware of subgrouping within the
Council and a conflict of goals.

For example, one group (led by a man) wanted to use Hunting Park
as the headquarters for the Townwatch while another group including
several women wanted an emphasis on youth activities, tutoring and educational programs. There was no resolution but strong feelings were
aired. Later, an exercise in cohesion pointed out an approach of compromise as a way of resolving conflict.

At the final regular meeting, the members of Hunting Park Action
Council and the PEP team had one last training session. Members were
encouraged to attend the Lewin Conference.

At the Conference, a round table discussion led by two graduate
students summarized the experiences of the PEP-H.P.A.C. group. Questions
were raised such as, "What were the things you learned as a result of
C.A.R.P.?" "What would you want to be done differently?" Responses
from H.P.A.C. members were almost unanimous in expressing gratitude
that they had become better community leaders, were more assertive as
individuals, and had gained other benefits from participation. Members
enjoyed the experiential method of training as opposed to the didactic.
We were implored to continue our efforts.

COMMENTS

Considering the time restraint the Temple team felt that the C.A.R.
P. project had been successful. We followed the Lewin model of action
research closely, using data collection, feedback, and action planning
in a participant mode. The feedback factors did not change a lot, on
the average, over the 6 weeks of data collection: "Productivity" rose
slightly; "Cohesion" rose and fell periodically; "Personal satisfaction"
went up some and then went back; "Tension" fell then rose. Our clients

testified as to the benefits of skills training in organizational leadership and they asked for more. There was, however, a feeling of incompleteness expressed by both the PEP team and H.P.A.C. members.

REFERENCES

Amidon, E., M. Greenberg, & J. Roth (1976). Group magic. St. Paul, Minn.: Paul Amidon and Associates.

Lewin, K. (1948). Resolving social conflict. New York: Harper Bros.

Lippitt, G. and Lippitt, R. (1978). The consulting process in action. University Associates, Inc., San Diego, Calif.

Marrow, A.J. (1969). The practical theorist: The life and work of Kurt Lewin. New York: Basic Books.

NOTES

The Temple University volunteer team consisted of Edmund Amidon, Jeannette Turner, Leigh Gordon, Edward Christian, Edward Manning, Theresa Randall, and Andrea Womack.

The Hunting Park Action Council group included Barbara Landers, Collie Landers, Bill Butler, Mercedes Martinez, Syed Haji, Dorothy Evans, Sunny McDonald, Lon Tubman, Norman Martin, Willie Russell, Josephine Hudson, Juanita Andrews, Mary Walke, Mamie Johnson, Harriet Ahmed and Bamaris Siqueros.

Report of an Action Research Project: The Hunting Park Community Leaders Survey – Problems and Prospects for Park Preservation

Stephanie Reynolds

Temple University

Introduction

The <u>field</u> of park planning and management in Philadelphia is undergoing major review city wide in the 1980's. A number of <u>forces</u> are evident in influencing new directions for the future of the city parks. The
changing <u>structure</u> of park financing is increasing the <u>needs</u> of park
users for an enhanced <u>relationship</u> with the park administration and with
civic organizations that can unite their power and facilitate forward
movement. Thus, education of community leaders and how they are taught
to identify the driving and restraining forces that enhance or bar the
way to further programs is critical in determining the quality and cost
effectiveness of park management.

Education of community leaders to meet the needs of park users requires comprehensive and dynamic concepts such as are suggested by the
underlined words in the first paragraph. These words are key ones in
the field theory of human behavior developed by Kurt Lewin. Essentially,
these words reflect Kurt Lewin's view that human action, feeling and
thinking, function in <u>relationships</u> with the persons and objects in the
environment. Everything with which a person is in <u>relationship</u> is a
part of his overall life space. The <u>life space</u> changes in response to
forces that operate within it with varying strength, direction, and
points of origin. Change can be brought about by increasing the tensions
within the life space produced by opposing forces or by decreasing tension in some key region of the life space. The first type of change
gives dissatisfaction; the second leads to some degree of satisfaction.
This paper represents one step toward identifying some of the most
salient driving and restraining forces in the life space of key members
of the Hunting Park (North Philadelphia) community leadership in regard
to the need for a safe, clean, equipped and well maintained park.

To undertake this preliminary step, a four-part questionnaire was
developed by members of a Temple University graduate course and given
to the Hunting Park leaders as part of an ongoing educational workshop
series (Community Action Research Project) which they were carrying out

with Temple University. The report lists each question and the answers, followed by a short summary with comments. This report was prepared as a preliminary form of feedback, recognizing that it might serve the greatest need if it sparked some further thoughts about future actions that might be attempted to bring about satisfying changes in the force field affecting the park.

Question I: What are the three major problems in the park?

Answers: The major problems in the park in descending order from most to least often mentioned are:

Drug dealing (5)	16%
Security of property (5)	16%
Sanitation (5)	16%
Lack of recreational equipment (5)	16%
Lack of community spirit (4)	13%
Vandalism (3)	10%
Personal safety (2)	6%
Landscaping (1)	3%
Other (1)	3%
TOTAL: (31)	99%

Summary and Comment

When viewed as basically eight major areas of park problems, there was a fairly strong consensus that one area, "security of property/vandalism" was the most important. This combination of problems received 26% of the vote. "Drug dealing," "sanitation," "lack of recreational equipment," and "lack of community spirit" received equal votes of 16% each. "Landscaping" and "personal safety" were the least often mentioned problems, receiving 3% each.

This response is significant in that it reflects an overriding concern with maintenance of existing facilities. This view is the same priority as was established in the National Urban Recreation Study of 1977. Based on the conclusions of the national study, Congress authorized $725 million dollars over five years for the Urban Parks and Recreation Recovery Program. This priority is also established in the "Fairmount Park Master Plan Summary" printed in December 1983: "The first priority for the next decade should be to preserve and enhance what is already in place." (p. 3) Sharing a top priority with the national and local top priorities may be significant in gaining access to any national and local funding or manpower commitment allocated to support it. Communication with government administrators and elected officials may be easier when it is clear that there is a basic agreement on priorities.

Additionally, it should be noted that actions taken to increase the security of park property and protect its buildings and equipment from vandalism could have a number of positive side effects on some of the other listed concerns. Drug dealing, for example, would become less likely in a more carefully watched park, and personal safety would be likely to improve. Even sanitation problems would be lessened if the primary problem of security could be successfully addressed.

Question II: What has been done to try to solve the major park problems?

Answers: There were seventeen responses to this question with the leading answer that nothing has been done. Sixty-four percent indicated that they were unaware of anything having been done in the past. Two people reported that attempts to organize a park advisory or action committee had been made but haven't yet been very successful. One person reported having attempted to correct some of the leading problems by contacting the City Sanitation, Drug Abuse and Police Departments but felt that no action was taken as a result of these contacts. One person, however, reported having resolved a lot of problems as a result of confrontation and meeting with the "Council."

Question III: What actions do you think you can take to try to help solve these problems?

Answers: There were nine types of actions listed in response to this question as follows:

. Organize an action group
. Increase community participation (3)
. Contact Park Personnel
. Contact Police (5)
. Get increased sanitation services
. Establish a "Town Watch"
. Contact persons in leadership positions: City Hall, the Mayor, Committee persons, and Community leaders (4)
. Speak out to raise awareness
. "Go out and do something"

Summary and Comment

Except for the last section, which is difficult to categorize, most of the proposed actions seem to involve actions designed to mobilize volunteer citizen groups and the City government through several departments by contacting community and City leaders. However, one of the proposed actions, organizing a "Town Watch," suggests a collaborative model in which the Police Department provides training, backup and radio equipment, but most of the work is carried out by neighborhood volunteers on a carefully coordinated schedule.

In view of the commonly shared perception in the group that past efforts to mobilize increased police, sanitation and drug busting action from City personnel have had little or no known success, there may be a great deal of special significance in the proposal to initiate a more collaborative model as is suggested by the concept of a "Town Watch."

Since the primary park problem identified was security of property and protection from vandalism, the "Town Watch" suggested would be top priority for involving a larger number of community members in the park with City Police supplying training, backup and equipment.

The second group of problems identified, however, might also be considered in the light of a collaborative model. For example, some neighborhood groups have organized volunteers for massive park "cleanup days" in which the City supplied trash bags, trucks and compactor for for litter removal. On other occasions, groups interested in the park have organized neighbors to plant donated bulbs, or "adopt" a tree or shrub to care for.

In addition to City departments, some groups have extended the collaborative model to get donated plants and trees from such groups as the Pennsylvania Horticultural Society and have added volunteer manpower from the Sierra Club, Junior League, Boy and Girl Scouts, and schools.

Question IV: If you did try to solve these problems, what do you think would help you or hinder you?

Answers: There were three hindrances identified:

. Petty differences between people, whether political, economic or personal
. Lack of help
. Apathy

Eight types of references to help were listed:

. More people would help
. Increased community participation
. City assistance
. Help from people in powerful positions
. Different approaches and ideas
. A good group
. Presenting problems to the Mayor
. Contacting the Sanitation Department

Summary and Comment

The particular items in this list of things that would help or hinder solving the park problems are consistent with the list of action already tried and those which were suggested for the future. There is one reference to something that would help that is totally new among the answers already given and that is the suggestion that it would be a help to have different approaches and ideas. To some extent, merely summarizing the variety of ideas which have already been tried may be informative for those who had not yet heard of them. For many people, these ideas <u>will</u> be new and different, because they haven't yet heard them. Developing additional answers to questions such as what <u>could</u> be done might also be a useful way to generate new ideas or approaches.

Conclusion

In terms of Kurt Lewin's field theory, the beginning of positive change is with the analysis of the <u>forces</u> for and against that change. This report has indicated some of these forces and hopefully will serve as a basis for the next step--returning the data to the individuals who supplied it, for validation.

Potentially, a third step would be agreement among the group about whether the data had any value in formulating an <u>action plan</u> to work on reducing the restraining forces so that the driving forces will have a greater influence in solving the problems in the park. This process of gathering data, reflecting on its relevance for future action and developing an action plan is the continuing process of "action research" which made Kurt Lewin's field theory uniquely suited to solving social problems.

REFERENCES

Clark, P.A. (1972). <u>Action research and organization change</u>. London, England: Harper & Row.

Eiben, R. <u>Force-field analysis: A tool for change</u>.

Evered, R. (1977). <u>An exploration of Kurt Lewin's contribution to the social sciences</u>. Unpublished paper, July.

<u>Fairmount Park Master Plan Summary</u>, Wallace Roberts and Todd, December, 1983.

Kelly, G. (1982). <u>Pioneer Park, American forests</u>, June.

Lewin, K. (1951). <u>Field theory in social science</u> (D. Cartwright, Ed.). New York: Harper & Row.

Spier, M.S. (1973). Kurt Lewin's "Force-Field Analysis". In J.E. Jones and J. William Pfeiffer (Eds.), <u>The 1973 annual handbook for group facilitators</u>. La Jolla, California: University Associates, pp. 111-113.

<u>Views from a Park Bench</u>, The Newsletter of Friends of Philadelphia Parks, 8801 Curtis Terrace, Wyndmoor, Pa. 19118.

<u>NOTE</u>: Members of the Temple University class active in the research were Leigh Gordon, Merri Baldus, Kim Hamilton, Barbara Masse, Stephanie Reynolds, Aileen Witzel, Gene Stivers and Ed Kies.

A Practical Theory for Optimal Intergroup Initiated Encounters: The Arab-Jewish Case

David Bargal

The Hebrew University of Jerusalem

and

Tsiyona Peled

The Israel Institute of Applied Social Research, Jerusalem

INTRODUCTION

The social, political and geographical reality in Israel dictates the inevitable coexistence of Arabs and Jews. Although the socio-political forces of the macro level have been crucial in shaping Arab-Jewish relations in Israel, the impact of occurrences at the micro level--in natural situations or in initiated, planned and manipulated settings--on Arab-Jewish interpersonal and intergroup relations, should not be ignored. Moreover, appropriate and constructive micro-level intervention programs aimed at improving Jewish-Arab relations should be considered as important means of counteracting the increasingly negative impact of the highly complex, unresolved political problems at the macro level. Such programs--if expanded in scope and properly handled--may change the attitudes and behavior of individual Arabs and Jews towards each other for the better. Mutual trust, respect and understanding, the main goals of the intervention programs, are necessary cornerstones for a working peaceful and normal coexistence between the people of the two nations destined to live together in the State of Israel.

The paper will advocate an interdisciplinary holistic approach to intergroup relations. An action research approach will be suggested as one of the main strategies for achieving significant long range results, which is the main concern of the intervention efforts. Therefore macro as well as micro issues will be addressed. These issues pertain to social action activities aimed at educational and policy changes for minority groups. However, the limits of social psychological theory in contributing to the solution of enduring political and ethnic conflicts will be pointed out and discussed.

General Theoretical Guidelines

According to Amir (1976) making individuals interact across ethnic lines seems to be a major difficulty because evidence suggests that, when given a choice, people prefer to interact within, rather between, ethnic groups. However, "there is also evidence to support that once contact is established between members of ethnic groups, it tends to produce changes in attitudes between these groups" (Lewin, 1948, p. 216). The direction of change depends largely on the conditions under which contact has taken place: "favorable" conditions tend to reduce prejudice, "unfavorable," ones may increase prejudice and group tensions (Amir, 1976, p. 277).

As regards the setting and interpersonal means of change, Lewin's (1948) contention is that: "Ideologies and stereotypes which govern intergroup relations should not be viewed as individual character traits, but they are anchored in cultural standards, that their stability and change depends largely on happenings in groups as groups" (p. 209). Taking into account the social nature of a person's ideologies and stereotypes concerning ethnic relations the change process is "functionally similar to change in culture." It is a process in which changes of knowledge and beliefs, changes of values and standards, changes of emotional attachments and needs, and changes of everyday conduct occur not piecemeal and independently of each other, but within the framework of the individual total life in the group" (Lewin, 1948, p. 58).

According to Lewin (1948) the intergroup intervention should not be perceived as a fixed institutional arrangement which utilizes a score of techniques to effect changes in participants. It is to be perceived as a dynamic, always changing operation, created for particular groups of participants who bring to the situation a certain set of characteristics as well as expectations, and who vary in their potential for change and for carrying over the effects of the intervention. The implications for intergroup encounters, as Lewin describes them, are that "social management proceeds in spiral steps, each of which is composed of a circle of planning, action and fact finding about the result of the action" (p. 206). In other words, each intervention should be perceived as a unique operation that requires a tailor made preparation, execution and evaluation, according to the participants' and their individualized needs and conditions.

It is an evident though neglected fact that a well planned and executed intergroup encounter experience is not sufficient to insure the transferability of the changes experienced by participants to real life situations, which is of course, the prime interest of the interventionists. Lewin (1948) expresses this notion as follows: "Even a good and successful workshop, however, seems seldom to have the chance to lead long range improvements in the field of intergroup relations--we are facing here a question which is of prime importance for any social change, namely, the problem of permanence" (p. 209). We will be referring later to measures that should be taken by interventionists to contribute to better transferability of intergroup initiated encounter results.

Summing up the main theoretical guidelines underlying intergroup-initiated encounters as introduced above, practicing interventionists assert that: (1) contact between parties involved in ethnic conflicts is essential; that (2) contact under favorable conditions will bring about (3) changes in attitudes and that in order to affect participants' values, emotions, and behavior they should undergo (4) a process of re-education which must (5) take place within the individual's total life in the group. Intergroup-initiated encounters are social arrangements which should be comprised of three main components dynamically inter-related to each other as an ongoing spiral. The components are (6) planning, action, and fact finding. However, in order to preserve the changes in individuals acquired within the group culture (7) follow-up measures should be adopted to carry over these effects to real life situations.

These seven theoretical guidelines will be elaborated and specified within the context of the operational model which we will suggest for the purpose of establishing intergroup initiated encounters.

Analytic Framework and Operational Implications

Intergroup initiated encounters or, as they are termed by Lewin, "intergroup workshops" would be perceived as open system organizational arrangements in order to meet the optimal conditions for effecting change in their participants. We suggest adopting Katz and Kahn's (1978) model of open systems to describe the structural components necessary for their operation. Our assumption is that the establishment of these subsystems will enhance considerably the functioning of organizations initiated for the purpose of intergroup encounters between Arabs and Jews. Open system theory, by formulating structural components, helps to sketch the organizational prerequisites for a continuous institutional activity and, if followed, will assure an important infrastructure for the organization's optimal performance.

The facts of organizational functioning, according to Katz and Kahn, (1978) can be described "with respect to five basic subsystems: (1) Production subsystems concerned with the work that gets done; (2) Supportive systems of procurement, disposal and institutional relations; (3) Maintenance subsystems for tying people to their functional roles; (4) Adaptive subsystems concerned with organizational change; (5) Managerial subsystems for the direction, adjudication and control of the many subsystems and activities of the structure (p. 52)." We are incorporating these five subsystems and their functions into the model of operation of intergroup encounters. Another operational dimension of intergroup initiated encounters that we suggest be considered is the dynamic component to these encounters. By "dynamic" we mean the sequence of activities which contribute to the accomplishment of the encounters. We perceive the dynamic dimension as comprised of the following phases: infrastructural inputs, input to encounter preparation, encounter processes, encounter outcomes and evaluation and follow-up to determine the transferability of encounter impacts. Underlying the dynamic dimension suggested here is the open system theory notion of the "cycle of events" (Katz and Kahn, 1978) which constitute the steps necessary for the organizational goals. Lewin's (1948) notion of "a spiral of steps each of which is composed by a circle of planning, action and fact finding about the result of the action" (p. 206), also contributes to the idea of the cycle of events.

Based on the seven theoretical guidelines formulated above, we have developed a model which incorporates the structural as well as the dynamic components necessary for an optimal intergroup initiated encounter. Here we will focus briefly on only four of the components, to illustrate and discuss the social science principles underlying them.

Input variables are very important components in the process of socialization, and they are the least addressed by Lewin's work (1948, 1958) regarding change. Perhaps we should consider his guidance for diagnosing each specific intervention as indicating his awareness of the importance of these input variables. However, students of adult socialization point to the importance of participants' initial characteristics (traits, attitudes, sociodemographic variables) in determining the scope of change they may attain following interpersonal contacts (Brim and Wheeler, 1966; Amir, 1976; Feldman and Newcomb, 1969). Generally speaking, an initially favorable attitude of participants toward change will bring about this change. At this phase of preparation for intergroup encounter, it is important to match members attitudes toward contact, not allowing a confrontation between very polarized groups.

The status of the two ethnic groups should also be matched. If possible, it is preferable (according to Amir, 1976) to bring together members of a majority group and higher status members of the minority group. Also of importance during this phase is preparing members of the two groups taking part in the encounter to be realistic about the prospective change, as well as possible pains and conflicts which might accompany these processes (anticipatory socialization).

The next component focuses on the main·interpersonal processes which take place in an intensive encounter between two parties. The theoretical literature contributes to outlining the major processes which take place under these conditions. Lewin's (1958) "unfreezing," "moving" and "refreezing" of attitudes are the dominant processes here. Receiving less attention in the literature are Sherif's (1958) suggestions for pursuing superordinate goals which are of importance for the coexistence of the two parties. There is hardly any systematic literature that deals with techniques and sequence of activities to be applied at the phase of encounter between two ethnic groups. Schein and Bennis' (1965) account of human relation training is not sufficient to cover an area of practice where the conflict among participants emanates not merely from communication difficulties, but from real ideological differences. Lewin's statement (1948) is appropriate here: "The research needed for social practice can best be characterized as research for social management or social engineering." More systematic knowledge concerning the conditions and effects of various forms of social action is badly needed to guide group leaders in constructing better encounters.

The last two components we discuss here deal with, perhaps, the most difficult issue of intergroup initiated encounters, namely, the problem of transferability of the latter effects to real life situations. The difficulty of carrying over the effect of intergroup contacts of real life situations and preserving it for considerable periods of time stems from two sources: theoretical and ideological/existential. From a theoretical point of view, it is difficult to preserve any achieved personal changes from the effects of attrition and devaluation. Lewin (1958) indicated the importance of what is termed "refreezing," but he did not specify conditions for achieving this phase of individual change. Activities to keep norms (which have been refrozen at the end of encounters) from fading away include (a) carrying over to real life situations meaningful intergroup activities like working for common ends, or (b) participating in social action projects which unite and bring former members of the two groups into intimate contact. This phase of intergroup initiated encounters is missing in most plannings of such programs.

It needs to be implemented even though it is very costly and very difficult to operate.

The second difficulty in transferring intergroup encounters to
real life situations is as indicated before: ideological/existential.
The reality regarding Jewish-Arab relations is that political polari-
zation between the two groups is increasing due to the Palestinian issue.
The Palestinian issue which has gradually come to the fore since 1967,
is of extreme importance and salience in the minds of both Arabs and
Jews in Israel. For the Arabs, recognition as a nation deserving independence and a state of its own, is an essential national aspiration.
For the Jews, a Palestinian state constitutes a tremendous threat to
security and the continued existence of their own state. Thus, this
issue divides the two peoples, and the division does not, of course,
help to reinforce the cooperation and trust which were practiced, in
"cultural islands," in day to day interactions between Arabs and Jews
in Israel.

Intervention to promote Jewish-Arab Relations

It seems obvious that Arabs and Jews in Israel who are brought up
under historical, socio-political and socio-psychological circumstances
of separation, divergence and growing radicalism, are not likely to have
in the foreseeable future a peaceful coexistence in the country unless
some sort of intervention is carried out to bridge the gap between the
two sectors. Steady and meaningful social contacts seems to be a promising avenue to bridging this gap. Yet currently--although considerable numbers of both Jews and Arabs declared (in public opinion surveys)
their readiness for such contacts with members of the other group--only
a minority among both populations actually maintain such contacts. Most
of the day-to-day encounters between Jews and Arabs in the Israeli society are impersonal and do not fulfill the basic conditions required
for socially and psychologically constructive contact, namely equal
status, common interest and institutional support.

Optimal intervention programs involving initiated contacts between
Jews and Arabs may perhaps pave the way for better relations between
the two people; however, as long as they are carried out on small scale
micro level interventions only, their potential as creators of meaningful
change is undoubtedly limited.

The number and variety of micro level intervention programs in Arab-
Jewish relations in Israel during the eighties is considerable, and have

been growing since last surveyed (Stock, 1968). Yet, their contribution
as against the counter effects of the social, political and religious
forces, seems to be like a drop in the ocean. Also, not always because
of program faults, these programs reveal the following weaknesses: (a)
lack of infrastructure and resources, and as a consequence instability
in their operation and low professional standards; (b) engagement with
relatively small and self-selected populations (i.e.: "Persuading the
already persuaded"); (c) lack of official institutional support as well
as public legitimation; (d) engagement in discrete and generally short
term interventions, which usually come too late in the participants'
stage of socialization (adolescence and adulthood).

Hence, it is unrealistic to believe that the goal of bridging the
intergroup gaps between Arabs and Jews in Israel is attainable without
institutionalizing comprehensive, obligatory and well-planned long term
interventions within the national educational system. Through the educational system, intervention should be a continuous long-term endeavor,
starting as early as the kindergarten level and continuing through all
levels of education, and on into adulthood; content and methods of intervention should be accommodated to specific age groups and environmental circumstances.

Four major kinds of target-populations should be approached: (a)
Pupils of all levels of the educational system (from kindergarten to
university); (b) teachers and other educators at all levels of the
formal and informal educational system (such as general supervisors and
school principals, social education coordinators, etc.); (c) public
opinion leaders and community gatekeepers such as journalists, community
workers, local officials, etc.; (d) the public at large, and especially
the parent population.

The channels through which each of these target populations are
to be approached are different. Getting through to the first and second
of the above target populations is relatively easy, since they constitute captive audiences of the educational system. The third is a rather
tough nut to crack, yet important as a mediator to the fourth target-
population. However, intervention activities should be carried out
simultaneously within all of these target populations, in both the Arab
and the Jewish sectors of the population.

Macro level interventions are extremely important in view of (a)
the sociocultural theories which indicate that discriminatory behavior
is acquired as a result of the interaction between the individual and
his socio-cultural environment; and (b) the sociological proposition
regarding the necessity of strong public consensus for the actualization

of policies aiming at the reduction of inequalities and related inter-group conflicts. Supplemented by optimally planned initiated contacts at the micro levels, long-term macro level interventions may meaningfully promote Arab-Jewish relations, under even the continuous existential conditions of the unresolved political conflict.

REFERENCES

Amir, Y. (1976). "The role of intergroup contact in change of prejudice and ethnic relations," in Katz, P.A. (Ed.), Toward the elimination of racism. New York: Pergamon, pp. 245-308.

Brim, O., Wheeler, S. (1966). Socialization after childhood: Two essays. New York: Wiley.

Cohen, S.P., Kelman, H.C., Miller, F.D., Smith, B.L. (1977). "Evolving intergroup techniques for conflict resolution: An Israeli-Palestinian workshop." Journal of Social Issues, 33, pp. 165-189.

Feldman, K.A., & Newcomb, T.M. (1969). The impact of college on students. San Francisco: Jossey, Bass.

Fischer, (1983). "Third party consultation as a method of inter-group conflict resolution." Journal of Conflict Resolution, 27, 2, pp. 301-334.

Katz, D. & Kahn, R.L. (1978). The social psychology of organizations. New York: Wiley.

Lewin, K. (1948). Resolving social conflicts: Selected papers on group dynamics. New York: Harper.

Lewin, K. (1958). "Group decision and social change," in E. Maccoby et. al., (Eds.), Readings in social psychology. New York: Holt Rinehart, pp. 197-211.

Peled, T. (1980a). On social distance between Jews and Arabs in Israel. The Israel Institute of Applied Social Research, Research Report, pp. 19-21.

Peled, T. (1980b). "In Israel, diminishing hopes for peace." Public Opinion, Aug/Sept., pp. 54-56.

Peled, T., Bargal, D. (1983). Intervention activities in Arab-Jewish relations: Conceptualization, classification and evaluation. Submitted to Ford Foundation through the Israel Foundation Trustees, Jerusalem.

Schein, E., & Bennis, W. (1965). Personal and organizational change through group methods: The laboratory approach. New York: Wiley.

Sherif, M. (1958). "Superordinate goals in the reduction of intergroup Conflicts". American Journal of Sociology, 63, pp. 349-356.

Smooha, S., & Peretz, D. (1982). "The Arabs in Israel". The Journal of conflict resolution, 26, 3, pp. 451-484.

Stock, E. (1968). From conflict to understanding. New York: American Jewish Committee, Institute of Human Relations Pamphlet, No. 10.

Zemach, M. (1980). Attitudes of the Jewish majority in Israel towards the Arab minority. Jerusalem: The Van Leer Foundation, (An Interim Report in Hebrew).

Part II: Practical Theory

Jeanne M. Plas, Kathleen Hoover-Dempsey and Barbara Strudler Wallston observe that increasingly large numbers of contemporary American women have developed career as well as family commitments. These dual
roles have created female lives that are very different from typical
ones of a generation ago. In order to develop a theoretical approach
capable of understanding these lives, the researchers turned to a synthesis of selected social-psychological thinkers from that era, notably
Kurt Lewin, John Dewey and Arthur Bentley, together with contemporary
theorist Carolyn Sherif. This synthesis they think is capable of responding to a number of issues that are of crucial importance for the
lives of today's career-committed women. They say, "We are beginning an
empirical program which uses the interpersonal field concept as a way of
directing observation of the lives of career-committed women and interpreting data which result from the observations. The first stage of the
research program has begun...."

Emmy A. Pepitone in a careful, interesting way describes the historical and theoretical threads that connect and distinguish her work in
cooperation and competition from that of other well known names. She
begins with Triplett's (1897) examination of bicycle races under different conditions! Then deals with more familiar researchers: F. Allport,
May, Doob, Festinger, Thibaut, Kelley, Kagan, and Deutsch--especially
Deutsch. Of her own research, she says that she has tried to remedy a
lack in the research on children's role-enactment skills in different
periods by the study of their interactions when placed into some of the
diverse cooperative and competitive conditions she describes in this
article.

Along a really different line, Jerome S. Allender develops and supports the radical assertion that the practice of scientific research
might be a small part of what educational researchers do, but relevant
educational inquiry from the viewpoint of certain ideas and practices
put forward in the last ten years requires something more and different
from its researchers. This assertion might have surprised Kurt Lewin,
who seemed to think that all research was scientific, and who probably
would not have made any distinction between educational and other research. But it is the departure of Lewin's thinking from the classic

Aristotelian model of science in the early part of the century, and later development of action research with his colleagues in this country that planted some of the seeds of the new paradigm espoused by Allender.

Eugene H. Stivers proposes the essential outlines of a Lewinian action research model that, again, goes somewhat beyond Lewin's work but not beyond his spirit. This model is collaborative, dialectic, and presents the outcomes of its work in metaphoric form.

Concluding this section, Rupert Nacoste presents research which is influenced by Lewin's philosophy of science, though not his field theory per se. And though Lewinian in having theoretical and practical implications, it is in particular in this tradition because it emphasizes the importance of understanding individual responses in relation to external and, or, situational variables. This emphasis is against the general tendency of research in social psychology (including work on affirmative action) to study psychological processes themselves without much concern for their relationship with other factors. Here again is an example of research that Kurt Lewin might be associated with if he were alive today.

Support, Reference, and Gatekeeping Functions Within the Interpersonal Field: Lewin Contributions

Jeanne M. Plas, Kathleen Hoover-Dempsey and Barbara Strudler Wallston

George Peabody College of Vanderbilt University

Increasingly large numbers of contemporary American women have developed career commitment as well as family commitment. These dual roles have created female lives that are very different from typical female lives of a generation ago. In order to develop a theoretical approach capable of understanding these lives we have turned to selected social-psychological thinkers from that era, notably Kurt Lewin, John Dewey and Arthur Bentley. We have crafted a synthesis of their work with that of a contemporary social psychologist, Carolyn Sherif. The result of this synthesis is promising; we think it capable of responding to a number of issues that are of crucial importance for the lives of today's career committed women.

The work of Kurt Lewin has been crucial to our thinking and it is the Lewinian influences that will be presented in detail here. Some of Lewin's empirical results, as well as significant portions of his theoretical work, have guided the development of the model; his legacy has been an important inspiration and we recognize our debt.

THE MODEL

The model was constructed for the purpose of providing a theoretical tool that could guide a major research program concerned with the relationship of social environment variables and patterns of experienced stress and nourishment to important physical and mental health outcome variables within the lives of women who have committed themselves to work outside the home. Preliminary empirical work (Plas & Wallston, 1983; Wallston, Hoover-Dempsey & Plas, 1984) had identified significant relationships between self-valuing and variables such as perceived level of support, number of persons within the field perceived as important, and encouragement given to others. Subsequently, during the process of attempting to uncover additional meaningful patterns within a large and rich data set, it became clear that, indeed, there is nothing so practical as a good theory, and that further attempts to understand the

social realities inherent in our data or to collect additional information would likely prove self-defeating in the absence of more adequate
theory.

The Interpersonal Field

We view the Lewinian concept of life space as a tool for the theoretical construal of all those physical and psychological dynamics from
which motivated behavior arises. The interpersonal field described in
our model can be thought of as a life space. In addition to the individual, the field contains three regions which we view as capable of representing the entire array of relationship functions that are important
within contemporary American lives.

We have concluded that the Lewinian life space concept is most flexible and theoretically strong when identified regions represent such
variables as functions or goals rather than persons. Sherif has contributed to our thinking here; when we consider the notions of social environment and attitudinal schemata, we are able to more clearly construe
an individual's transaction with another person as a transaction at any
point in time with but one aspect of the person or, put another way, a
transaction involving one function of a person-person relation. Lewin
himself gave some direction to this interpretation of his work when he
wrote of the general life situation which serves as a remote background
for the momentary situation which is held in consciousness (Lewin, 1936,
18 ff.) With reference to our model, we see engagement with a single
relational function (such as support) as momentary while recognizing
the consistent potential for bringing other functions to the fore. In
our view, if one sees the life space primarily in terms of individuals
or regions of persons identified by virtue of conventionally defined
independent variables (e.g., race, gender, SES), a great deal of flexibility is lost. It is more useful to incorporate life space regions
that represent functions so that it is possible to think in terms of the
locomotion of the person or environmental "others" from one region to
another depending on the situation being viewed.

Thus, while the regions identified within the model are named as if
they contain persons (support persons, reference persons, and persons-
to-be-reckoned-with), it is important to remember that our emphasis is
on function rather than individual identity. For example, a person who
is inhabiting the support region is there by virtue of the support func-

tion which characterizes the person-environment relationship at the time of interest. It is not that a given individual is always a support person; rather, person X at times provides the function of support and in so doing is part of the support person region--while at other times he or she may fill other functions, thus appearing as a part of other regions. Thus, unlike conventional independent variables, the functional variables we think important to emphasize represent much more momentary characteristics. Such a construal allows us to capture more fully the social-psychological aspects of the life space at any point in time.

Support persons. Support functions within a relationship through the exchange of instrumental or affective resources of a personal or work-related nature. There may or may not be reciprocity of exchange, at any given time or across time, with respect to type and amount of supportive resource; however, as long as one of the involved persons is giving support on some dimension and the other is receiving it, the relation is characterized as supportive. The two persons may be involved in offering supportive resources on different dimensions (i.e., one offers affective support, the other instrumental) and the amount of support may vary as defined by frequency or intensity. As an illustration of one possible variation of a supportive relation, consider the transaction involving person A who infrequently offers substantial support, such as auto repair work and gutter cleaning, to person B, who quite frequently offers to person A small bits of encouragement for a variety of career-oriented tasks. A person is classified as a support person only during the time that he or she is exchanging support with the individual whose interpersonal field is of identified interest.

We have explicated the subcategories of instrumental and affective support based on extant literature (e.g., Bell, 1981; Sarason, Levine, Basham & Sarason, 1983) and pilot work of our own, though we shall not present them here.

Reference Persons. The reference function is fulfilled by persons whose professional or personal characteristics provide standards for evaluative comparison. Reciprocity may or may not exist in reference functions; thus, an individual in the reference group of person A may or may not find person A in his or her own reference group. An individual is considered a reference person only during those times when the reference function has been activated within a relation involving the person whose interpersonal field is being plotted.

We have divided the reference person region of the interpersonal field conceptually into three areas of reference possibility: general resources, personal, and professional. The general resources category

incorporates assets perceived in themselves to be at least somewhat
self-generative: financial resources, personal background, social support system, intellectual resources, and physical resources (e.g., health,
energy). The personal category includes any of the following dimensions:
interpersonal skills, personality characteristics, values and attitudes,
physical appearance, life style, and physical skills. Finally, professional reference dimensions include standards for competence, status
and recognition, productivity, and professional style.

Four qualities of a reference relationship have been identified;
these qualities are characteristic of all three subcategories of this
interpersonal field component. The first of these is the degree to which
the reference person is viewed as similar to the self (e.g., Bleda &
Castore, 1973; Gruder, 1971). The second concerns the direction of
the evaluative judgment (i.e., the person viewed as "worse," "same,"
or "better" on the given dimension). The third quality represents the
degree to which the reference dimension is considered to be important
by the perceiving person. The fourth quality concerns reciprocity. The
theoretical construction of this region of the interpersonal field allows
us to capture in a logical fashion the wide variety of reference relationships that are important for daily living. Use of the model permits
the specification of targeted professional reference relationships.
For example, one such relationship may operate on the dimensions of
productivity and professional style with little reciprocity of reference,
within a relationship where the reference person is viewed as dissimilar
to the self and "better" on the specific dimensions, both of which are
seen as highly important by the perceiving person.

Persons-to-be-reckoned-with. When individuals act as persons-to-be-
reckoned-with they are functioning as gatekeepers who modulate the flow
of resources available to the individual; these resources may include
such things as time, finances, energy, information and other important
material and non-material contingencies. Persons-to-be-reckoned-with
relations are characterized by power (either direct or indirect), and
reciprocity of influence may be unequal.

The concept of the gatekeeper within the classic Lewin food study
(1951) has inspired our development of this region of the interpersonal
field. In that study, Lewin identified the housewife as the person who
controlled the channels through which food reached the table. He was
interested in the psychological factors which influenced the gatekeeper
and he identified cognitive and value-oriented variables associated with
gatekeepers which guided the flow of food resources within the American
home during World War II.

The persons-to-be-reckoned-with region of the interpersonal field contains persons who function as gatekeepers in much the same sense. However, a difference of emphasis should be noted between our work and that of Lewin. Whereas he was interested almost exclusively in representing the psychological factors influencing the person who acts as gatekeeper, we are equally interested in understanding the factors that are salient for the person whose access to resources is being controlled by a gatekeeper.

Of the four regions of the interpersonal field, the persons-to-be-reckoned-with function has been the least studied within the literature. Yet, we believe that relationships of this type represent a sizable proportion of daily transactions, especially for career-committed women. These relationships are required and contain power, either direct or indirect. Relationships with these persons are required in that we may not choose to be involved in persons-to-be-reckoned-with functions but feel we must be; the gatekeeping role that an individual occupies is one that we are somehow bound to honor. Our relationship with such persons is characterized by power in that we have direct or indirect influence upon them or they upon us; or, there is mutuality of power and impact. By direct power, we mean control over needed resources; indirect power refers to influence that is not coercive. Often, persons-to-be-reckoned-with influence us because they influence others who are close to us. The following list provides examples of required influential roles that may be characterized by gatekeeping functions from time to time: boss, secretary, sister-in-law, spouse's best friend, landlord, tenant, colleague, client, neighbor, child's teacher, auto repairperson, the ex-wife of a husband or significant other, and so forth.

Explication of this interpersonal field region is still at a preliminary stage of development. Currently, we are investigating several aspects of the region (for example, the individual's awareness of the presence of these function within her personal and professional spheres; attitudes towards self in relation to individuals who are functioning as persons-to-be-reckoned-with; and perceptions of the behavioral and attitudinal styles of persons who are viewed as often exhibiting the gatekeeping function). A person's description of this function may reveal, for example, that she is aware of this interpersonal field region; recognizes that most of her relations within it tend to involve direct power functions; tends to perceive herself as highly capable of participating effectively in such relations within the professional but not the personal sphere; that relatively few of the gatekeeping relations she considers relevant are located within the professional sphere; and that reciprocity of relation is generally equal in the professional sphere but not in her personal sphere, where she perceives persons-to-be-reckoned-with as having power over her.

We consider our understanding of the persons-to-be-reckoned-with region to be less satisfactory than our knowledge of the support and reference regions, at present, perhaps because this area of interpersonal functioning has received little attention in the theoretical and empirical literature. Like Lewin, we perceive the gatekeeping function to be fundamentally important for the conduct of daily living—both in the workplace and in the home. For example, we suspect that the work-oriented woman's experience of stress and nourishment is linked closely to the ways in which she deals effectively and ineffectively with individuals who are functioning as persons-to-be-reckoned-with, particularly as she finds herself moving toward or away from sources of reference possibility and support. A wide variety of specific hypotheses emerge from a consideration of this region relative to the functioning of the total interpersonal field; several of those which currently intrigue us are presented below as we discuss use of the model.

Functional relationships among regions. This model of the interpersonal field is indebted heavily to the Lewinian notion of a dynamic life space. The full model is to be viewed as dynamic rather than static, allowing for shifts of environmental individuals from one region to another as well as shifts of P (person who is being studied) from region to region. In addition, with respect to size, we regard the expansion and shrinkage of a region across time to be of observational importance. For Lewin, topographical geometry considerations prevented a full appreciation of changes in size of various life space regions. However, we are persuaded that it may be quite important to plot these size shifts in order to capture such information as the relative size and weighted importance of a support region for an individual who experiences great stress on an almost continual basis emerging from the other two regions. Issues related to the nature of the flux of the interpersonal field for specific groups of persons, such as professional or blue collar workers, can be addressed best through longitudinal research. It is quite conceivable that the nature of such flux is related in a significant way to mental and physical outcome variables.

It is expected that overlap of functions may occur within any one relationship; an individual may be perceived as providing support, reference, and gatekeeping functions, or some combination of two or three. As Lewin suggests, when a person within the environment is operating within overlapped regions, a relative weighting of the various regional functions is in operation. One function predominates during any selected time period.

We conjecture that the degree of region overlap may constitute a measure of intimacy and further, that the degree of overlap to be found in the professional sphere may be related to experiences of stress and nourishment as well as measures of mental and physical well-being. We further hypothesize that the extent to which overlapped personal sphere relationships contain frequent functioning within the reference and persons-to-be-reckoned-with regions (relative to less frequent functioning in the support region) may be related importantly to indicators of depressed levels of mental and physical health.

GENERAL CONSIDERATIONS AND USES OF THE MODEL

The explanatory potential of the interpersonal field model is strengthened as a result of its ability to capture current and relevant person-environment transactions at the same time that the influences of the past and future can be taken into account. While some of Lewin's contemporaries accused him of ahistorical thinking, we agree with his interpretation of his work as quite concerned with historical data and its indirect influences on current behavior (Lewin, 1938). He makes the point that anyone who is concerned with psychological data is ultimately concerned with history since such data are the product of historical influences. We view the Lewinian approach to the variable of time as a transactional approach that recognizes that past experiences and future aspirations always inform the present moment and that any representation of motivated behavior requires that time-based influences be included. Through use of two approaches, the interpersonal field concept allows for such inclusion while at the same time focusing attention on present functioning. The first approach recognizes that the specific representation of regions for any individual is dependent upon the phenomenology of P and that the experience of P is significantly dependent upon her view of past and future as well as present. The second approach requires that shifts of regions be inspected across time in order to provide a richer understanding of the influence of support, reference, and gate-keeping functions on the lives of career-committed women. Thus, the life space concept allows for consideration of time in both a linear and non-linear fashion.

We are beginning an empirical program which uses the interpersonal field concept as a way of directing observation of the lives of career-

committed women and interpreting data which result from the observations.
The first stage of the research program has begun and involves empirically based description of the persons-to-be-reckoned-with region.
When sufficient knowledge is available for all three regions--support,
reference, and gatekeeping functions--we will inspect the patterns of
interpersonal fields for three cohorts of career women (entry level,
early-established, mid career-established). We think it important to
observe the interpersonal fields of cohorts from three gender-associated
work categories: female-dominated, male-dominated, and mixed. Research
questions call for a longitudinal look at issues such as the relative
size and weight of the various interpersonal field regions vis-a-vis
stress, nourishment, mental and physical outcome variables, and levels
of personal and career success. We suspect that the ways in which different groups of career-oriented women compare themselves to others, seek
and use various sources and types of social support, and deal with gatekeeping functions will create identifiable patterns which can distinguish
highly successful women from less successful women on both personal and
professional dimensions.

REFERENCES

Bell, R.R. (1981). Friendships of women and of men. Psychology of
    Women Quarterly, 5, 402-417.

Bleda, P.R., & Castore, C.H. (1973). Social comparison, attraction
    and choice of a comparison other. Memory and Cognition, 1, 420-424.

Cobb, S. (1979). Social support and health through the life course.
    In M. W. Riley (Eds.), Aging from birth to death: Interdisciplinary
    perspectives. New York: American Association for the Advancement
    of Science.

Dewey, J., & Bentley, A. (1949). Knowing and the known. Reprinted in
    R. Handy & E.C. Harwood (Eds., 1973), Useful procedures of inquiry.
    Great Barrington, MA: Behavior Research Council.

Gibbs, J.C. (1979). The meaning of ecologically oriented inquiry in
    contemporary psychology. American Psychologist, 34(2), 127-140.

Gruder, C.L. (1971). Determinants of social comparison choices. Jour-
    nal of Experimental Social Psychology, 1, 473-489.

Hoover-Dempsey, K. (in press). Stress and coping among teachers:
    Experience in search of theory and science.

House, J.S. (1981). Work stress and social support. Reading, MA:
    Addison-Wesley.

Lewin, K. (1936). Principles of topological psychology. New York:
    McGraw-Hill.

Lewin, K. (1938). The conceptual representation and measurement of psychological forces. Contributions to psychological theory, I(4). Durham: Duke University Press.

Lewin, K. (1951). Field theory in social science. New York: Harper & Bros.

Liem, R., & Liem, Jr. (1978). Social class and mental illness reconsidered. The role of economic stress and social support. Journal of Health and Social Behavior, 19, 139-156.

Marrow, A.J. (1969). The practical theorist: The life of Kurt Lewin. New York: Basic Books.

Mueller, D.P. (1980). Social networks: A promising direction for research on the relationship of the social environment to psychiatric disorder. Social Science and Medicine, 14A, 145-161.

Plas, J.M., & Wallston, B.S. (1983). Women oriented toward male dominated careers: Is the reference group male or female? Journal of Counseling Psychology, 30, 46-54.

Plas, J.M., Hoover-Dempsey, K.V., & Wallston, B.S. (in press). A conceptualization of professional women's interpersonal fields: Social support, reference groups, and persons-to-be-reckoned-with. In I.G. Sarason & B.P. Sarason (Eds.), Social support: Theory research and application. The Hague: Martinus Nijhof.

Russo, N.F., & Vanden Bos, G.R. (1981). Women in the mental health delivery system. In W.H. Silverman (Ed.), A community mental health sourcebook for board and professional action. New York: Prager.

Sarason, I.G., Levine, H.H., Basham, R.B., & Sarason, B.R. (1983). Assessing social support: The social support questionnaire. Journal of Personality and Social Psychology, 44, 127-139.

Sherif, C.W. (1982). Needed concepts in the study of gender identity. Psychology of Women Quarterly, 6, 375-398.

Wallston, B.S., Alagna, S.W., DeVellis, B.M., & DeVellis, R.F. (1983). Social support and physical health. Health Psychology, Vol. 2, 367-392.

Wallston, B.S., Hoover-Dempsey, K.V., & Plas, J.M. (1984). Psychosocial variables and self-valuing among women in traditionally male and traditionally female career fields. (Manuscript submitted for publication).

A Continuation of Lewinian Research in the Study of Cooperation and Competition

Emmy A. Pepitone

Bryn Mawr College

Lewinian research most relevant to my own sort of investigations into cooperation and competition includes Lewin, Dembo, Festinger & Sears' (1944) study of level of aspiration, and Morton Deutsch's (1949 a, b) research on cooperation and competition. In the present paper I will touch on this confluence and how it relates to my work.*

A. Distinctions between and within Competitive and Cooperation Conditions

Of course one can date the experimental study of competition and cooperation to Triplett's (1897) examination of bicycle races under different conditions, closely followed by Mayer's (1903) studies of quantity and quality of German school children's performance in the thriving German public school system; F.H. Allport's (1924) face-to-face groups and coaction, or May and Doob's (1937) inventory of the status of the field in this area. Over those three decades, each one of the studies addressed an increasingly greater number of theoretical issues in that area. But none were as profoundly influential as Deutsch's (1949) conceptualization and accompanying study carried out at MIT. It rested on the assumption that competition and cooperation constitute conditions of interdependence. That cooperation meant promotive interdependence could be readily seen; that competition may be as powerful a condition of interdependence, albeit contrient, was a considerable conceptual lead indeed. The source of both of these interdependencies was attributed solely to the goal relations inherent in both conditions.

During the subsequent decade, numerous studies appeared, documenting differing kinds of behaviors under the two goal conditions (Hammond & Goldman, 1961; Raven & Eachus, 1963), not to mention Deutsch's (1957, 1958, 1962) continued involvement. Interestingly, and yet perhaps pre-

*Her own investigations are reported in a companion article, in section IIB, "Children in Cooperation and Competition: The Role of Entitlement and Deservedness."

dictably, it was Deutsch himself, as well as two former Lewin students (Thibaut & Kelley, 1959) who were at the forefront in changing the direction of this research from emphasis on the type of behavior displayed in the two respective conditions, to personal preferences for being in either of these situations. That is, based on the increasingly prevalent exchange theoretical formulations of the 60's and 70's, dyadic interpersonal relations came to be studied almost exclusively within experimental gaming models. Gone were the large live interacting groups, and the corresponding numbers of assorted experimenters and interaction and process observers; the model almost exclusively involved two subjects, confronted with a rational matrix of gaming strategies offering different combinations of relative gains and losses to the two players who had to choose between them to benefit themselves and the partner in various ways. In game theoretical research, the choice from among several limited options in fact is the sole behavior that is studied; self-orientations or other-orientations respectively, are inferred. Interest is not in the varieties of behavior, but merely in a choice within the matrix that presumably indicates the subjects preference for, or motivational orientation toward, a given reward distribution. Note here, too, that the conceptualization of motivation has also changed drastically from activities aimed at reaching contrient or common goals, to individually distributed rewards that may at best be divided and shared between two or more persons. The counterpart in developmental research employed methodologies scaled down to children's games, that also required a child to choose--often quite ingeniously--between several alternatives benefiting him/herself or the other child (e.g. Nelson & Madsen, 1969; Kagan & Madsen, 1972; Kagan & Knight, 1980).

When I began my series of studies of children's cooperation and competition in the early seventies, it was clearly not mainstream research. In fact, I build on Deutsch's earliest conceptualizations of interdependence, though with a difference: I considered two sources of interdependence: not only those created by different goal structures, but also interdependencies created by different task structures, each varying along a dimension of similarity and of required contact. Deutsch's (1982) latest theoretical analysis is relevant here: it continues his concern with types of cooperation-competition. However, he conceives of this dimension as bi-polar, as a pro-con distribution, ranging from relations such as close friends, team-mates, co-workers and the like, at the cooperative end, to personal enemies, divorced couples, political opponents and so forth, on the other end. Of course he readily admits to oversimplification inherent in such dichotomizations. I take issue with this categorization not so much on these grounds, but rather because it sets up false opposites. Based on research evidence presented later, it would appear conceptually more correct, and empirically more useful, to consider cooperative and competitive situations as two distinctly different social fields. Different constellations of forces are created--the degree of difference being a function of particular patterns of goal and task interdependence as is described below--and the respective force fields giving rise to qualitatively different kinds of social behaviors. The research implication here is that each of these social conditions demands separate study, with finer distinctions made within each, and emphasis on the resulting behaviors within each. It follows further that concepts and theories that have been found useful in determining directions for, and analysis of, research into competitive conditions have at best a limited usefulness when considering problems of interaction under cooperative conditions.

Over the years, we have begun to build a categorization scheme of different types of competitive and cooperative conditions, respectively. It rests on differences resulting from variously combined dimensions of goal relationships and task relationships, as shown in figure 1.

FIGURE 1

Dimensional Bases for

Conditions of Cooperation and Competition

Goal Characteristics

    Goal Similarity   0% _____ 100%
                   No Commonality   Identity

    Goal Interdependence
            Contriency   0% _____ 100%

            Promotivity   0% _____ 100%

Task Characteristics

    Task Similarity   0% _____ 100%
                   No Commonality   Identity

    Task Interdependence   0% _____ 100%
                No Interaction   Continuous
                                             Interaction

The major patterns, with major differences both within and between competitive and cooperative conditions are outlined next.

Distinctions within competitive conditions

Coaction

In coaction, each person works on an unconnected task; by definition, no contact is required. Thus, task interdependence is zero. Activities may vary in degree of similarity as well as in degree of goal contriency. A classroom during a period of "seat work" may serve as a prototype: each child sits in her/his seat, side by side, filling out pages in workbooks. Assume the teacher created what is generally known as an "individualized learning situation": each child works at her own unique level of proficiency and speed, trying to fill in answers on a particular page that is different from her neighbor. From the teacher's viewpoint, and also that of some social psychologists (Johnson & Johnson, 1974) this is a wholly individualistic achievement situation; the child is concerned with his own progress only. Hence this is a non-competitive situation; at most the pupil is competing against himself, trying to best his previous record. From our point of view, there are a number of task- and goal similarities (activities around filling out the page, including similar workbooks, use of pencil, working within a limited time period, being "checked" and eventually evaluated by the teachers, etc.) to make it more correct to consider this condition as a minimal competitive learning situation. It represents exactly what Allport (1924) referred to as coaction, with "the sights and sounds of others doing something" constituting the minimal conditions for the occurrence of competition. Given a minimum of achievement motivation such as is likely to be present in most school rooms, some similarity of activities and individual goals will turn this presumably non-interdependent situation into one of competition. The dynamic process involved is that of social comparison.[1]

---

[1] Since our focus here is on Lewin and those associated with him, let me remind us of a bit of history that we may all know, but is rarely acknowledged: namely, that the seeds of social comparison theory were sown by Festinger (1942a,b) well over a decade before appearance of his landmark Human Relations article by that name in 1954. I am, of course, referring to his demonstrations and interpretation of shifts in levels of aspiration, including the role of normative group standards and the unique case of unidirectional upward striving in the case of abilities.

Our series of studies support the assumption of a tripartite process of social comparison that is postulated to occur whenever two or more persons perceive each other as relevant in achievement settings (Pepitone, 1972). First, in order to assess oneself or another in terms of progress made, relative success and so on, attentional processes must be engaged so that others or their performance outcomes may be observed. Second, these processes are closely followed, and often intermingle with, evaluational processes which allow inferences about relative standings, about the level of opponents' abilities, strengths and weaknesses, tactics and so forth. Third, motivational processes are aroused in form of achievement-related motives as a result of conclusions drawn from these inferences. One of the salient characteristics of this process is that it may be initiated at any point in the cycle, by any one of the three subprocesses. Thus, highly motivated persons may wish to assess progress of their competitors, hence attend to the others' performance, conclude that the neighbor is about to finish, and increase their own speed. Yet a child's mere attention to another for some point of information about their similar assignments may evoke the other two processes as well.[2] As similarity of activities in which various children engage increases, so does the amount of non-verbal attention paid to others (Pepitone & Hannah, 1980). Social comparison is increased still more as similarity of goals is increased and goal contriency becomes explicit.

In coactive situations--aside from the level of motivation brought to the situation--the degree of competition present is a function of degree of similarity between individual task assignments and similarity of contrient goals. By definition, in coaction, task interdependence is zero; hence, physical and verbal interaction is generally absent in coaction, and nonverbal social comparison the prevalent dynamic process.

---

[2]Here again, a similarity may be noted between this conceptualization of a circular relationship between the three behavioral processes and Deutsch's (1982) postulating different cognitive, motivational and moral dispositions people bring to their social relationships and the cyclic process existing between these psychological orientations and social relations such that any orientations can induce or be induced by a given type of interdependency.

Competitive counteraction

Some competition, however, does require interaction. In what we call competitive counteraction contact is required. In some games such as chess, tennis, wrestling or other "contact" sports, maximal task interdependence exists in that each move by A requires B's countermove. Competitive counteraction is differentiated from coaction not only because it requires overt task-related interaction, but also because of its implied demands for interactive skills necessary to execute these tasks. These skills tend to require a certain level of development and experience in anticipating behavior of others that is not demanded in coaction. In the latter condition, by definition, interaction is not required, individuals need only to possess simple assessment skills to evaluate their own and their competitor's status. Is he ahead? If so, I must speed up; he has made four wagons--I must get more blocks to make a longer train than he, etc.

To be sure, there are coactive situations in which more complex inferential skills are also required. But it is typically in counteraction that formal reasoning and emphatic understanding are required, since one competitor must anticipate the other's move, prepare his/her own defense, and the likely response and counter-response, and so on. This is important because, as contrasted with cooperation, competition is often considered a more "natural" response in small children. Not only is there crosscultural evidence that casts some doubt on this assertion (Graves, 1976; Graves & Graves, 1983), but in fact competitive situations may be highly complex, even though research-wise we have almost exclusively studied behaviors in simple counteractive situations.

Distinctions within cooperative conditions

A somewhat different mix of task and goal characteristics yields different patterns of cooperation. As a beginning, three major types are distinguished.

Colabor

    We refer to situations that seem to constitute the minimal coopera-
tive condition as that of <u>colabor</u>. In fact, it corresponds to coaction
in that no interpersonal contact is required--i.e. task interdependence
is zero. Task similarity may vary anywhere from zero (or none) to task
identity; the difference resides in presence of similar or shared goals.
A typical example is that of an assembly line, where each worker may have
to perform a different task which ultimately gets combined into one product. It should be apparent that in situations where individuals are
cut off from access to this common goal experience the situation will in
fact resemble coactive competition from the worker's perspective. Thus,
these conditions of minimal interdependence can--and we believe do--easi-
ly fluctuate between coaction and colabor. The difference is in the
goal structure which, in colabor, may vary from various degrees to identity of goal structure.

    Permit me here another small digression on the concept of group
goal, since in the early post-Lewinian period at the Research Center for
Group Dynamics it certainly constituted a lively topic of inquiry, if
not of equal all-consuming interest to all researchers present. Some
are content to refer to identity of individual goals as a "group goal."
Just how, theoretically, individual goals may be transformed into a
group goal still remains as much of an unsolved conceptual issue as it
did then. Deutsch in his early writings emphasized substitutability of
members' goal strivings as the essence of promotive interdependence.
In the increasingly behavioristic climate of the 50's, the concept of
group goal was imperceptibly being replaced by that of group reward. A
current refinement was provided by Slavin (1983), who distinguishes among
cooperative incentive structures between those given for performance of
the "group-as-a-whole" vs. group rewards based on each person's individual performance in their contribution to the group. This is a useful
conceptual clarification; yet, to my mind, there is a significant difference between the meaning of group rewards as it refers to an external
evaluation of one sort or another placed on a group's accomplishment it-
self--be it based on a group score or a summed score--as contrasted with
the <u>objectives</u> of the group and goal strivings inherent in the original
concept of a group goal. This distinction may be particularly relevant
to learning settings, considering the important literature on extrinsic
vs. intrinsic motivation (e.g. Condry, 1977; Deci et al, 1981).

    As far as the minimal cooperative situations of colabor are concern-
ed, presence of such a common objective tends to be accompanied by some

interpersonal interaction, even if none is required. One is reminded here of the old Hartshorne and May (1928) workroom situation, where a small group of women started out in a coactive situation that, through creation of shared goals, was effectively turned into one of colabor, and, by increased contact, showed signs of the more complex types of cooperations that are next examined.

Coordinative collaboration

We single out as the next minimal interactive cooperative situation one in which interaction toward a common goal is not required, but at least minimal task-interdependence exists in a mutual exchange relation that satisfies participants' individual goals. Personal goals may be entirely different, may overlap, or vary anywhere along a continuum of goal similarity. In these situations, task relationships are established along lines of reciprocal assistance. This is most apt to occur in dyads--a "tit-for 'tat'" helping characterized by the proverbial "you scratch my back and I scratch yours."

An example of an experimental task developed for the study of children's behaviors in competitive and cooperative situations that falls into this category is Nelson & Madsen's (1969) marble pull game. Here, a desirable object in the middle of a table could be obtained by one child pulling the object on an attached string toward him/herself only if the child on the opposite end of the table let go of his/hers. This is the prototype of so many relationships that occur in school, at work, or in presumably "intimate" relationships, that I felt it constituted a separate category. These situations are in fact an analogue to competitive counteractive situations, differing only on the simple goal dimension: contrient in the one case, promotive in the other.

This "coordination of activities in order for individuals to obtain what they want" (Bryan, 1975) is frequently accepted as the standard definition of cooperation. Indeed, if such collaborative exchange relationships become formalized, they may assume characteristics of task role division. However, we prefer a separate category for situations to be described next where the dynamics of role-relationships assume such complexities as to deserve a separate study.

Role-related cooperation

In colabor, the only source of interdependence is, by definition, goal commonality; in coordinative collaboration it is the interdependent task relationship. In role-related cooperation each of the two sources of interdependence combine to make this the condition of greatest potential member interdependence. The stress is on potential, because there is no assurance that in each situation where strong role enactment requirements exist, individual persons involved will be able and/or willing to carry them out. The label emphasizes the dominant function of both task roles and group roles, a distinction that has been made by Benne and Sheets back in 1948. The model of differential member assignment to fulfill diverse task requirements is exemplified by Aronson's (1978) "jigsaw program," in which each pupil is assigned one part of a learning problem, the solution of which is needed by all members in a small group. The concept of group roles figured prominently in the early days of the Bethel laboratory. It has subsequently and almost inexplicably been largely neglected both in research and practice; yet it is inconceivable that a work group engaged in tackling anything but the simplest kind of collaborative situations could get very far without participants that could mediate disputes, draw out silent members, and otherwise engage in what used to be referred to as "socio-emotional roles."

If the study of adult role-related cooperation has all but disappeared, investigation of children's role enactment skills at different periods in their development may be said to have never really gotten off the ground; the "role taking skills" discussed by developmental psychologists such as Flavell (1968), Selman (1971) and others, while tangentially related, are basically conceptually different. Some of my research tries to remedy this lack by the study of children's interactions when placed into some of the diverse competitive and cooperative conditions that I have described.

REFERENCES

Allport, F.H. (1924). Social psychology. Boston: Houghton Mifflin.

Aronson, E. (1978). The jigsaw classroom. Beverly Hills, CA: Sage Publications.

Benne, K., & Sheats, P. (1948). Functional roles of group members. Journal of Social Issues, 4, 41-49.

Bryan, J.H. (1975). Children's cooperation and helping behavior. In E.M. Hetherington (Ed.), _Review of child development research_, 5. Chicago: University of Chicago Press.

Condry, J. (1977). Enemies of exploration: Self-initiated vs. other-initiated learnings. _Journal of Personality and Social Psychology_, 35, No. 7.

Deci, E.L., Betley, G., Kahle, Jr., Abrams, L., & Porac, J. (1981). When trying to win: Competition and intrinsic motivation. _Personality and Social Psychology Bulletin_, 7, 1, pp. 79-83.

Deutsch, M. (1949a). A theory of competition and cooperation. _Human Relations_, 2, 129-151.

_____. (1949b). An experimental study of the effect of cooperation and competition upon group process. _Human Relations_, 2, 199-231.

Deutsch, M. (1957). Conditions affecting cooperation: I. Factors related to the initiation of cooperation. II. Trust and cooperation. Final technical report for the office of Naval Research.

Deutsch, M. (1962). Cooperation and trust: Some theoretical notes. In _Nebraska Symposium on Motivation_, M.R. Jones (Ed.) University of Nebraska Press.

Deutsch, M. (1982). _Interdependence and psychological orientation_. In Derlega, V. J. & Grzelak, J. _Cooperation and helping behavior_. New York: Academic Press.

Festinger, L. (1942a). Wish, expectation and group standards as factors influencing level of aspiration. _Journal of Abnormal Social Psychology_, 37, 184-200.

Festinger, L. (1942b). A theoretical interpretation of shifts of level of aspiration. _Psychological Review_, 49, 235-250.

Flavell, J.H. (1968). _The development of role-taking and communication skills in children_. New York: Wiley.

Graves, N.B. (1976). _Egocentrism and cultural deprivation: Empirical evidence for the ethnocentric bias of Piagetian theory_. Aukland, New Zealand: South Pacific Research Institute, Inc., 12.

Graves, N.B. & Graves, T.D. (1983). The culture context of prosocial development: An ecological model. In D. Bridgeman (Ed.), _The nature of prosocial development: Interdisciplinary theories and strategies_. New York: Academic Press.

Hammond, L. K. & Goldman, M. (1961). Competition and non-competition and its relationship to individual and group productivity. _Sociometry_, 24, 46-70.

Hartshorne, H. & May, M.A. (1928). _Studies in the nature of character_. Vol. I. Studies in deceit. New York: MacMillan.

Johnson, D.W. & Johnson, R.T. (1974). Instructional goal structure: Cooperative, competitive, or individualistic. _Review of Educational Research_, 4, 2, 213-240.

Kagan, S. & Knight, G.P. (1980--in press). Cooperation--competition and self-esteem: A case of cultural relativism. _Journal of Cross-Cultural Psychology_.

Kagan, S. & Madsen, D.C. (1972). Experimental analyses of cooperation and competition of Anglo-American children and Mexican children. _Developmental Psychology_, 6, 49-59.

Lewin, K., Dembo, T., Festinger, L. & Sears, R. (1944). Level of aspiration. In J. McV. Hunt (Ed.), Handbook of personality and the behavior disorders. New York: The Ronald Press.

May, M. & Doob, L. (1937). Competition and cooperation. New York: Social Science Research Council.

Mayer, A. (1903). Uber Einzel-und Gesamtleistung des Schulkindes. Archiv fur die Gesamte Psychologie, 1, 276-416.

Nelson, L.I. & Madsen, M.C. (1969). Cooperation and competition in four year olds as a function of reward contingency and subculture. Developmental Psychology, 1, 340-344.

Pepitone, E.A. (1972). Comparison behavior in elementary school children. American Educational Research Journal, 9, 1, 45-63.

Pepitone, E.A. (1980). Children in cooperation and competition: Toward a developmental social psychology. Lexington, MA: D.C. Heath & Co.

Pepitone, E.A. & B.H. Hannah (1980). Exploration of comparison behaviors in third-grade children. In Pepitone, E.A. (Ed.), Children in cooperation and competition: Toward a developmental social psychology. Lexington, MA: D.C. Heath & Co.

Raven, B.H.& Eachus, H.T. (1963). Cooperation and competition in means-interdependent triads. Journal of Abnormal and Social Psychology, 67, 307-316.

Selman, R.L. (1971). Taking another's perspective: Role-taking development in early childhood. Child Development, 42, 1721-1734.

Slavin, R. (1983). Cooperative learning. New York: Longman.

Thibaut, J.W. & Kelley, H.H. (1959). The social psychology of groups. New York: John Wiley and Sons.

Triplett, N. (1897). The dynamogenic factor in pacemaking and competition. American Journal of Psychology, 9, 507-533.

New Paradigm Research

Jerome S. Allender

Temple University

The Evolution of Research Methods

In striving for quality methods, educational research as a whole
has never come close to the demands of an ideal empirical science. The
paradigm of which these strivings are a part has had the germ within it
for the developments that are now occurring. Partly, the research techniques of historians, astronomers, archeologists, biologists, psychologists, etc., although dissimilar because of their radically different
focuses, have had influences that cross over into education. Within
the paradigm of educational research as a regular science as well, there
have always been a variety of novel approaches to some degree.

* * *

Taken together, the ideas proposed and used in the last ten years
of educational research would constitute a major change in the rules of
research. For the moment, though, they are more of a signal that the
traditional paradigm is shifting (as opposed to an actual shift itself).
Arguments about validity, control groups, statistical significance,
case study methods, and noncausal research are relatively isolated and
have effects in different spheres. From a larger perspective, however,
they do show a current sentiment that increasing the meaningfulness of
research is more important than protecting the ideals of traditional
scientific method.

There are also proposals for radical changes in the total structure
of the methods and purposes of educational research. For these proposals,
traditional scientific methods are not the main focus or concern. Testing theories with facts or looking for the cause of phenomena, although
acceptable, are not of prime importance. It is in no way assumed that
necessary knowledge is created by building up facts with one added to
another patiently over time as one would build a wall out of bricks.

* * *

The overall changes that are proposed by Eisner (1981), Shubert
(1980), and Manicas and Secord (1983), for example, have significant
implications for an understanding of where educational research methodology might be headed. Both Eisner and Schubert extend the boundaries

far beyond what is considered to be scientific inquiry. They do this un-
apologetically and with arguments of necessary and good purpose. Eisner
is concerned with the creation of meaning as opposed to the discovery
of predictable knowledge. He argues for a polystructural bases for
methodology. His position supports the conscious consideration of personal views in the research process. Schubert is concerned with the
immediate practical value of research as opposed to the development of
theory. His position too is polystructural. It allows for scientific
research, but more importance is given to methods that lend themselves
to the social responsibility of educational researchers. Manicas and
Secord, in contrast, are arguing that a real science of psychology is
outside the domain of the practioner. The usual quest for cause and
effect relationships is relegated to studies where closed systems are
created. In open systems, there are too many specific factors involved
to allow for finding meaningful, predictable relationships. These papers
taken together support my proposition that educational research ≠ science. The practice of science might be a small part of what educational
researchers do, but relevant educational inquiry from these views requires something more and different from its researchers.

New Paradigm Research

Concurrently with the changes occuring within education, new paradigm research methods have been developing as separate fields--the most
prominent of which is humanistic psychology. Humanistic psychology as
a whole is itself a new paradigm and is often considered outside the
pale of acceptable psychological science. The separateness has actually
facilitated the methodological developments because the paradigm in
general is geared toward avoiding the placement of scientific ideals
over human concerns.

* * *

These newer developments in humanistic psychology fit easily into
the perspectives created by Polanyi (1962) and Kuhn (1970). There has
been a conscious rethinking of the basic assumptions and a recognition
that the humanistic view of reality is substantially different. New
kinds of data are relevant along with a different spectrum of methods
for collecting the data. Greater regard is given to methods which are
reliant on intrapersonal processes such as introspection and self-re-
ports. The emphasis is on personal meaning, holistic explanations, and
societal change. Because of these differences and emphases, humanistic

psychological methods are often not acceptable to those working inside
the traditional framework. From Kuhn's view, their practice is a press-
ing influence on the academic community, and I am sure that this influence extends to the domain of educational research.

It must be noted that the research methods used for the study of
humanistic psychology, although in need of refinement, not entirely consistent, and sometimes vague, are presently in use. Their influence on
other researchers stems more from their practice than from arguments
about their necessity and relevance. The previous discussions related
to changes within and beyond the traditional structure of educational
research are more in connection with arguments about the need for change.
Against the background of these arguments, the majority of journals,
texts, and dissertations reflect the directions of traditional scientific inquiry. The practice of humanistic methods, however, with the
parallel publication of the research in humanistic journals, texts, and
dissertations is direct evidence of the existence of the new paradigm.
One can hope for refinement of the methods as part of the process, but
meanwhile, this new paradigm is here to be reckoned with.

Some of the influence lies outside humanistic psychology and is
incorporated within the academic community without regard to fit. For
example, Bogdan and Taylor (1975) published a text to guide researchers
in qualitative research methods based on principles of phenomenology,
symbolic interactionism, and ethnomethodology. Their approach is related to participant observation, personal documents, unstructured inter-
viewing, and the creative invention of new methods. Their position simply assumes that the methods they present are part of rigorous scientific
inquiry. Another intriguing example is a text edited by Amabile and
Stubbs (1982). Traditional research methods are juxtaposed with humanistic methods without discussion of the underlying conflicts that exist
between them. A researcher who follows their guidance is likely to be
confused when his or her work is rejected as outside the pale of scientific research. In these ways, there is a slow shifting from one paradigm
to the other. The wide variety of methodologies that are considered today reflect generally increased attention to qualitative research methods.
Even so, these kinds of examples for the time being are only of minor
significance.

There are a number of recent texts that begin to define the boundaries of the new paradigm. Without such a definition, it is reasonable
to expect fears of rampant relativism and nihilism. The texts bring no
coordinated definition but they do make the picture clearer. Even

though they embody significant conflicts, they are consistent in their newness. This is not traditional scientific method slightly reworked.

Laing's (1982) book, The Voice of Experience, is the most radical and one that has disturbing elements. He discusses the practice of psychoanalysis within and without the context of science and objectivity. Laing lucidly shows how the scientific version of objectivity and the information gained through this lens have a deleterious effect on human relations. His examples are the stories of the lives of people who get help that is objective for their own good--necessarily unfeeling and lacking in deep empathy. The consequences are disasterous. As well, he writes of cultural biases, deep within all of us, that are the result of this orientation. It is not only objective research itself that is so onerous, but the attitude that pervades our culture. Our value of objectivity is out of balance, and he points to the distancing between people that this attitude brings and the societal ills it fosters. What is needed is the recognition that reality is determined in so many ways by how we look at it. He has made this point before, and the examples he provides are extraordinarily convincing. Laing challenges us to the lessons of experience--where life is experienced as directly as possible. I timidly interpret the trouble he describes as one of unbridled objectivity.

Laing's ideas represent for me the outer boundaries of the new paradigm. They are not central in humanistic psychology and hardly a whisper in the world of educational research. But his views are not just argument; they are part of his practice of an aspect of psychology. He has clients, he researches, he is published, and he is read. We might wonder about the extremes to which he pushes us--I found the reading of his examples scary. Here in his methods lies the basis for understanding research as a personal process. Whatever stance we take and use, still his insights will haunt us. So we will (sometimes) say to ourselves, "I create reality by how I look at it." Caveat emptor.

Argyris' (1980) ideas, firmly rooted in Lewinian theory, writes of Inner Contradictions of Rigorous Research with an eye to group dynamics and organizational development. What he calls "action science" is intended to apply to the study of human experience in general and is meant to replace the traditional paradigm. The focus is on the practical world and the study of people's actions in everyday life. Far from Laing's view, there is still significant concern for the individual. His basic concerns, however, are more pointed at relationships from dyads to complex systems. He argues that the methodology of rigorous research by following its own rules detracts from its actual validity and by studying the universe as it exists serves to maintain the status quo. About his notions of objectivity he says (p. 3), "I adhere as strictly as I can to the underlying notions of science, namely: public disconfirmability, some notion of causality, and the idea of elegance (i.e., theories that have the greatest comprehension with the least number of concepts and untestable axioms)." It is research, though, where investigators and the investigated interact, where researchers do not distance themselves or unilaterally control the methods of investigation, and where the constraints of everyday life encounters are considered relevant. The goal is to find knowledge that people can use to design and execute their actions in their daily relationships at all levels. The methods are focused on generating alternative possibilities.

Argyris systematically develops the Lewinian concept of action research. It too is not central to humanistic psychology, although it is more familiar to educational researchers. As part of the evolution of the new paradigm, he offers more specific direction than most others. He also departs less radically from traditional science than do others, certainly Laing. In consequence, the methodology admits a narrower range of new kinds of data, analyses, and interpretation into its purview. Yet it forms a solid basis for doing research in the framework of a social process. As a refinement of action research, it brings with it a tradition of inquiry-oriented human interaction and cooperative problem solving.

The potentially most influential addition to the literature is the publication of Human Inquiry: A Sourcebook of New Paradigm Research edited by Reason and Rowan (1981). It is a collection of 40 articles all relating to methodological developments and representing 35 researchers. It is an unusual book of readings because the editors' mark is very much apparent, editorially, as authors of four of the articles, and in reviews of books. The strongest influence is humanistic psychology; other influences include Kelly, Rogers, Laing, Jung, Sullivan, Bion, and Lewin as well as phenomenology, existentialism, and Marxism. It is a broadly-based text drawing on many roots. The editors regard themselves as outside the pale of traditional methodology. In their words (p. xxi),

> So maybe our work must be seen as directly in opposition
> to orthodox work, a kind of antithesis, if that sort of
> language helps. But if this is true then we are in trou-
> ble, because as dialectic thinking shows, to be opposed to
> something is still to be bound to it. If we were simply
> against orthodox research, we would not be saying anything
> new, and we could easily be seen as simply 'anti-science'.

The issue of anti-science is resolved mainly by concentrating on new philosophical and methodological approaches accompanied by examples and some discussion about implementation. Reason and Rowan briefly describe aspects of the old paradigm to which they object, namely, positivism, reductionism, reification, undue emphasis on quantification, deception, debriefing, determinism, and plus a few others. For the most part, though, the articles and the discussion are related to specific methodological ideas for doing new paradigm research. It should not be assumed that this is a single model of research. A variety of models are presented including collaborative inquiry, experiential research, action research, personal construct theory, heuristic research, illuminative evaluation, and endogenous research--which are the ones that can be named easily. They are certainly not all precisely different from each other, but they do reflect specific emphases that might be useful for a particular researcher's goals. As well, there are aspects of research presented that are just alternative methods and not complete models.

So this is not a unified approach. There are, though, basic underlying concerns for personal integrity and social values. For all the differences, these concerns are shared throughout. It is strongly evident that this text represents a developing new paradigm where agreement is more prominent than disagreement. There seems to be a common belief that further development and refinement is leading to a reputable approach to research that is better suited to our present times.

More recently, another text appeared edited by Morgan (1983) under the title, Beyond Method. The title is misleading, though, because the book is in fact a compilation of new paradigm approaches to research. Here, another group of 25 authors write of their experiences outside the realm of orthodox methodology and only one overlaps with Reason and Rowan's book. The text is not as differentiated from old paradigm research as is the latter. There is some overlap among the positions, but common assumptions among them are not as apparent. Nor is humanistic psychology a salient influence. From the editor's view, differences in methodology are more apparent than sameness from author to author. "Reflective exploration" is the common theme he identifies somewhat more as an organizing hope than as a reality. Still, the text is part of the ever clearer picture that is evolving for new paradigm research.

We might well worry that new paradigm research brings with it the difficult problem of relativism. Does this mean that anything goes? Are there no criteria for quality? How can we decide on the appropriate rules for research? If we don't know, doesn't this undermine the use-

fulness of the findings? What part can research play in human experience with this starting point? And how would it be possible to teach
research skills? Judging from the range of discussions that have been
generated, we might also worry that a Tower of Babel is being built.
It's a long way through the field of humanistic psychology from Laing to
Argyris. Just as there are arguments between old and new paradigmers,
there is a lot of room for difficult disagreements among the different
alternative approaches to research, Reason and Rowan's "synthesis" not-
withstanding. As well, the old paradigm is not just going to lie down
and die (see, for example, a response to Eisner by Phillips, 1983, "After
the Wake: Postpositivistic Educational Thought"). These are real problems some of which have solutions and some do not. In good part, as we
learn from Kuhn, it's a process that carries us in its own currents.

From my view, whatever the difficulties that new paradigm research
brings with its development, they will have to be confronted. We are
in the middle of what I call the "lamplight phenomena." It is abundantly
clear to many that old paradigm methods are the lamplight under which we
are looking for answers to important human concerns. The key, however,
that was lost by the drunk in the proverbial joke is not under the light
of the lamp. It's elsewhere. The key in this retelling is the primary
concern for the person and for social relevance. The light represents
the highly technical scientific methods of old paradigm research. Those
who are practicing new paradigm methods, for all the problems yet unsolved, are saying that however intense the light, it cannot illuminate
answers to our questions. They are looking where they think the key was
lost.

Personal Inquiry and Connection

As I described earlier, there are different kinds of paradigm
shifts. Some are not major disruptions, and when complete have not left
casualties in their wake as in the case of the shift from behaviorism
to cognition. What Reason and Rowan call new paradigm research, in contrast, appears to be part of a difficult paradigm shift. If more and
more researchers openly turn to the use of these methods, the consumers--
the larger world of education in general--will find themselves in the
middle of a battle over what is real and what is to be believed.

Research from this alternative can be a passionately personal process. Moustakas (1967, reprinted in 1981) writing about a method he
calls "heuristic research" describes his study of loneliness. The begin-

ning was an intense personal experience connected with the serious illness of his daughter. This was followed by engaging in a variety of
other life experiences that felt connected with the initial experience.
He relates (p. 102), "Experiences in meditation and self-searching, in
intuitive and mystical reachings, and in hours and hours of silent mid-
night walking paved the way to a formulation of my study of loneliness,
a formulation which emerged clearly during my observations of hospitaliz-
ed children." He then immersed himself in related literature, and
finally he articulated a number of concepts which culminated in a book
entitled <u>Loneliness</u> (Moustakas, 1961). Letters from 500 readers served
as a validation of the study.

This is strikingly different from the model of educational research
we normally expect. The researcher as a person is deeply involved and
concerned with every part of the process--with the children he studied,
with himself, and with all those who might be affected by the results.
The approach draws strong support from phenomenology even though this
branch of psychology hasn't been central in the development of the new
paradigm. The main tenet is that human behavior can only be understood
in reference to the perceptual field of the behaving person. There is
a commitment to understanding human behavior as it relates to individuals' specific life experiences, and a commitment for a researcher's
understanding that is personal as well. In restating these concepts
in an updated edition of the Snygg and Combs' texts, Combs, Richards,
and Richards (1976), in fact, subtitle their work as a humanistic approach to the study of persons: What we see is a potential revitali-
zation of the field of phenomenology, a rethinking and a reconsideration
of past research, and its general application to the study of human
psychology and education.

The irony of a new paradigm is that the evidence for its validity
is busy poking holes in the old paradigm for everyone to see (but somehow not see). That the researcher's personality is a major determinant
involved in any investigation is really no surprise. Using Freud and
Adler as case studies, Riebel (1982) shows how their theories act as a
kind of self-portrait. As a consequence, their notions of objectivity
reflect their underlying personality dyanmics. Not only do we as researchers choose and conceptualize our problems, choose and design our
methods, and creatively generalize from our results, we cannot help but
determine our standards of objectivity. This is why, of course, Polanyi
argues the need to consider the subjective elements of the research process. As an extreme example, Morrow (1984) documents how writings by
James and Dewey on consciousness were suppressed. He feels that members

of the predominant paradigm didn't want all aspects of their personalities fully recognized. I wonder whether these kinds of pressures have a bearing on how our awareness is kept down? This starting point, when taken seriously, means that it is the responsibility of researchers to use their self-knowledge in relevant and sensible ways and to bring it to bear on the results of one's studies.

Further support and more difficulties regarding the persona of the researcher come from the field of physics. In an article cited earlier and in a second by Keutzer (1982, 1984), she describes three paradoxical discoveries and their implications for psychology. For her, Godel's incompleteness theorem implies "that every encompassing system of logic must have at least one premise that cannot be proved or verified without contradicting itself" (1984, p. 83). Extrapolating from Bohr's principle of complementarity, she proposes the possibility that there can be two opposite explanations of all phenomena--as in the wave-particle nature of an electron. And from Heisenberg's uncertainty principle, we know that the reality we observe is changed by our observation. These kinds of principles are usually considered too remote to worry about their application to the study of human experience. In the new paradigm, however, they have particular relevance. As we let go of the previous primary focus on the establishment of cause and effect relationships and the logical framework it requires, these principles from modern physics give new direction. The contradictions within ourselves are admissible; we don't need to pretend singularity of purpose, nor must we pretend that there is a completely logical basis for our research. We don't assume we will find single consistent answers to complicated problems. And finally we can recognize and work with the fact that we interact and are an integral part of what we study.

To view educational research primarily as a personal process in a narrow sense is not sufficient. More is implied than the concept that all research is fundamentally subjective. The shift from one paradigm to another would not be so difficult for this reason alone. That the basis of research is subjective is not new, and accepting it does not particularly require a new paradigm. However, the personal process under discussion also requires responsible, personal inquiry. This is inquiry which by its nature entails risk and has the potential for significant self development. This kind of research fosters personal growth and learning for the researcher as well as everyone else who is involved in the process. In addition, the learning is not likely to be isolated to single aspects of experience; it is holistically related to life experience in general.

The nature of objectivity in new paradigm research is the one element that receives the least amount of discussion. It is possible to imagine that objectivity has no place in research oriented as a personal inquiry. It is difficult to know, too, whether some traditional methods are totally inappropriate or whether there are limits to the creative invention of alternative methods. From my experience doing new paradigm research, I have created metaphors for objectivity and think of it as a wand, or a stick, or a screen by which aspects of reality are viewed in search of interesting and helpful patterns. In teaching research skills, I begin by asking students to delineate the context of their research, to relate their ideas to a relevant, small body of literature, and to specify some problems and questions about which they want to achieve some clarity. With this in mind, I then ask them to create a design that specifies a source of data and a lens through which to look at the data. All considerations of old paradigm notions of objectivity are secondary. Of primary importance is the total sense of the design, and the critical test of sense is the researcher's belief that putting an analytic tool into the data or that looking at the data through a specified screen will produce meaningful results.

The range of designs is limited only by common sense and the regard for the integrity of others. Highly technical and sophisticated designs are not ruled out, but it is more difficult to get them to meet the basic criteria. Simple designs are usually all that is required for carrying out meaningful educational research in the new paradigm. Reality viewed in this way connects subjectivity and objectivity to self and suggests generalizations that include intuitive perspective.

What remains to consider is educational research as a social process. It goes without saying that personally-oriented research which lacks support of an academic community is a lonely endeavor. Within the new paradigm, the academic community ordinarily would not have reason to inhibit any investigator from carrying out his or her research. Still, as in the old paradigm, assistance, interpersonal interactions, publication, and application are aspects of the process. Research can be done without this support, but its utility for others is likely to be minimized. The consensual aspects of research continue to operate as in any paradigm.

Not striving to discover traditional objective knowledge about reality makes for further complications. I believe that there are only two kinds of knowledge towards which to strive: personal and consensual. In the new paradigm, the activity of the lone researcher is not discouraged because the process itself is deemed valuable. The knowledge derived necessarily furthers a relevant inquiry which in essence is personal growth. And yet, another important goal of research that remains is to add to the understanding of human experience in useful ways for others. Its achievement is based on consensual knowledge. Because of this goal, a body of new theories and new rules for research are evolving. For students particularly, there is no option to finding professors who agreed with their proposals. For a dissertation, a student must find the minimum required number of professors to accept it. The experience of students parallels the whole of the academic process. What is new, though, is the conscious recognition that this is how general knowledge is supposed to be formed--by consensus. Making this a normal, conscious activity leaves room for changes to develop continuously.

There is more to the role of social process in research though. Sanford's (1982) consideration of the interview as an intervention gave me the first clue. Basing his discussion on the Lewinian concept of action research, he notes the effects that interviews have had in several studies, and asks the question, "how do people benefit from being interviewed?" He weaves a case for thinking about the interview as a tool for helping people think and talk about relevant aspects of their lives. Used in this way, the process and outcomes of such research benefit both the interviewers and the interviewees.

Torbett (1981) added a piece to my thinking with his concept of educational research as a collaborative inquiry. He criticizes designs of research that are unilaterally controlled by the researchers. From this view, colleagues, administrators, teachers, students, and anyone else that is in the purview of a study, have important interactive roles in guiding the progress of the research. The necessary attitude as I see it is one of believing that everyone is involved in an endeavor together and should stand to benefit from each different relevant viewpoint.

Another clue came to me from Tyler, Pargament, and Gatz (1983) with their model for a resource collaborator role for psychologists. They see psychologists--as teachers, investigators, consultants, therapists, and change agents--predominantly using a unidirectional model of influence. They propose the resource collaboratory role, as an alternative for the expert-nonexpert model, to be used in a more interactive relationship with clients.

With Sanford, Torbett, and Tyler et al. in mind, I find that, as is the personal process in research more than a matter of subjectivity, so too is the social process more than the recognition of the role of consensus. Beyond the role of consensus is a concern for connecting people

with each other in positive, mutually benefiting interactions. This
means that educational research must serve, by the nature of the process,
to improve the quality of human relationships. This is certainly what
Lewin meant when he conceived of action research. Two further conclusions loom out for me: the connections establish a greater objectivity,
and achieving objectivity is a way of connecting in a relationship.
The first is relatively easy to argue because making connections is the
natural part of establishing a consensus. For arguing the second, one
might say that objectivity is a common wavelength on which to communicate. However unconvincing the final conclusions are, I feel that it
has been established that, in the new paradigm, educational research
is primarily a personal and a social process. In the long run, these
concepts will need more explication and refinement.

One misconception of the traditional paradigm is that the big problems of education can be solved by research. This is a frustrating
mythical promise that educational research as science has created for
itself. The myth is probably perpetrated any time someone proposes
that action should be deferred until a complete investigation can be
undertaken. As if the only intelligent way to act is on the basis of
scientific knowledge. Sarason (1978) points to the need for greater
awareness of what he terms, intractable problems. He argues that there
is an underlying assumption of science that all problems are potentially
solvable. Saying this outloud should convince anyone that it is obviously untrue. The insights of Manicas and Secord (1983) cited earlier add
to the argument. Scientific information from experiments in closed systems can provide thought-provoking help, but they are not methods for
using in the open, on-going practical world of everyday problems. Only
some form of action research is really applicable. The role of the researcher is, at best, a coequal partner in the problem-solving process.
Arrogance is intolerable and defensiveness is unnecessary. There is an
alternative myth to believe: If we all work together, maybe we can
solve some of the problems and improve the educational process a little
from week to week, month to month, and year to year.

I do not think that the new paradigm attitude toward research is
brand new, just that it is now coming more into its own right. Through
Moustakas (1967), I discovered the Sea of Cortez by Steinbeck and Ricketts (1941). John Steinbeck and his friend Ed Ricketts, a marine biologist, went on a scientific expedition together to catalogue and write
about the sea life in the Gulf of California around the time of the onset of World War II. In "A Leisurely Journal of Travel and Research,"
they wrote of their starting points (pp. 3-4):

We suppose this was the mental provisioning of our expedition.
We said, "Let's go wide open. Let's see what we see, record
what we find, and not fool ourselves with conventional scientific strictures. We could not observe a completely objective
Sea of Cortez anyway, for in that lonely and uninhabited
Gulf our boat and ourselves would change it the moment we
entered. By going there, we would bring a new factor to the
Gulf. Let us consider that factor and not be betrayed by
this myth of permanent objective reality. If it exists at
all, it is only available in pickled tatters or in distorted
flashes. Let us go," we said, "into the Sea of Cortez, rea-
lizing that we become forever a part of it; that our rubber
boots slogging through a flat of eel-grass, that the rocks
we turn over in a tide pool, make us truly and permanently
a factor in the ecology of the region. We shall take something away from it, but we shall leave something too." And
if we seem a small factor in the huge pattern, nevertheless
it is of relative importance. We take a tiny colony of soft
corals from a rock in a little water world. And that isn't
terribly important to the tide pool. Fifty miles away the
Japanese shrimp boats are dredging with overlapping scoops,
bringing up tons of shrimps, rapidly destroying the species
so that it may never come back, and with the species destroying the ecological balance of the whole region. That isn't
very important in the world. And six thousand miles away the
great bombs are falling on London and the stars are not moved
thereby. None of it is important or all of it is.

The log together with its scientific appendix sets an examples of new
paradigm research for education. It's not their methods, though, that
are so exemplary, it's their attitude. The starting points were impressive to me, considering the field and the year, and only more so, when
I discovered that Rickett's partner was, for sure, the John Steinbeck,
the novelist.

REFERENCES

Amabile, T.M., & Stubbs, M.L. (1982). Psychological research in the
    classroom: Issues for educators and researchers. New York: Perg-
    amon Press.

Argyris, C. (1980). Inner contradictions of rigorous research. New
    York: Academic Press.

Bogdan, R., & Taylor, S.J. (1975). Introduction to qualitative research
    methods: A phenomenological approach to the social sciences. New
    York: John Wiley & Sons.

Combs, A.W., Richards, A.C., & Richards, F. (1976). Perceptual psycho-
    logy: A humanistic approach to the study of persons. New York:
    Harper & Row.

Dunkel, H.B.   (1972).   Wanted: New paradigms and a normative base for
    research. In L.B. Thomas (Ed.), Philosophical redirection of edu-
    cational research: The seventy-first yearbook of the National Soci-
    ety for the Study of Education, Part I (pp. 77-93). Chicago: Uni-
    versity of Chicago Press.

Eisner, E.W.   (1981).   On the differences between scientific and artistic
    approaches to qualitative research. Educational Researcher, 10(4),
    5-9.

Keutzer, C.S.   (1982).   Physics and consciousness. Journal of Humanistic
    Psychology, 22(2), 74-90.

Keutzer, C.S.   (1984).   The power of meaning: From quantum mechanics
    to synchronicity. Journal of Humanistic Psychology, 24(1), 80-94.

Kuhn, T.S.   (1970).   The structure of scientific revolutions (2nd ed.).
    Chicago: University of Chicago Press.

Laing, R.D.   (1982).   The voice of experience. New York: Pantheon Books.
    Books.

Lewin, K.   (1948).   Resolving social conflicts: Selected papers on group
    dynamics. London: Souvenir Press.

Lewin, K.   (1951).   Field theory in social science: Selected theoretical
    papers. New York: Harper & Row.

Manicas, P.T., & Secord, P.F.   (1983).   Implications for psychology of
    the new philosophy of science. American Psychologist, 38, 399-413.

Morgan, G.   (Ed.).   (1983).   Beyond method: Strategies for social re-
    search. Beverly Hills, CA: Sage.

Morrow, F.   (1984).   William James and John Dewey on consciousness: Sup-
    pressed writings. Journal of Humanistic Psychology, 24(1), 69-79.

Moustakas, C.   (1961).   Loneliness. Englewood Cliffs, NJ: Prentice-
    Hall.

Moustakas, C.   (1967).   Heuristic research. In J.F.T. Bugental (Ed.),
    Challenges of humanistic psychology (pp. 101-107). New York: Mc-
    Graw-Hill.

Moustakas, C.   (1981).   Heuristic research. In P. Reason & J. Rowan
    (Eds.), Human inquiry: A sourcebook of new paradigm research (pp.
    207-217). New York: John Wiley & Sons.

Phillips, D.C.   (1983).   After the wake: Postpositivitic educational
    thought. Educational Researcher, 12(5), 4-12.

Polanyi, M.   (1962).   Personal knowledge: Toward a post-critical philo-
    sophy. Chicago: University of Chicago Press.

Polanyi, M.   (1966).   The tacit dimension. Garden City, NY: Doubleday.

Polanyi, M.   (1968).   Logic and psychology. American Psychologist, 23,
    27-43.

Reason, P., & Rowan, J.   (Eds.).   (1981).   Human inquiry: A sourcebook
    of new paradigm research. New York: John Wiley & Sons.

Riebel, L.   (1982).   Theory as self-portrait and the ideal of objecti-
    vity. Journal of Humanistic Psychology, 22(2), 91-110.

Sanford, N.   (1982).   Social psychology: Its place in personology.
    American Psychologist, 37, 896-903.

Sarason, S.B.   (1978).   The nature of problem solving in social action.
    American Psychologist, 33, 370-380.

Schubert, W.H.   (1980).   Recalibrating educational research: Toward
     a focus on practice. Educational Researcher, 9(1), 17-24, 31.

Steinbeck, J., & Ricketts, E.F.   (1941).   Sea of Cortez: A leisurely
     journal of travel and research. New York: Viking Press.

Torbert, W.R.   (1981).   Why educational research has been so uneduca-
     tional: The case for a new model of social science based on colla-
     borative inquiry.   In P. Reason & J. Rowan (Eds.), Human inquiry:
     A sourcebook of new paradigm research (pp. 141-151). New York:
     John Wiley & Sons.

Tyler, F.B., Pargament, K.I., & Gatz, M.   (1983).   The resource colla-
     borator role: A model of interactions involving psychologists.
     American Psychologist, 38, 388-398.

A Neo-Lewinian Action Research Method

Eugene Stivers

Temple University

Though Kurt Lewin's action research has never had a recognized place in psychological research methodology, it has a proud history among its users. In recent years, the basis of this special status has broadened, as intervention inquiry has taken new forms. In Reason and Rowan's book on new paradigm research, for example, R. Tandon gives Lewin credit for originating a forerunner, and says, "However, there is beginning to emerge some consensus among action researchers and participatory researchers that inquiry can be conceptualized and practiced as an intervention process" (Tandon, 1981).

A new Lewinian paradigm

In this paper I will describe a research paradigm, new in ways familiar to Reason and Rowan's work, though clearly in the Lewinian tradition (Lewin, 1946). My purpose is to encourage this emerging consensus that "inquiry can be conceptualized and practiced as an intervention process" and so contribute to the development of an action research method that will have a place in psychological research methodology.

This paradigm is also new in the sense that it belongs to a relatively unfamiliar methodological tradition. Not part of the logical positivist group, of course, nor the school of realism, it is more related to the constructionists' position (Scarr, 1985) than the phenomenologists'. More directly, it is a method that Lewin himself might have developed had he decided to become again a philosopher of science and turned to a version of John Dewey's thought (Dewey, 1933), enlarged by some features of psychological humanism, for help in building a thorough action research method.

Rather than presenting a thorough version of the method, I will describe a research story-line and comment on it. This story features (a) the familiar Lewinian action research cycle of data collection and action, guided by a developing local model of the problem situation, (b) a less familiar, for research methodology purposes, focus on the dynamics of the research consultant-client collaboration, (c) use of the notions of knowledge as "opposing metaphors," and research as "language development," and (d) decision-making processes in which consensus rather than "general trend of evidence" plays the central role.

The running narrative of this research plan is presented in a familiar outline for describing research.

A) Problem formulation

A group has serious work to do. It is part of an organization (choose: a class, a training group, a team, a crew, a department, or a task force). The group feels put-upon, stretched, awed, disorganized, threatened, excited. Or it has other complex, strong inner and outer feelings. The situation is compelling and indeterminate. The members are ready to do something and ready to do nothing. So, they get an expert consultant who is a qualified leader and a researcher. This consultant does not formulate the problem, however--neither theirs nor an objective one. As a result, their sense of problem is heightened.

B) Conceptualization

The consultant does not conceptualize the problem, either. In fact, it is not formulated or formally conceptualized at this time, though a cycle of data collection and conceptualization-formulation is begun which leads to major constructions.

At this point, what the consultant does do is encourage and organize the persons in the group, who have been relieved of part of their regular duties, to collaboratively construct a tentative model of the important elements in their work situation, especially those that are problematic. This graphic and verbal model gives them impetus and direction as they form teams to make the preliminary gathering of information. They go ahead to make a "literature review" of formal and informal documents that will altogether offer a history of the problem situation, its context and peculiarities; they survey most of the people involved in the situation about their views of the problematic elements; and interview a few persons about both problem history and issues.

The group is flushed with pleasure about the various personal and technical accomplishments that have been a part of their data collection. But by the time this information is collated, the first real arguments have taken place, because the consultant has not taken the role of a strong expert leader, and has not tried directly to resolve the social antagonism that has resulted. Further, the consultant has encouraged the formation of advocate sides about the meaning of the information collected.

Time and argument bring out informal group leaders who then play a part in the formation, through extended discussion, of a second consensual model of the problem situation. In this work, the consultant is largely a technical adviser about verbal expression, listening, forceful argument, consensual decision making, and representative model construction.

This new model has gradually been taking shape in the language of the group as they regularly argued about the research work, about the many personal arrangements involved in carrying it out, and about its meaning.

Time, human and objective requirements, careful expert attention of the consultant, effectiveness of the natural leaders, and a little luck, result in an impressive second model. It takes the form of an organic representation of the sharp vital necessities and contrasts in the problem situation: The cast of characters, the plot, the situation, and, the quantitatively-weighted features of the organizational setting. The model is a double metaphor--a complex "figure of speech" made up of the symbols and phrases of the consensual language they use when they systematically describe the problem situation in an informed way.

The group at the same time reaches a very satisfying state of relations among themselves.

COMMENT

The consultant, as expert, has offered advice on several matters that the group has dealt with so far. He has explained that a good model is (a) couched in a familiar language that has authority, (b) presents in dynamic form the essentials of the situation it represents, and (c) suggests lines of effective action. He has patiently coached them in the routines of formal and informal data collection, and initiated them into the use of the special terms of these domains. He has trained them in some basic skills of verbal expression, listening, and forceful argument. He has spent a lot of time, all told, explaining and training them in the consensual decision process--intellectual and personal expression by every member, attention to clarification and understanding of each view, development of main opposing views, and work toward a common position that is viable for all members. He has discussed with the group the difference between this process and the majority-vote process. He has talked them into trying out the idea that consensus is essentially a matter of reaching agreement upon the words and other symbols that represent their world of work.

To introduce the metaphor device, which was new to most, he used a chart (Figure 1) and remarks along the line of the following:

"Natural and physical scientists have frequently chosen analogies and similar comparisons to extend and develop theories: Black Hole, gene splicing, particle/wave theory, survival of the fittest. Further, scientific theories have usually developed from a root metaphor about the nature of reality--that it is (like) a well-arranged library, or a mechanism, or a dramatic event, or a dynamic system (e.g., a whirlpool, the solar system)."

"We are going to construct a double metaphor, not as a supporting device but as the main object of our work. Our metaphors constitute a complex model--an especially effective container for both subjective and objective information, in complementary tension. The model will be characterized by the cohesion of opposites that are related or belong to the same system, such as: Historical past vs. present, feeling vs. thought, being here vs. being there, qualitative vs. quantitative, probability vs. occurrence, primary process thought vs. secondary process, experiential vs. empirical, group vs. individual. Our metaphor/model will have the potential to embrace a range of evidence in a way that other descriptive devices can not, with impact and with the pragmatic quality characteristic of scientific work. It will serve very well our purposes of collating, organizing, understanding and acting on our research data."

FIGURE 1 EXPLANATION

The metaphor/model features a main outer interactive tension and correspondence--between the actual situation and the representation--and a main inner interactive tension and correspondence--between (A) the more abstract and (B) the more concrete parts of the representation. It is the argument among these aspects, as it is carried on in the data collection, collation, and discussion by the researchers, that produces authentic and useful findings.

    (A)   The more abstract objective analytic part of the metaphor/model is in this case a mathematical coordinate system. Variables important to the research are assigned to each axis. These variables could be, for example, "Power" and "Social distance."

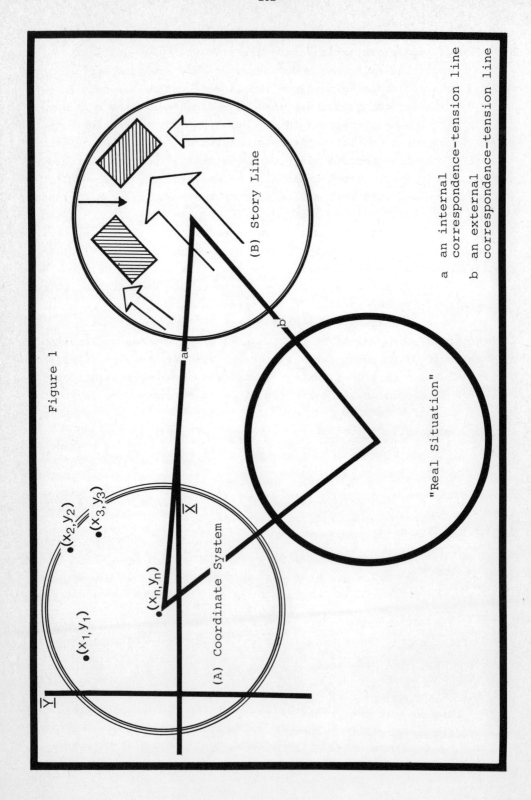

Figure 1

(A) Coordinate System

$\overline{Y}$

$\overline{X}$

$\bullet(x_1, y_1)$

$\bullet(x_2, y_2)$

$\bullet(x_3, y_3)$

$\bullet(x_n, y_n)$

(B) Story Line

a

b

"Real Situation"

a   an internal
    correspondence-tension line

b   an external
    correspondence-tension line

The major concentrations representing the group and the rest of the organization are plotted. (The information for this plotting will come mostly from precise empirical collection.) An accompanying succinct verbal description, in this case, answers the question: What is the placement and configuration of the main organizational concentrations of people in terms of two essential variables?

(B) The more concrete subjective qualitative part of the metaphor/ model is a sketch or diagram of the group. The group, for ex- ample, could be "on a journey." The graphics are supplemented by an elaborate verbal description. The description answers the questions: Who are the persons? What are the surrounding circumstances? What is happening? What lead up to this situa- tion? What is being thought? What is wanted? By whom? What will happen? What will be done by these persons and others in the situation? (The information to answer these questions is collected in a variety of ways.)

When the group was actually trying to construct the metaphor/model, the consultant used some of the "immersion in data" techniques of Sprad- ley (1979) and "creative thinking" techniques of Synectics (Gordon, 1961). This was an enjoyable, difficult and confusing time in their work.

C. Operationalization

From the metaphoric representations, the group derives an action hypothesis--a series of actions planned to "upset the equilibrium" of the present system enough for the problem to be resolved and the work to proceed well. The consultant and the informal leaders guide the group in the development of this plan, which is based on a "force-field analysis" of the total metaphor/model (Eiben, 1976). They also work carefully to organize the extensive qualitative and quantitative "feed- back" data collection which will accompany the intervention.

When the action is implemented for the agreed-upon time, and data are collected and collated, the group returns to the state of conceptual- ization for extensive argument and consensual revision of the formal metaphor/model. This is done in order to decide whether the work situa- tion has changed significantly and for the general purpose of understand- ing the organizational system better. They also have some questions of their own to answer.

The group now argues less on social or personal grounds of various sorts, and more on the basis of the roles and skills they have learned and refined with the help of the consultant. (There have been times when the consultant did not think that they would make it to this stage, and considered how some membership changes would work, and whether he should offer his resignation.)

The results are satisfying, but the group wants to be surer and decides to make one more intervention. So they proceed to Operational-ization again, to consensually derive a second action hypothesis and implement it.

Then the group makes a final data collection, because a deadline for completion of the entire operation is approaching, and the special resources are almost used up.

COMMENT

It is clear at this stage that the consultant views knowledge in an unusual way. He sees theoretical knowledge as _not_ most fully express-ed in precise abstract form (as in principle, formula or law), but in informed social record (as in scientific oral tradition, focussed nar-rative, and diagrams). Further, practical knowledge is _not_ viewed as the product of converging lines of evidence developed by a researcher, but as the product of argument by researchers about contrasting lines of evidence.

Accordingly, it is natural for the action plan to be framed through use of an analysis of opposing forces in the recorded field, though contrary to usual practice, action is not the outcome of algebraically summed forces but is based on a consensus about the essential nature of the force system. It might be said that a new, minimal single meta-phor of choice is formed--usually it is a mixture of abstractness and concreteness--just for the purpose of developing an action hypothesis at this time.

Though the action hypothesis is called a plan of action, it is usually more like a catalytic agent than it is a direct intervention. Especially in regards to the larger organization to which the group be-longs, the group does not have the access or influence to be a direct change agent.

D.   Decision making

Now the consultant works quietly but intensively to make group mem-bers more aware of their own dynamics and of the research process they have carried out. With this awareness, the final formulation of this cycle of action research is made: Not primarily a decision about the action hypothesis (for the research purposes, it has played an heuristic role), but about the form and details of the concluding four-fold metaphor/model. This formulation--the product of extended, turbulent, satisfying consensual decision-making--not only tells whether the work situation has improved, but reflects the essential human and objective urgencies and other realities of the group and organizational system.

Because the action research is ending, the group becomes on their own more aware of their processes and of their place and goals in the organization. This is only partially satisfying, but it gives them a more confident basis for thinking and action than they had before.

E. Conclusions

The group prepares a formal written report, and a more informal widely distributed one. These reports present the models of the organizational situation, showing the changes that have been accomplished, with some features of the last model accentuated as lines for future change, though no action hypothesis is offered.

With the consultant's help, the group manages to arrange for a smaller version of the action research team to continue on a trial basis for another year, as part of the regular operations of the organization.

Otherwise, the consultant leaves and the group members go back to their basic work, having overcome their immediate work obstacle, and changed themselves and the situation somewhat.

Later, a visiting team from another organization comes to ask the group about what they did, and at the following yearly Conference two of the group leaders direct a small seminar on action research.

COMMENT

In the most formal sense, it is the final metaphor/model that is the outcome of the action research. This model is the representation of the refined consciousness of the group about themselves and their situation, out of which analysis, diagnosis, action plans and assessments can be made. The knowledge implicit in this model may take written form ("systematic essential narrative theory"), or diagram form (a real model), or exist primarily as spoken language and be disseminated as part of scientific oral tradition by those who experienced the research.

The place of this paradigm in research methodology

Can this neo-Lewinian method have a recognized place in psychological research methodology? What would this place be?

To consider these questions, I will describe in what ways the method responds to the demands of the traditional criteria of validity, reliability, generalizability, and potential usefulness, as it carries out the stages of inquiry and draws conclusions.

a. Validity depends on correspondence between research language and operations, especially in the conclusions. (The correspondence may also be between the research language and some other language in which we already have confidence about its meaning.) The neo-Lewinian paradigm I have presented is greatly concerned with validity, and accomplishes it mainly through the process of those persons who are actually engaged in the operations also developing the language of the conceptualizations. The language in which conclusions are expressed has a high meaning quotient, its words and phrases having been drawn mostly from the language of discourse in an area of human activity.

b. Reliability depends on repeated operations (or a simulation of them) with corresponding outcomes. This quality is of less importance to the paradigm, which highlights contextual and developmental (time) changes in operational outcomes rather than seeking for precise constant relationships. The metaphor/model which is the formal conclusion of action research is by its nature a representation of a real situation, not a statistical probability for a real occurrence. The reliability that the paradigm might have comes from the cycle of repeated data collections. This reliability has more to do with the type of outcome than with a specific effect.

c. Generalizability depends upon the functional (or critical) similarity between the research setting and other settings that seem similar and invite comparison. Action researchers are often concerned about generalization of their results. Emphasis is on discussion with researcher/practitioners in the similar setting and adaptation of the research procedures and outcomes, however, and not with the direct application of the formal conclusions. A "similar" setting is more likely to be defined by urgency and perceived commonalities than by sampling procedures.

d. Potential usefulness depends on the attractiveness of the research conclusion to practitioners and the correspondence of the language and procedures to their own--that is, the potential ease and economy of application. For users of Lewinian research outcomes there is not much

research-technology gap. When the action-research cycle has been completed, what is obtained has come from a concrete situation and has the
potential appeal of real operations.

Conclusion

I propose that such a research paradigm as this neo-Lewinian one
can fill a present vacancy in the panoply of research methods in psychology. Whether it <u>does</u> assume that place, time will tell. Support and
use have a small base, but a growing one. The paradigm has value. It
will encourage the consolidation of quantitative and qualitative evidence, and deepen the base for research decision making. It will supplement the familiar linear-convergent majority-of-evidence view of
knowledge with one that is dialectic and consensual. It adds to the
social and political meaning of research by including in the production
of knowledge those who will use it. It helps close the theory-techno-
logy gap. By no means last, use of the paradigm will broaden the oral-
interactive tradition of knowledge--a powerful but underrated part of
the scientific enterprise.

BIBLIOGRAPHY

Dewey, J. (1933). <u>How we think</u> (Rev. Ed.). New York: Heath.
Eiben, R. (1976). Force field analysis: A tool for change. In Eiben,
     R. and A. Milliren, (Eds.), <u>Educational change: A humanistic ap-
     proach</u>. LaJolla, Calif.: University Associates.
Gordon, W. J. (1961). <u>Synectics</u>. New York: Colber-MacMillan.
Lewin, K. (1946). Action research and minority problems. <u>Journal of
     Social Issues</u>, 2, 34-46.
Scarr, S. (1985). Constructing psychology: Making facts and fables.
     <u>American Psychologist</u>, May, 499-412.
Spradley, J.P. (1979). <u>The ethnographic interview</u>. New York: Holt,
     Rinehart and Winston.
Tandon, R. (1981). Dialogue as inquiry and intervention. In Reason,
     P. and J. Rowan (Eds.), <u>Human inquiry: A sourcebook of new paradigm
     research</u>. New York: John Wiley and Sons.

The Effects of Affirmative Action on Minority Persons: Research in the Lewinian Tradition

Rupert W. Nacoste

University of North Carolina

Kurt Lewin's philosophy of science, and not his field theory <u>per se</u>, is what has influenced my work as a social psychologist. Being a third generation Lewinian, I did not have the pleasure or privilege to be taught by Kurt Lewin. Thus, I am not privy to the unrecorded assumptions and inner workings specific to Lewin's field theory. But because I have worked with one of his students, John Thibaut, and have studied Lewin's writings I approach the investigation of social psychological phenomena in a way that is Lewinian in heritage. In this paper, I will outline the characteristics of Lewin's philosophy of science which are important in my orientation as a researcher. Then I will attempt to show how those characteristics are integrated into my research on minority responses to the social policy of affirmative action.

Before I go into Lewin's philosophy of science, I must first call your attention to an important point. The research I will describe is classifiable as of the Lewinian tradition in a number of ways. For example, a focus on the responses of minority group individuals is a focus that appears often in the work of Kurt Lewin (for a review, see Lewin, 1976). Also, like much of Lewin's work, my research has implications for both theory and practice. I do not think that there is anything important about the similarity of my research to Lewin's on the basis of my focus on minority group individuals. Although social psychologists should pay more attention to the psychology of minority individuals, that focus bears only a superficial similarity to the Lewinian tradition of research. However, the fact that the research does have theoretical and practical implications is a central part of the Lewinian tradition. That parallel between my research and the work of Lewin is not the result of chance, but is a direct product of my adherence to Lewin's philosophy, which emphasized the importance of understanding individual responses in relation to external and, or, situational variables.

The General Approach

The features of Kurt Lewin's philosophy of science that are important in my research are those put forth in his paper on conceptual modes
of thought in psychology (Lewin, 1935, pp. 1-42). In that paper, Lewin
distinguished Aristotelian from Galilean concepts and modes of thought.
He characterized Aristotelian concepts as those derived from a way of
thinking which presumes that factors that cause some phenomenon lie
within the organism; environmental factors, factors external to the organism, are viewed as nuisance factors. On the other hand, Lewin argued
that the use of Galilean concepts presumes that the cause of some phenomenon is to be found in the relationship between the organism and its
environment; here, both organismic and environmental factors are the
subject of conceptual analysis. According to Lewin, the goal for the
psychologists of his day was to move from an Aristotilean conceptualization of perception, and other psychological phenomena, to a Galilean
mode of concept formation. He put it very strongly by arguing that:

> "The dynamics of perception is not to be understood by ...
> excluding all fortuitous situations, but...only by the
> establishment of a definite form of structure in a definite
> sort of environment" (p. 40, emphasis in the original).

Lewin was saying that to study psychological phenomena appropriately,
we--psychologists--needed to develop concepts for both individual-level
factors, factors within the organism, and environmental factors, factors
external to the organism.

Although Lewin has had a strong influence on research in social
psychology, that influence has not been consistent over time. Reflecting a continuing problem in social psychology (Pepitone, 1981), there
has been a re-emergence, among social psychologists, of the tendency
to study psychological processes themselves without much concern for
their relationship with other factors. Thus, external or situational
variables to which individual-level variables may be related go unexam-
ined. Not surprisingly, that tendency has influenced the research on
the social psychology of affirmative action.

Affirmative action is the title given to the government's equal
opportunity decree that is aimed at increasing the participation of
racial minorities and women in all levels of American society. As a
directive to organizations and institutions, it is designed to induce
them to adopt some means of increasing the numerical representation of
the target groups among their personnel. When hiring or promoting, and
so on, organizations are required to be sensitive to the need to take

positive, affirmative steps to include members of a target group. The implication is that organizations must find ways to increase the chance that members of racial minority groups and women are selected hired, promoted, admitted, etc.

A number of questions have been raised about affirmative action as a policy. All of the questions center on how to select individuals to receive the relevant outcomes, and the questions intimate that selections associated with the policy of affirmative action may have negative consequences. For example, concern has been expressed that being chosen for a job or promotion when an affirmative action policy operates, devalues the achievement for the minority individual. It has also been suggested that when there is an affirmative action policy and a minority group individual is selected to receive some outcome, majority group individuals' perceptions of the minority person are affected negatively.

Even though social psychologists have studied attitudes towards affirmative action (Kluegel & Smith, 1983), as well as affective (Austin, Friedman, Martz, Hooe and Ball, 1977) and attributional outcomes (Garcia, Erskine, Hawn and Casmay, 1981), no comprehensive understanding has emerged. A central problem is that none of the research has moved beyond sole reliance on the assumption, drawn from the equity literature, that individuals prefer pure merit-based distributions. The assumption is well founded, theoretically and empirically (for recent reviews, see Greenberg & Cohen, 1982). Yet, the merit-preference assumption is limited in where it leads research on the psychological ramifications of affirmative action. By itself, the merit-preference assumption implies that we only need to assess differences in individual responses to the mere presence or absence of affirmative action. Since affirmative action selection cannot be said to be purely merit-based, individual responses should differ on the basis of the presence or absence of affirmative action because of a preference match or nonmatch. Any researcher, would expect to find different responses to merit vs. nonmerit selections and would expect those differences to occur across types of outcomes. If we followed this approach, however, we would also be accepting the hidden assumption that the cause of phenomena related to affirmative action is located within individuals, because of our reliance on individual preferences as the explanatory concept.

While the approach I have taken to studying the social psychology of affirmative action acknowledges the importance of the merit-preference assumption, the search for explanatory variables goes beyond factors inherent to the individual. As I have implied, my approach is informed by Kurt Lewin's metatheory, especially the emphasis he placed on the notion that to understand fully the operation of individual-level factors (e.g. preferences), it is necessary to develop concepts and operational definitions not only of those factors, but also of relevant external factors. In that light, I have found the work on procedural justice (Thibaut & Walker, 1975) to be quite germane to the social psychological issues connected with affirmative action.

Research in the procedural justice tradition indicates that we may hamper our ability to understand how preferences operate, when we confine our analysis to the question of whether the individual's preferences were or were not met in the situation. The work on procedural justice focuses on determinants of responses to the use of different procedures for the resolution of conflicts and disputes. The preferred procedure for dispute resolution takes equity claims--the particulars of each individual's position--or more generally, equity units, into account.

In a variety of experiments, dispute resolution procedures have been varied on the basis of the degree to which they took account of each disputant's equity claims. The results of those experiments demonstrate clearly that an individual's perceptions of the resolution of a conflict, and their affective reactions to the resolution, were related to how much the procedure used differed from the preferred procedure (Houlden, LaTour, Walker, and Thibaut, 1978; Lind, Erickson, Friedland, and Dickenberger, 1978). The research I will review is based on the argument that responses to affirmative action are determined not merely by an individual's preferences for merit selection, but also by the nature of the affirmative action decision rule used to make a selection. The notion is that responses to affirmative action are a function of the degree to which an implementation selection procedure differs from a purely merit-based procedure.

To make workable the notion that responses to affirmative action are the result of the type of selection procedure used to implement affirmative action, requires that we determine and classify potentially relevant components of selection procedures. The most straightforward analysis points to merit and group membership as important factors. The policy of affirmative action brings together principles that direct the use of merit criteria for selection, with principles that direct the use of group based criteria. How these criteria are weighted into a selection procedure as selection criteria is probably what determines responses to affirmative action. Thus, I have argued that selection procedure, defined in terms of how much weight merit and group membership receive as selection criteria, is a variable critical to developing an understanding of responses to affirmative action.

Using the weight given to merit and group membership as selection criteria to differentiate types of affirmative action selections, gives us the means to make predictions about a variety of outcomes. Rather than go into all the possibilities, I will review research which is completed. That research was designed to investigate the effects of selection procedures on those individuals whose chances of selection are enhanced through affirmative action-beneficiaries. For them, consideration of group membership is in their favor. I was concerned, in particular, with the effects of selection procedure on psychological processes which might be related to the adjustment of beneficiaries.

Review of Research

The completed research focused on the question of whether different descriptions of selection procedures affect beneficiaries perceptions of their selection and their emotional state, even though each procedure used group membership as a selection factor. Two descriptions of the selection mechanism constituted the manipulation of selection procedure. The difference between the descriptions of the procedures was in the degree merit (i.e. qualifications) and group membership were used as selection criteria. In one instance, equal or more weight apparently was given to qualification, but in the other instance more weight apparently was given to group membership.

That manipulation of selection procedures relates to dispute resolution procedures conceptually, in that qualifications are considered to fall into a general category of equity inputs or units. Equity units are those factors which the individual holds in the situation through their own past actions, or those actions concurrent to the present situation. Demographic group memberships, such as race or sex, are not then considered as equity units. On that basis, I label the procedure giving weight to qualifications while also taking group membership into account, equity-based. The equity-based procedure was expected to be preferred to the selection procedure which gave more weight to group membership. The latter procedure I refer to as nonequity-based.

An equity-based procedure, and outcomes received through it, should be perceived as fairer by beneficiaries (and others). Likewise, beneficiaries' emotional state should be more positive when they are chosen by way of an equity-based procedure. One of the reasons this effect on emotional responses is expected, is that individuals generally feel more satisfied with outcomes obtained when the procedure allows them to feel that they have had some control over what occurs (Musante, Gilbert & Thibaut, 1983).

These basic predictions were investigated in two runs of a role-play experiment. Participants in the experiment read a vignette which described a situation. The situation involved a competition for grant money, sponsored by a university. According to the scenario, it was during a time when universities in general were under pressure to allocate funds proportionately on the basis of sex. The finalists in the competition were a male and a female. All participants in the experiment were female and they each imagined themselves to be the female finalist. In every case, the female finalist received the grant. Relative qualifications of the finalists, the selection committee's history of discrimination and the selection procedures were the variables manipulated.

To manipulate the qualifications of the finalists, it was indicated in the scenario that the selection committee felt that one or the other finalist had superior qualifications. History of discrimination was manipulated in the scenario by sometimes saying the selection committee either had disproportinately allocated funds in favor of males in the past (Clear history) or by not giving any history information (Ambiguous history). Finally, selection procedure was manipulated by suggesting that the final selection decision was based mainly on sex (nonequity-based procedure) or on consideration of qualifications and sex (equity-based procedure).

Since the variable of major interest is selection procedure, I will focus here on results having to do with that manipulation. Results of the first run of the experiment, experiment A (Nacoste, in press), generally confirmed the predictions. Table 1 shows that estimates of the importance given to qualifications were higher when an equity-based procedure was used, relative to a nonequity-based procedure. Perceived fairness of the procedure and the outcome of the selection process was higher when an equity-based procedure was used. Emotional responses were also more positive when the equity-based procedure was used.

These results, of course, raised additional questions. A relatively important one was whether selection procedure, since it did influence affective responding, might not be relevant to the psychological adjustment of affirmative action beneficiaries. Others have suggested that because of the uncertainty it instills about competency, affirmative action may negatively influence the self-esteem of beneficiaries. I became interested in whether selection procedure might serve to moderate feelings of uncertainty. Both the reasoning behind experiment A as

Table 1

Basic Effects of Selection Procedure from Experiment A

	Importance given to Qualifications Qualifications		Fairness of Procedure Qualifications		Fairness of Decision Qualifications		General Affect Qualifications	
	Higher	Lower	Higher	Lower	Higher	Lower	Higher	Lower
Equity	81.9	56.0	67.0	51.1	74.3	38.1	81.0	51.4
Nonequity	48.5	28.8	45.0	33.3	42.9	23.2	64.4	53.3

All dependent variables were measured on a continuous 100 point scale. Higher numbers mean more of the dimension being measured. General affect is a composite measure which includes responses to bipolar feeling scales: good/bad, pleased/displeased, competent/incompetent, etc. For general affect higher scores mean more positive responses.

The main effects of procedure and qualifications were significant for each of the dependent variables shown:

Importance given to qualifications:
  Qualifications, $F(1,88)=17.25$, $p < .001$
  Procedure, $F(1,88)=32.45$, $p < .001$
Fairness of Procedure:
  Qualifications, $F(1,88)=5.47$, $p < .02$
  Procedure, $F(1,88)=11.2$, $p < .001$
Fairness of Decision:
  Qualifications, $F(1,88)=27.6$, $p < .001$
  Procedure, $F(1,88)=19.1$, $p < .001$
General Affect:
  Qualifications, $F(1,88)=21.6$, $p < .001$
  Procedure, $F(1,88)=11.5$, $p < .001$
Adapted from Nacoste (in press).

well as the results of that experiment (experiment A), imply that the
structure of a selection procedure may well have something to do with
adjustment.

Keep in mind that in my work the major difference between selection
procedures is the degree to which a procedure incorporates equity units
as selection criteria, when a nonequity criterion is required. I thought
this relevant to the issue of negative effects on psychological adjustment because the structure of a selection procedure might influence psychological processes related to self-esteem. For example, when qualifications are given equal or more weight relative to group membership as
a selection criterion, then individuals may be better able (and more
likely) to make internal (competency) attributions about their selection.
These internal attributions should influence self-esteem and related
emotions, positively. Of course, the more weight given to group membership, the less able will beneficiaries be to make an internal attribution, since they have had no control over their demographic group membership. That should make them uncertain about the legitimacy of their
being chosen. Thus, their self-esteem and related emotions should either
be unaffected or negatively affected. Selection procedure, then, was
expected to affect emotional responses related to self-esteem through
an impact on attributions about being selected. I will refer to this
as the attribution hypothesis.

The likelihood that affirmative action beneficiaries might make a
successful adjustment to their new circumstance may be influenced by
factors unrelated to their self-doubts. Being selected partially on the
basis of a nonequity criterion may cause beneficiaries to expect that
other individuals will view them differentially. They may feel stig-
matized, and expect that those who know of the conditions of their selection, will have a biased view of them. Consequently, beneficiaries
may anticipate biased and negative evaluations of their work. These
expectations, in and of themselves, may contribute to a lowered probability of the individual making a successful adjustment. No one who
anticipates receiving negative evaluations can be expected to feel opti-
mistic about how much they will be able to control their own outcomes
in the relevant situation. But the potential magnitude of the stigma
should be related to the type of selection procedure. There will be
more possibility of stigma, and a stronger stigma, associated with a
nonequity-based selection procedure. The type of selection procedure,
then, should affect the prevalence of negative expectations about evaluations. I hypothesized that how a beneficiary expects to be evaluated
will be more or less positive depending on the type of selection

procedure they think was used. I refer to this hypothesis as the selection stigma hypothesis.

Both the attribution and the selection stigma hypotheses were investigated in a replication (experiment B) of experiment A. No change in the experimental method or independent variables was made. To investigate the attribution hypothesis, following Weiner (1982), I made a distinction between esteem-related emotions and general emotions. Esteem-related emotions included subjects' self-reported experience of feelings of Tension (e.g. anxiety, uneasiness) and Depression (e.g. hopelessness, unhappiness). General emotions included self-reported experience of feelings of Vigor (e.g. alert, energetic) and Anger (e.g. angry, annoyed).

The results of Experiment B (Nacoste & Lehman, 1985) confirmed our predictions. Figure 1 is a graph of selected findings, and provides a sense of how the results are patterned. Once again, estimates of the importance given to qualifications were highest in the equity-based procedure condition. Beneficiaries in the equity-based procedure condition felt that their individual characteristics had more impact on their being selected than those in the nonequity-based condition. Apparently, those in the equity-based condition made an internal attribution about their selection. In line with that attribution, beneficiaries in the equity-based procedure conditions reported more positive esteem-related affect than those in the nonequity-based condition. Figure 1 shows that they felt less tension; they also reported less depression and confusion. Selection procedure did not influence general emotions (see result for Vigor in Figure 1). It does appear then, that the structure of a selection procedure can influence psychological factors related to adjustment by affecting cognitive (attributional) processes related to emotions.

I have used the notion of selection stigma to indicate that beneficiaries of affirmative action might anticipate the inevitable evaluations of their work to be more or less biased and negative depending upon the selection procedure. The results of experiment B partially support those predictions. In this case, the history of discrimination variable conditioned the impact of selection procedure. Figure 2 shows that for both how objectively and how positively they expected to be evaluated, selection procedure did not influence beneficiaries' responses when it was apparent that there had been some relevant past discrimination (Clear history). However, when it was unclear that there had been discrimination, selection procedure did influence responses. Figure 3 shows that the use of a nonequity-based procedure led beneficiaries to expect less objective and less positive evaluations, relative to when an equity-

Figure 1 Selection Procedure Effects : Attributions and Emotions

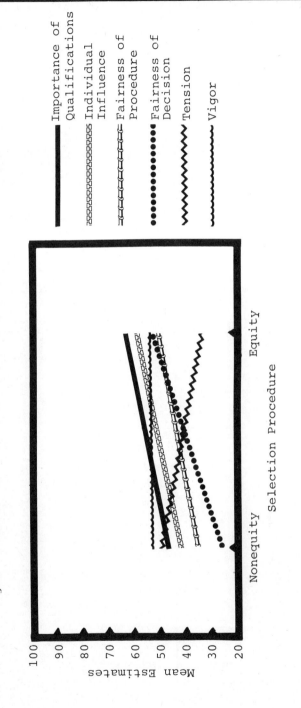

The differences shown between mean ratings for the individuals' perceptions of the importance given to qualifications, influence of individual characteristics, fairness of procedure and decision, and experienced Tension are all significant ($p < .05$). The slope of the line for experienced Tension is opposite in direction from the lines for importance given to qualifications, etc. In line with the hypothesis, when more importance is given to merit, individuals believe their individual characteristics influence their selection (internal attribution), and they experience more positive affect. The mean ratings for experienced Vigor did not differ by procedure.

Adapted from Nacoste and Lehman (1984).

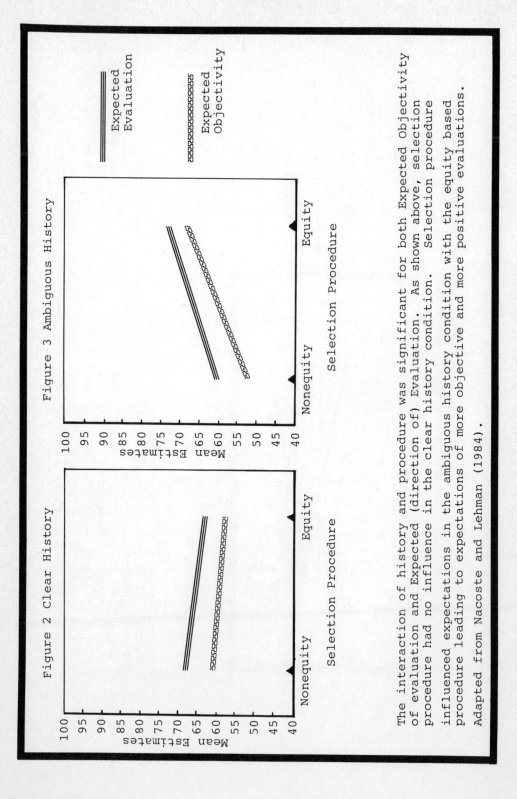

Figure 2 Clear History

Figure 3 Ambiguous History

Expected Evaluation

Expected Objectivity

Mean Estimates

Nonequity   Equity

Selection Procedure

The interaction of history and procedure was significant for both Expected Objectivity of evaluation and Expected (direction of) Evaluation. As shown above, selection procedure had no influence in the clear history condition. Selection procedure influenced expectations in the ambiguous history condition with the equity based procedure leading to expectations of more objective and more positive evaluations.

Adapted from Nacoste and Lehman (1984).

based procedure was used. These findings suggest that selection procedure may influence psychological adjustment through processes other than self-attributions. Under certain conditions, when a nonequity-based procedure is involved in their selection, beneficiaries apparently will generate expectations that others will look at their work with a jaundiced eye and probably denigrate what they accomplish.

Implications of the Research

In view of the results obtained from experiments A and B, I and my colleagues (Nacoste, in press; Nacoste & Lehman, 1985) have made suggestions concerning both theoretical and applied issues. Because of the nature of the selection procedures represented in the research, it was possible, and necessary, to indicate what the results implied about the social policy of affirmative action. Each selection procedure described in the studies took group membership (sex) into account, with some advantage given to females. In those terms, these procedures were in line with the list of affirmative action mandates. Thus, the comparisons were between different types of affirmative-action-like procedures and not comparisons between a pure merit procedure and affirmative action. Differences in psychological responding then, were the result of the nature of the affirmative-action-like procedure.

The results suggests that when greater weight is given to group membership relative to merit as selection criteria, beneficiaries may be affected negatively. The research showed that beneficiaries perceived their selection as less fair, they experienced more negative affect related to self-esteem (e.g. tension) and they were sometimes more likely to expect negative evaluations of their work from others. Not only is this relevant to an individual's psychological well being, but also to their adjustment to a new circumstance or setting. Organizations with a serious commitment to increasing and maintaining their number of minority and women employees should be interested in information that suggests factors that might influence the adjustment of those employees.

On the theoretical end, our research has introduced for further theoretical exploration the whole of a psychology of selection. What goes into how we respond to being chosen to receive good outcomes, or having someone chosen instead of us? We have identified selection procedure as one factor and have developed lines of thought that connect selection procedure with both cognitive and affective outcomes. New conceptual developments such as that embodied in our notion of selection stigma are bound to come along as responses to selections are studied by others.

CONCLUSION

What has made it possible for me to draw both theoretical and practical implications from the research is a product of the Lewinian approach. No matter the specific topic of our interests as social psychologists, using Lewin's philosophy of science as a guide requires that when developing an explanatory scheme, we attend to both individual-level psychological factors and factors external to the individual. Lewin felt this important because it would mean that psychologists would gain knowledge of how psychological processes operated at various points along some continuum and not merely in isolated instances. From that type of knowledge he hoped would develop theories about the dynamics of psychological processes.

The research I have reviewed supports the notion that one ought to be concerned with more than individual-level characteristics as influences on equity (or any social psychological) phenomena. The results indicate that researchers who investigate phenomena related to affirmative action, or any selection-related phenomena, should be equally concerned with conceptualizing factors of the social environment. Had I relied on individual preferences alone as an explanatory concept, my research would not go beyond demonstrating differences in responses to merit vs nonmerit selection. However interesting that may seem, knowledge of those differences would not move us far theoretically or practically. Taking seriously the task of conceptualizing both individual and situational variables has led us to a position where the research has both theoretical and practical implications.

Although what I am about to say may be obvious to some, it needs reiteration for individuals now being trained as social psychologists. One reason that the basic and applied divisions still persist in social psychology, is that a certain component of Lewin's position has not been understood. To do work that has applied implications does not require necessarily studying behavior in specific settings. It is more a matter of what is brought into the conceptual apparatus. As I see it, when social psychological phenomena are conceptualized in terms of individual-level processes _and_ their relation to situational factors, basic research will enhance efforts towards application.

REFERENCES

Austin, W., Friedman, J.S., Martz, R.A., Hooe, G.S. and Ball, K.P. (1977). Responses to favorable sex discrimination. _Law and Human Behavior_, 1: 283-298.

Garcia, L.T., Erskine, N., Hawn, K. and Casmay, S.R. (1981). The effect of affirmative action on attributions about minority group members. _Journal of Personality_, 49: 427-437.

Greenberg, J. and Cohen, R.L. (Eds.) (1982). _Equity and Justice in Social Behavior_. New York: Academic Press.

Houlden, P., LaTour, S., Walker, L. and Thibaut, J. (1978). Preference for modes of dispute resolution as a function of process and decision control. _Journal of Experimental Social Psychology_, 14: 13-30.

Kluegel, J.R. and Smith, E.R. (1983). Affirmative action attitudes: Effects of self-interest, racial affect, and stratification beliefs on whites' views. _Social Forces_, 61: 797-823.

Lewin, K. (1935). The conflict between Aristotelian and Galilean modes of thought in contemporary psychology. In K. Lewin, (Ed.), _A dynamic theory of personality_. New York: McGraw Hill.

Lewin, M.A. (1976). Psychological aspects of minority group membership. In T. Blass (Ed.), _Contemporary social psychology: Representative readings_. Itasca, Illinois: Peacock.

Lind, E.A., Erickson, B.E., Friedland, N. and Dickenberger, M. (1978). Reactions to procedural models for adjudicative conflict resolution: A cross national study. _Journal of Conflict Resolution_, 20: 319-356.

Musante, L., Gilbert, M. and Thibaut, J.W. (1983). The effects of control on perceived fairness of procedures and outcomes. _Journal of Experimental Social Psychology_, 19: 223-238.

Nacoste, R.W. (in press). Selection procedure and responses to affirmative action: The case of favorable treatment. _Law and Human Behavior_.

Nacoste, R.W. and Lehman, D.R. (1985). Selection procedures: A link to beneficiaries affective and cognitive responses to affirmative action. Manuscript submitted for publication.

Pepitone, A. (1981). Lessons from the history of social psychology. _Journal of Personality and Social Psychology_, 34: 641-653.

Thibaut, J.W. and Walker, L. (1975). _Procedural justice: A psychological analysis_. New Jersey: Erlbaum.

Weiner, B. (1982). An attributionally-based theory of motivation and emotion: Focus, range and issues. In N.T. Feather (Ed.), _Expectations and actions: Expectancy-value models in psychology_. New Jersey: Erlbaum.